JULES SIMON

JULES SIMON

Republican Anticlericalism and

Cultural Politics in France, 1848–1886

Philip A. Bertocci

UNIVERSITY OF MISSOURI PRESS

COLUMBIA & LONDON, 1978

39881

Library of Congress Cataloging in Publication Data

Bertocci, Philip A.   1940–
    Jules Simon: Republican Anticlericalism and
Cultural Politics in France, 1848–1886.

    Bibliography: p. 219
    1. Simon, Jules, 1814–1896. 2. Anti-clericalism—
France. 3. France—Politics and government—19th
century.
DC255.S5B47   320.5   77–14668
ISBN 0–8262–0239–X

Grateful acknowledgment is given to the Bibliothèque nationale,
Paris, for granting permission to use the photograph of Jules Simon,
which was taken by Félix Nadar (ca. 1859), a celebrated early
French photographer.

This book is biographical in theme and topical in subject. In these pages, the political and intellectual biography of Jules Simon offers successive points of reference from which to view republican anticlericalism and cultural politics between 1848 and 1886.

A prominent nineteenth-century French moral philosopher and republican politician, Simon, in both his thinking and his politics, gave his primary attention to matters involving the relations of Church, State, and School. The portrait of Simon that emerges from the examination of these persistent public and personal concerns is not the conventional image of the overly ambitious, indecisive, and sanctimonious rival of Léon Gambetta and Jules Ferry but rather that of a high-minded, tenacious, and professorial republican committed to a complex if somewhat narrow ideal of liberal civilization. His reputation for untrustworthiness, widespread among both contemporaries and subsequent historians, stems less from his actual character than from his principled political moderation, which, in the French context especially, was bound to generate frequent misunderstanding on both the Left and Right.

The study of Simon's efforts on behalf of his particular political and cultural ideals sheds new light on the internal divisions within the democratic movement on the question of anticlericalism. On this issue, I hope I have shown, republicans were deeply divided, not merely by political temperament, as is commonly believed, but by more fundamental differences in attitude toward Catholicism, Christianity, and positive religion.

In this space, I can never sufficiently thank all those who have aided me in the conception, research, and composition of this book. I owe a special debt of gratitude to Stanley S. Mellon, whose persistent questioning aided in the clarification of my objectives and who taught me how to give a hearing to nineteenth-century middle-class Frenchmen. I also thank Franklin Le Van Baumer and Henri Peyre for advice and support at the beginning.

In France, I was particularly fortunate to have received the gracious aid of the late Mme. Delorme-Jules Simon, who granted me permission to consult the Jules Simon Papers in the Archives nationales and showed me other papers that, at the time, were still in her possession. I also thank M. Rémy Buffet for allowing me to consult the correspondence of Jules Simon with his teacher Jean-Philibert Damiron. Louis Hachette and Company readily put at my disposal materials that illuminated Simon's relationship with the great publishing house. And I am indebted to the staffs of the Bibliothèque nationale and the Archives nationales for their competent assistance.

This book is better than it might have been because of much friendly criticism. I thank my father, Angelo P. Bertocci, for his stylistic aid and his paternal enthusiasm and encouragement. I wish also to thank Edward T. Gargan and Robert R. Palmer for the attention they have given my work, and whose remarks and questions have helped me immeasurably. I am especially grateful to my friends Robert J. Bezucha, Mark U. Edwards, Hester Eisenstein, E. Peter Fitzgerald, C. Alan Grubb, Eugenia P. Janis, Michael R. Marrus, Martin A. Miller, Karen Offen, Laurence Romero and Christiane Z. Romero, and Dale Van Kley for their wise suggestions and stimulating conversation. Also, I was privileged to benefit from the skillful and responsive assistance of the staff at the University of Missouri Press.

Finally, I wish to thank the generous Early Leave Program of Wellesley College, which made completion of this book possible.

P. A. B.
August 1977
Cambridge, Mass.

Contents

Abbreviations in Footnotes, viii

I. Introduction, 1

II. Republican Varieties of Anticlerical Imagination, 10

III. The Making of a Philosopher, 33
    A Quiet *Crise de Conscience*

IV. The Making of a Republican, 55
    Early Encounters with Democracy, Voltairianism, and
    Reaction

V. *La Religion naturelle*, 78
    Simon's Religious Consciousness

VI. The Politics of *La Religion naturelle*, 93

VII. Republican but Respectable Opposition, 1857–1870, 118

VIII. The Ministry of Public Instruction,
    Worship, and Fine Arts, 1871–1873, 151

IX. The Campaign for the Conservative Republic, 1873–1886, 181

X. Epilogue, 212

Selected Bibliography, 219

Index, 239

Abbreviations in Footnotes

A.N.—Archives nationales
A.P.P.—Archives de la Préfecture de police
Bib. VC—Bibliothèque Victor Cousin
JS—Jules Simon
LP—*La Liberté de penser*
n.a.fr.—Bibliothèque nationale, nouvelles acquisitions françaises
RDM—*Revue des Deux Mondes*
RIP—*Revue de l'Instruction Publique*
R.N.—*La Religion naturelle*, 2d edition
87 AP 1–21—Archives nationales (Archives Privées), Jules Simon
    Papers
Annales—Annales du Sénat et de la Chambre des Députés

CHAPTER I

INTRODUCTION

Among the founders of the Third Republic, the tenacious, professorial figure of Jules Simon (1814–1896) has faded into shadow, obscured by the popular eloquence of Léon Gambetta and by the parliamentary achievements of the grand bourgeois Jules Ferry. Although Simon left no monuments like Gambetta's republican and anticlerical *mystique* or Ferry's *école laïque*, this historical eclipse is quite undeserved. In a political career that spanned almost half a century and that included terms as minister of public instruction and worship (1871–1873) and president of the council of ministers (1876–1877), Simon won general recognition for his far-reaching republican vision, his intellectual versatility, his tactical skills, especially in parliament, and his indefatigable industry. A philosopher by training, who entered politics from the Sorbonne, Simon quickly grasped the importance of education for the future of parliamentary democracy, and his book *L'École* (1865) established him as one of the foremost advocates of the reform and expansion of French public instruction. The Liberal Charles de Rémusat expressed a broad consensus when he described Simon as a formidable force in French parliamentary politics in the last years of the Second Empire and the early years of the Third Republic:

Jules Simon stood out from the start among the new deputies whom the Opposition recruited. He knew how to hold the ear of his audience . . . for although his ideas were bold, his language was not violent. He is a man of distinction, with a variety of abilities. I pass on his philosophical works which may not seem particularly profound or original, but which show real qualities of understanding, fairness, high-mindedness and style. Especially as a moralist, he has written excellent books. These earlier writings turned his interest toward political questions which involved the improvement and happiness of the human race. . . . He speaks the language of "democratic philanthropy" but without falling into tomfoolery or flattery. His language is vivid, clever, measured; he is captivating, and moderates his deep convictions on matters of principle with a highly personal sort of unction.[1]

Simon's career is noteworthy, however, not only because of the prominence that he achieved but also because of the light that its study sheds upon the character and development of middle-class republican anticlericalism.

The story of the republican battle with the Church between 1848 and 1905 has become a commonplace in the standard histories of the republican movement and of the early Third Republic. In these accounts, democratic preferences and anticlerical convictions are depicted as twin facets of a single republican movement. The "laic laws" of the 1880s and the Law on Separation of Church and State of 1905 appear in these narratives as the historical and even logical conclusion of a long and continuous republican struggle against the Church. In this kind of description, the republican campaigns against the Falloux Law under the Second Republic, against French support for the temporal power of the Roman Catholic Papacy under the Second Empire, and against the "clerical" coup of 16 May 1877 in the early years of the Third Republic were based on the same spirit and intent that produced later anticlerical legislation. This way of thinking, with its marked teleological overtones, has sustained the view that French republicans, inspired by a single anticlerical animus, were bound to express their distrust of the Church only in the way that they did.

This image of a kind of republican anticlerical fatality has been the work of both the friends and foes of the *esprit laïque*. Catholics, then and now, in their hostility to the secular movement, have minimized the differences between anticlericals. The prisoners of their own fears, they often viewed republicans who expressed apprehensions about the Church in firm but moderate terms as only the wily advance guard of an impla-

1. Charles de Rémusat, *Mémoires de ma vie*, 5:165. Throughout this work, the translations from the French are mine, unless otherwise indicated.

cable anticlerical army. On the other side, republican historians, with the *universitaire*'s conviction of the virtues of the laic ideal, have viewed anticlericalism and the scientific spirit as constituent elements of the secular consensus underpinning the republican movement and the Third Republic itself. This tendency to pass over the differences between republican anticlericals is evident in the classical treatments of republican anticlericalism written by the Catholic scholar Father Louis Capéran and by the orthodox republican Georges Weill.[2] Even when they acknowledge that republican anticlericals disagreed among themselves about the nature of the danger to the republican cause posed by the Church, they emphasize what was shared in common by grouping them together as exponents, some more mature than others, of a single laic spirit or idea.

The study of Simon offers a fresh vantage point from which to view republican anticlericalism. Unlike the unqualified opponents or the principal architects of the anticlerical legislation of the Third Republic, he was, by the special nature of his position in the republican movement, more inclined to appreciate the differences among republicans on anticlerical questions, than to exaggerate the range of consensus. An examination of his outlook provides insights that should help historians to explain the development of republican anticlericalism not in terms of *laïcité en marche* but rather in terms of a real and ongoing struggle within the republican movement on policy toward the Church.

Why is Simon such a valuable observer for the student of anticlericalism? First, because of his relationship with republican anticlericals in the period between 1848 and 1886. Students of nineteenth-century republican anticlericalism, perhaps misled by the men they study, have often used the term *anticlerical* rather loosely and have neglected to distinguish sufficiently between anticlericalism (in its various forms) and an intolerant anti-Catholicism. In the strictest sense, Émile Littré has suggested, anticlericalism was not a philosophic or religious attitude but a political one. The term denoted hostility to the efforts of the Catholic clergy or laity to maintain and expand by

---

2. Louis Capéran, *Histoire contemporaine de la laïcité française;* Georges Weill, *Histoire de l'idée laïque au XIXe siècle.*

political action a network of legislation that almost exclusively served the institutional interests and doctrines of the Church; the anticlerical opposed the Roman Catholic Church's attempts to subordinate temporal authorities to ecclesiastical ones. Throughout his adult life, Simon, "republican of 1848" and stalwart freethinker, shared a visceral anticlericalism with his fellow republicans.[3] Yet, although he was a convinced anti-clerical, Simon was nevertheless often at odds with other republican anticlericals. While admitting that the Church con-stituted an ever-present danger to the republican cause, he was critical of many republican interpretations of the nature of the threat and often considered the favorite anticlerical strategies as contrary to the rights of conscience and politically inap-propriate, even self-defeating.

Unlike militant anticlericals, Simon minimized the sup-posedly inherent clericalism of the Church and of the laymen, priests, monks, and nuns who served it. Catholics, he argued, were not immune from the political temptations that beset all people of deep conviction and extensive organization; but they were not bound by the nature of their faith to support those political forces, invariably authoritarian, which favored mea-sures tending to subordinate secular authorities to ecclesias-tical ones. With their sense of involvement in a mortal combat with an implacable enemy, militant anticlericals, he believed, had lost their sense of perspective. In their eagerness to anni-hilate clericalism, they disregarded the legitimate rights of the religious conscience. Thus, on the premise that Catholicism was not irremediably authoritarian and clerical in cultural and political matters, Simon resisted pressures originating among militantly anticlerical republicans to enact preventive legisla-tion against powerful religious orders especially active in the field of education. Although he had no great affection for the Society of Jesus and certain other orders of regular clergy, he did not believe that the safety of the French Republic re-

3. In my use of the term *freethinker* or *libre penseur*, I am following the broad eighteenth-century definition cited in the *Oxford English Dictionary* and Robert's *Dictionnaire alphabétique*. According to this usage, the term designates one who refuses to submit his reason to the control of authority in matters of religious belief. It consequently re-fers to both religious skeptics and theists who reject the authority of revelation.

quired that they be banished from French public and private education, let alone from the national territory. In a more general way, he continually resisted the tendency of these same anticlericals to transform the struggle against monarchism and Bonapartism into a war on clericalism.

Intent upon forging a republican alliance of Catholics and freethinkers committed to the principle of liberty of conscience, and determined to oppose both the "exaggerations" of republican anticlericals and the "pretensions" of authoritarian clericals, Simon had particular interest in discriminating among the anticlericalisms of his republican colleagues. With a philosopher's capacity for making distinctions, the subtle-minded Simon knew how to look beyond the stock anticlerical formulas of his colleagues in republicanism, beyond the standard references to the "clerical danger," insinuated or denounced, as circumstances required, to the more indirect reservations and qualifications that revealed a measured and deliberate attitude toward religious questions of great complexity. Throughout the Second Empire, Simon struggled, with some successes, to rally men of moderate temperament like Jules Ferry and to put a damper on the anticlerical militancy of such new younger recruits to the republican cause as Léon Gambetta, Henri Allain-Targé, and Henri Brisson.

This tempered anticlericalism, a constant source of tension between Simon and certain elements in the republican movement, was not part of a mere family quarrel, but rather involved a struggle for the power to determine the character of the French republican movement. For Simon was a man with a grand design, who pictured himself as a prospective leader of a moderate Republic based on a centrist alliance of middle-class freethinkers and Catholic notables committed to the principles of parliamentary democracy and liberty of conscience. With the benefit of hindsight, it now appears that Simon was overly sanguine about the possibility of constructing a Republic with such a cultural core. As Gambetta knew well, the popular fear of "government of priests" constituted a reservoir of exploitable passion with sufficient weight to counteract all Simon's efforts to separate republican anticlericals who sharply distinguished between clericalism and Catholicism, from those who did not.

Yet at the time, to his own misfortune, Simon was willing

to stake his political career on his own vision of the potentiali-
ties of the situaton. Thus, in 1877, he sought, through the
exercise of the powers of president of the council, to build the
credibility of the moderate line in Church-State relations. This
policy led, in May, to a conflict with the more militant Gambetta in the Chamber of Deputies. Denouncing Simon's sup-
posedly soft attitude toward the political activities of the clergy,
the tribune uttered a virtual declaration of war on the Church.
With the great republican battle cry, "*Le cléricalisme, voilà
l'ennemi!*" Gambetta set in motion a chain of events that led
to President MacMahon's dismissal of Simon and to the famous constitutional crisis, the "16th of May."

In 1879, when republicans gained control of the Senate and
the presidency of the Republic, with anticlericalism as the
order of the day, it was again the republican Simon who opposed the more militantly anticlerical aspects of the laic legislation proposed by his republican colleague and long-time
political associate Jules Ferry. Supported by a portion of the
Left Center, the most conservative republican group in the
Senate, and by Catholic and monarchist authoritarians, Simon
opposed key measures in that body of legislation known as
the Ferry Laws, which sought to establish an expanded and
secular system of public education in France. The Ferry Laws,
he believed, attacked not only clericalism but also Catholicism.
The legislation was a direct affront to the large number of
Frenchmen who were Catholic, for it sought to obstruct the
Church's efforts, through its teaching, to propagate and fortify
the faith. It violated the principle of liberty of conscience, the
wellspring, in Simon's view, of all free political institutions.
In these confrontations with Gambetta and Ferry, Simon lost
his political wagers and irreparably damaged his career in public life. Yet, although he erred in his judgments, his observations and political activities are replete with acute commentary
on the structure of republican anticlerical opinion.

Second, Simon is a particularly valuable witness not only
because of the political interest he brought to his observations
but also because of the high importance that he attached to
the cultural issues involved in questions concerning the relation
of Church, State, and School. A graduate of the *École normale
supérieure,* where he studied under the philosopher Victor
Cousin, and a former professor of philosophy at the Sorbonne,

Simon brought to public life the conviction that "moral formation and religious belief, whether based on positive religion, natural religion or philosophy, are the *souverains des moeurs*," the determining force in social relations. Convinced of this priority of manners, he believed that a society without a deepseated respect for classical and Christian virtue could not support free political institutions.[4] Virtue, as Montesquieu had observed, was the principle of republics. If Frenchmen were to achieve liberty, they needed to learn self-control. French Catholics and freethinkers, with the human propensity to civil intolerance, needed to learn to respect the natural rights of all to liberty of conscience. French workers, when tempted by the promises of socialist utopians, needed to remain firm in their commitment to the principle of self-help. In defense of these views, Simon published, during the Second Empire, a series of popular philosophic works that attracted a wide readership. Indeed, one contemporary estimated, in 1860, that over two hundred thousand people had read Simon's works *Le Devoir* (1854) and *La Religion naturelle* (1856), not to mention *La Liberté de conscience* (1857), *La Liberté* (1859), and a prominent series of articles that would appear later as *L'Ouvrière* (1861).[5] Thus, for Simon, who was elected to the Academy of Moral and Political Sciences in 1863, the politics of culture, the political questions raised by the forces of anticlericalism, secularization, and dechristianization, were the primary concern. What has recently been written of John Stuart Mill's *On Liberty* applies equally to Simon: his principal writings were "early specimens of a mode of thought which has only recently become prominent, the tendency to think in terms of 'cultural politics' rather than politics *per se*, to find political reality more accurately reflected in opinions, attitudes, perceptions, ways of thought and behavior, than in the more conventional arena of institutions, legislation and electoral arrangements."[6]

4. Amédée Jacques [JS], "La Liberté de penser," *LP* 1 (15 December 1847): 3 (see Abbreviations, p. viii). Jacques, the legal director of the journal, signed the article, but Simon wrote it. JS to Jean-Philibert Damiron, 21 July 1847, Jean-Philibert Damiron Papers; JS, "Une Révolution dans un verre d'eau," *Nouveaux mémoires des autres*, p. 186.

5. Hippolyte Taine, "*La Liberté* de M. Jules Simon," *Le Journal des débats*, 1 February 1860.

6. Gertrude Himmelfarb, *On Liberty and Liberalism: The Case of John Stuart Mill*, pp. 302–3.

In Simon's writings and speeches, these questions, too often dismissed as mere bourgeois ideology, receive unusually detailed discussion. Wide ranging in subject matter and rich in description of attitude, Simon's works provide a promising entrée into the mentality of a highly esteemed middle-class moralist. They reveal with a singular poignancy, even in their reticences, hesitations and qualifications, the kinds of moral tensions, the conflicts of principle and self-interest, of hope and fear, which nineteenth-century republicans faced. For the political hopes of Simon and his colleagues rested on the eighteenth-century faith that truth and history were on the side of science, representative government, and natural virtue. Their perceptions of the social realities of nineteenth-century France, however, raised conflicting fears in which the Church loomed large. Did the principle of religious liberty obligate them to grant liberty to a disciplined Catholicism that seemed likely to use its right to preach, teach, and engage in charitable activities as a base for a political campaign to deny the same liberty to non-believers? Did the principle of free thought require them to use public education to seek to undermine the restraining and consoling force of Catholic ideas among the lower orders in a society where the words *civilized* and *barbarous* often seemed best to sum up the differences between a prosperous, literate elite and a people perceived as illiterate, wretched, savage, ferocious, almost inhuman? In his responses to these questions, Simon took a number of positions that, throughout his career, set him apart from his republican colleagues. His answers are not only of intrinsic interest but they also shed light upon the attitudes of the men who, under the leadership of Ferry, waged the first anticlerical campaign of the Third Republic.

Although this book is biographical in theme, republican cultural politics remain its topical focus. The figure of Jules Simon serves as a kind of *catalyst,* in the presence of which the varieties of republican attitude toward the Roman Catholic Church, Christianity, and positive religion acquire sharper definition. This approach requires, therefore, special attention to the universe of discourse within which Simon sought recognition for his views. To study the republican debate over cultural policies from the inside, to view the prolonged nineteenth-century debate through Simon's eyes, one must learn to recognize some of the contours of the anticlerical landscape and to grasp the basic elements of its topography. The next chapter attempts to sketch out the principal landmarks that were part of Simon's daily experience.

CHAPTER II

REPUBLICAN VARIETIES OF ANTICLERICAL IMAGINATION

Most republican activists, after the experiences of the Second Republic, viewed the Roman Catholic Church as a threat, in some degree, to the republican cause. With the apprehension of confirmed freethinkers, they expected the Church to act in a clerical manner. This clericalism consisted in the tendency of Catholic priests and laymen to seek to subordinate temporal to ecclesiastical authorities, to pressure the civil power to accord the Church privileges that would favor both its spiritual and material interests, and to support politically authoritarian and anti-republican movements in France. Republican anticlericals were determined to opposed this clerical spirit, but they differed markedly among themselves about the nature and the gravity of this threat and about the measures that might effectively counter the political influence of priests. At the root of these disagreements, there often lay differing presuppositions about the nature of Catholicism, Christianity, and of positive religions in general, presuppositions that were often consciously understood only in part, and that took the form of various images of the Church as enemy. The term *image* or *imagination* seems appropriate here not because the threat was imaginary but because the Church, like any large and multifarious organization, was often understood through an act of imagination—through a metaphor or model that helped men to make sense of their encounters with Roman Catholicism in their passage from cradle to grave.

Forms of anticlerical imagination fall into two major categories. The most militant form was the Voltairean, which tended, in theory and practice, to make no distinction between Catholicism and clericalism. In republican circles, this attitude found expression in the Second Empire republican newspapers *Le Siècle* and *L'Avenir national,* and on a more literary level in Jules Michelet's republican classics. The second category, occasionally anti-Voltairean, and always consciously un-Voltairean, distrusted the clerical tendencies of Churchmen and their zealous supporters but conscientiously sought to distinguish both in theory and practice between clericalism and Catholicism, "political Catholicism" and "religious Catholicism." Centers of this kind of tempered anticlericalism were the newspaper *Le Temps*, the journal *La Philosophie positive* of Émile Littré, and, finally, the milieu that exercised a formative influence on Simon, the philosophic establishment of the French University.

I

When nineteenth-century Frenchmen used the term *Voltairean* with precision, they referred to a particularly harsh form of irreligion that the positivist Littré described as an "attitude of mocking incredulity toward Christianity." In these pages, we will use the term *Voltairean* in this specific and rather circumscribed sense, although many nineteenth-century Frenchmen were not so careful. Indeed, in the religious polemics of the period, the term was often used in a number of misleading, polemical senses. Thus, Catholics used the term to designate all freethinkers and to underscore what they regarded to be the inherent hypocrisy in their thought; freethinkers, in turn, even when they were not Voltaireans in the strictest sense, accepted the Voltairean label when Voltaire's name was linked to the Enlightenment in general, and to the principle of liberty of conscience in particular. Properly speaking, however, Voltaireans, like the Voltaire of the *Dictionnaire philosophique*, viewed the priest not merely as a representative of ignorance and superstition but also as a "charlatan puffed up with pride, self-interest and pretense." In this vein, nineteenth-century Voltaireans habitually interpreted much of present and past Catholic behavior as that of men more often hypocrites than dupes and looked upon the Church as an instrument of domination in the service of the worldly interests of priestly imposters.[1]

1. Voltaire, "Préjugés," *Dictionnaire philosophique*, edited by René Etiemble (Paris: Garnier, 1967), p. 352. On nineteenth-century Voltair-

The foremost representative of this Voltairean spirit during the Second Empire was the widely read republican newspaper *Le Siècle*, edited by the shrewd and irreverent Léonor Havin. Press laws forbidding "outrage" to a religion recognized by the State and to "public and religious morality" made it a crime to impute religious fraud or imposture to Pope Pius IX, ecclesiastical authorities as a group, or to the founders of the Catholic religion.[2] Although they might attack the Society of Jesus and obscure, deceased clergymen with impunity, Havin and such journalists as Louis Jourdan, Émile de La Bédollière and Eugène Ténot were obliged to work between the lines to get their Voltairean message through to their middle-class readership. Their most dramatic tactic was the popular subscription that they sponsored in 1867 to erect a statue of Voltaire, not merely the Voltaire characterized by "a profound passion, an ardent love for justice and humanity," but the Voltaire of Houdon, the Voltaire of Catholic nightmares, with his famed *rictus*, "his biting irony, his mocking verse, his Gallic laugh." "Voltaire's laugh," Havin asked pointedly, "was there ever a more powerful weapon against stupidity, hypocrisy and lies?"[3] At the same time, *Le Siècle* announced the publication of a new eight-volume popular edition of Voltaire, at a

---

ianism, see Étienne Vacherot, *La Religion*, p. 411; Jean Nourrisson, *Voltaire et le voltairianisme*, pp. 656–57; Pierre Guiral, "Quelques notes sur le retour de faveur de Voltaire sous le Second Empire," *Hommage au Doyen Étienne Gros*; Claude Pichois, "Voltaire devant le XIXᵉ siècle," *L'École*.
    2. Article 1, Law of 25 March 1822, *Bulletin des lois du royaume de France*, No. 514, 14:7 (1822), pp. 249–50; Article 8, Law of 17 May 1819, *Bulletin des lois du royaume de France*, No. 278, 8:7 (1819), pp. 466–67. For the best discussion of this legislation, see Gustave Rousset, *Code général des lois sur la presse*, pp. 161–63, 167–71, 176–77. The term *outrage* never received formal juridical definition. In practice, judges were more likely to convict for outrage if the passages were part of a discussion sarcastic and mocking in tone. In the five cases I have studied, the imputation of fraud or imposture was always an issue. See the *Gazette des tribunaux*, 16 September, 12 October 1855 (Erdan, *La France mystique*); 18 May 1862 (*Le Travail*); 19 August 1865 (*Le Candide*); 28 January 1866 (Proudhon, *Les Évangiles annotés*); also A.N. BB¹⁸ 1657 (see Abbreviations, p. viii).
    3. Léonor Havin, "Souscription pour élever une statue à Voltaire," *Le Siècle*, 25 January 1867. See also Louis Jourdan, "Souscription pour élever une statue à Voltaire," *Le Siècle*, 22 February 1867.

"price fabulously reduced and unprecedented in publishing history"; in this work, edited by La Bédollière and Georges Avenel, the works of Voltaire would be arranged in order of importance, with the *Dictionnaire philosophique,* offering a "Voltairean idea on everything," in the place of honor.

In their discussions of political questions involving the Roman Catholic Church, the journalists of *Le Siècle* were prolific in stratagems designed to communicate the Voltairean idea that the Church was not a spiritual power but a worldly power, existing for worldly ends and run by all too worldly men. The bias was mostly in the day-to-day emphasis of the paper. Although *Le Siècle* formally proclaimed itself "Christian, independent of everyone but God," respectful of sincere religious sentiment in both laymen and priests, such declarations were merely precautionary.[4] About the only good priests or good Christians who appeared in the pages of *Le Siècle* were either heretics or the anonymous parish priest who, caught in the grip of episcopal tyranny, pathetically sent in a few *sous* to the subscription for Voltaire. In this view of the Church, faith, love, charity, and humility were conspicuously lacking. "You are the clergy," Jourdan addressed the bishop of Poitiers, "that is a powerful, rich, influential, learned corporation; you want to dominate body and soul; you want to manage spiritual and temporal goods."[5]

To elaborate on this theme, *Le Siècle* constantly alerted its readers against the clergy's "thirst for domination."[6] When the Church demands liberty, Bédollière warned, do not be deceived—"What they call the liberty of the Church, is the *compelle intrare,* the oppression of everyone who does not agree with them."[7] The refusal of Pope Pius IX to give up the temporal power in the Papal States reveals that the real goal of

4. Louis Jourdan, "Christianisme et Catholicisme," *Le Siècle,* 9 July 1856; Léonor Havin, Eugène Pelletan, "Profession de foi," *Le Siècle,* 27 January 1855.

5. Quoted in Louis Veuillot, "France. Paris, — 2 décembre, 1855," *L'Univers,* 3 December 1855; see also Émile de La Bédollière, "France. Paris, — 18 mai, 1858," *Le Siècle,* 19 May 1858.

6. Eugène Ténot, "France. Paris, — 7 décembre, 1867," *Le Siècle,* 8 December 1867.

7. Émile de La Bédollière, "France. Paris, — 17 janvier, 1867," *Le Siècle,* 18 January 1867.

the Church everywhere is "theocracy"—the "ancien regime of material despotism and intellectual oppression,"[8] a government by priests. The Church's power, like the power of other worldly organizations, rests on wealth. For the reader's edification, *Le Siècle* monitored the varied fund-raising efforts of Churchmen, the "miracle trade," the practice of "*cumul*" among priests, efforts to "grab" fat inheritances, the formation of the budget of the state Direction of Worship.[9] "He's a Machiavelli doubling as a cardinal," commented Jourdan on the ingenious fund-raising schemes of the cardinal-archbishop of Besançon.[10] There are no limits to the Church's thirst for power. It seeks not only to control men's thoughts but also through the confessional to appropriate men's will power. In Rome, Vilbort reminded his readers, where the Pope can get what he really wants everywhere, "the Roman citizen must go to *la confesse* every year. And if he does not hand over his conscience in the confessional," his punishment is prison.[11] The Church wants everything—"mind and conscience," "body and soul"—its aim is to *abrutir* and *abêtir*, to brutalize and stupefy the masses, to rob them of their moral being.[12]

It was not just the emphasis upon the clergy's "thirst for domination" that gave *Le Siècle*'s anticlericalism its particular edge. Treading the line between the legally outrageous and the legally permissible, the newspaper constantly called attention to the possibility of religious fraud, prevarication, charlatanry, hypocrisy, and swindle. In its "Profession of faith," written in response to a query from the Catholic *La Gazette*

8. Eugène Ténot, "France. Paris, — 17 octobre, 1867," *Le Siècle*, 18 October 1867.

9. Pierre Veron, "Le Docteur Tartufe," *Le Siècle*, 18 November 1867; Émile de La Bédollière, "France. Paris, — 14 septembre, 1867," *Le Siècle*, 15 September 1867; Hippolyte Lucas, "Revue bibliographique," *Le Siècle*, 17 January 1864; Louis Jourdan, "Une très bonne année," *Le Siècle*, 7 January 1858.

10. Louis Jourdan, "Un pauvre," *Le Siècle*, 2 August 1867.

11. J. Vilbort, "Les Réformes à Rome," *Le Siècle*, 8 October 1867.

12. Émile de La Bédollière, "France. Paris, — 17 septembre, 1867," *Le Siècle*, 18 September 1867; Louis Jourdan, "*La Morale de l'Église et la morale naturelle*, par M. Boutteville," *Le Siècle*, 20 September 1867; Eugène Ténot, "France. Paris, — 5 décembre, 1867," *Le Siècle*, 6 December 1867; Émile de La Bédollière, "France. Paris, — 19 mai, 1867," *Le Siècle*, 20 May 1867.

de France, Le Siècle utilized a page from Chateaubriand's *Génie du christianisme* to insinuate that the the faith was more a pretext than a reality for the clerical enemy:

> I am not a Christian because of any license to peddle religion: my letters patent is only my baptismal certificate . . . I do not make a career and a commodity of my opinions . . . I am not a sceptic disguised as a Christian who offers religion as a useful bridle for the people. I do not interpret the Gospel for the benefit of despotism, but for that of misfortune.[13]

From the moral point of view, as clerical "lies" and "pious frauds" prove, the "ultracatholics" seem less wedded to the golden rule than to the jesuitical doctrine that "the ends justify the means."[14] The debates over the accreditation of such miracles as La Salette and Lourdes gave the journalists of *Le Siècle* an unparalleled opportunity to dwell on "godly hallucinations," "wretched deceptions," "pious frauds," and "trickeries and ways to make dupes." Miracles like that of La Salette, Jourdan wrote, "always leave me incredulous; there is too much at stake for those who accredit them." As another journalist remarked, "As far as miracles are concerned, we prefer those which, like the laying of the transatlantic cable, have palpable results."[15] Finally, *Le Siècle* was always ready to suggest that most Catholics are only "lukewarm Catholics," and that their faith is "emaciated," "short-winded," more a matter of material convenience than of spiritual conviction.[16] In the work of Voltairean propaganda, *Le Siècle* was seconded by the efforts of the forbidding and irascible veteran of republican journalism, Jean-Alphonse Peyrat (1812–1890).

13. Havin, Pelletan, "Profession de foi," *Le Siècle*, 27 January 1855.

14. Eugène Ténot, "France. Paris, — 8 octobre, 1867," *Le Siècle*, 9 October 1867; Émile de La Bédollière, "Les Hostilités utiles," *Le Siècle*, 24 March 1867; Émile de La Bédollière, "France. Paris, — 14 janvier," *Le Siècle*, 15 January 1858.

15. Émile de La Bédollière, "France. Paris, — 6 septembre," *Le Siècle*, 7 September 1858; Louis Jourdan, "Le Miracle de Lourdes et les spiritualistes," *Le Siècle*, 18 September 1858; Louis Jourdan, "Un Miracle imminent," *Le Siècle*, 27 August 1858; T. N. Benard, "France. Paris, — 30 août, 1858," *Le Siècle*, 31 August 1858.

16. Edmond Texier, "Revue hebdomadaire," *Le Siècle*, 17 November 1867; Eugène Ténot, "France. Paris, — 6 octobre, 1867," *Le Siècle*, 7 October 1867.

Peyrat, who became the editor-in-chief of the Jacobin *L'Avenir national* in 1865 after a long journalistic career at the liberal *La Presse*, supposedly began each new year by reading *Candide*. He was known both for his Voltairean crudity and his vast knowledge of the Enlightenment, the French Revolution, and the history of Christianity. Graceless and humorless in argumentation, he punctuated his political conversations with the phrase, later immortalized by Gambetta, *"Le cléricalisme, voilà l'ennemi!"* Committed to the experimental method, he was as distrustful of the "abstractions" of metaphysics as of the "chimeras" of theology.[17]

For Peyrat, Renan's controversial *Vie de Jésus* (1863), which combined an illusive idealism with the techniques of modern biblical criticism, was a step backwards away from an eighteenth-century tradition that excelled at cutting through "hypotheses, lies, and dreams." In his own *Histoire élémentaire et critique de Jésus* (1864), Peyrat insisted on the historical unreliability of the four Gospels and stressed the number of "frauds, some pious, some pre-meditated," often undetected, which marred the texts.[18] While protesting his admiration for Jesus and his respect for the sincerity of the apostles, Peyrat depicted Jesus as a moral reformer who, driven by a megalomania unsurpassed even by the prophets, compromised a good cause with demagogy. The Galilean died, abandoned by apostles whose lethargy in his defense was only matched by their agility in exploiting for their profit the myths that circulated after the body turned up missing.[19] In his newspaper articles at *La Presse* and at *L'Avenir national*, Peyrat sounded the same Voltairean note as *Le Siècle*. Indeed, when *Le Siècle* announced its subscription for a statue of Voltaire, Peyrat enthusiastically threw his support behind the effort and announced that the spirit of Voltaire would, as the philosophe had prophesied,

---

17. On Peyrat's Voltairianism, see Jules Levallois, "Souvenirs littéraires," *Revue politique et littéraire*, p. 330; Henri Brisson, "Les Idées," Marie Arconati-Visconti Papers, 37:8547, Bib. VC.

For Peyrat's philosophic views, see "Le Discours de M. Favre," *L'Avenir national*, 25 April 1868.

18. Alphonse Peyrat, *Histoire élémentaire et critique de Jésus*, pp. vi–viii, 4, 65, 68–69.

19. Ibid., pp. 159–70, 176–77, 180–81, 320, 332–33.

provide "scissors and files to file the teeth and clip the nails of the monstrous" *infâme.*[20]

Although this republican, journalistic Voltairianism usually rested on rationalistic and scientistic assumptions, for some, like the former Saint-Simonian Jourdan, at *Le Siècle*, the defense of reason retained a certain romantic religiosity. The God of Jesus, who had revealed Himself through the Word, had in modern times, descended into the individual rational conscience; the Spirit that vivified was now in the forces of enlightenment and not in the moribund Church. Such was also the view of the most prominent literary contributor to the current of republican Voltairianism, the historian Jules Michelet. In his course *Les Jésuites* (1844) and his polemical *Du prêtre, de la femme et de la famille* (1845), Michelet inaugurated what one contemporary observer called a "renaissance of Voltairianism."[21] Written at a time when Michelet had broken with the Church to return to his eighteenth-century origins, these attacks focused on the jesuitical spirit that, the historian implied, was an ineradicable and terminal cancer on the Church.[22] In *Du prêtre, de la femme et de la famille*, Michelet described how the quietistic ideas of seventeenth-century churchmen like François de Sales and Miguel de Molinos were synthesized by the Jesuits in a technique of spiritual direction ideally suited to the Society's drive for worldly domination. This spiritual method, in universal use in the confessionals of the nineteenth-century Church, constituted "the vital part of ecclesiastic power."[23] In a text rich in imagery, Michelet described the march of the clerical army, Jesuits, clergy, and laymen, "arrogant machinators with fawning countenances," advancing

20. Alphonse Peyrat, "Voltaire," *L'Avenir national*, 28 January 1867; see also Alphonse Peyrat, "Épitre aux Romains," *L'Avenir national*, 15 October 1867.

21. Émile Saisset, "Renaissance du voltairianisme. *Du prêtre, de la femme et de la famille*, par J. Michelet," *RDM*, n.s., 9 (1 February 1845): 377–408.

22. Jules Michelet, "A monsieur le rédacteur en chef du *Siècle*," *Le Siècle*, 3 February 1845; Jules Michelet to Eugène Noël, 3 August 1854, Jules Michelet, *Lettres inédites à Alfred Dumesnil et à Eugène Noël* (1841–1871), p. 222.

23. Jules Michelet, "Préface de la troisième édition," *Le Prêtre, la femme et la famille*, pp. 323–24.

"sometimes in broad daylight, and more often underground," incomparable "slanderers," patiently spinning their webs to "win a soul, to gain an ascendancy over a certain woman, to get into a certain family."[24] For Michelet, quietism was ideally suited to this task, for it stressed the annihilation of the will, the cultivation of a state of utter passivity in preparation ostensibly for the entrance into the soul of the Holy Spirit. This "theory of somnolence," this "doctrine of torpor," where the person lost the "habit, inclination and power to act," was a "murder machine" that destroyed a person's moral being.[25] More often than not, Michelet insisted, the moral vacuum in this human shell was filled not by the Holy Spirit but by the will of the spiritual director in a process that the historian graphically described as "transhumation."[26] This form of direction, aimed at women, gave the priest entrance into the home, and even into the conjugal bed. That priest who passed you in the street, Michelet warned his readers, specialized in domestic secrets. His humility was a mask, which, behind the back, turned into a fiendish laugh.[27] The carrier of a plague worse than death, the priest was also a threat to *bonnes moeurs* and to the sanctity of the family; he was a mortal peril to society.

During the Second Empire, Michelet supported the Voltairean cause and even spoke of himself as part of the hard core of the Voltairean party.[28] In these years, when he was working on his *Histoire de France* from the Renaissance to the Revolution, he concluded that his *Du prêtre* had not been polemical enough, that he had concentrated on the history of spiritual direction at a "decent moment," while in reality the "learned corruption of casuistry" went back to the Middle Ages.[29] In 1861, at the time of the publication of a new edition of *Du prêtre*, Michelet confided to one of the Goncourts: "We romantics . . . have poeticized, idealized the country curé. We should have always depicted him as ridiculous and filthy. . . .

24. Michelet, *Le Prêtre*, pp. 20, 82, 190, 209.
25. Ibid., pp. 63, 147, 163.
26. Ibid., pp. 248–50.
27. Ibid., p. 218.
28. Eugène Noël, "Variétés. Opinion de Michelet sur Jésus en 1854," *Revue politique et littéraire*, p. 731.
29. Michelet, "Préface," *Le Prêtre*, pp. iv–v.

Look at the great philosophes of the eighteenth century, Voltaire: he always drew a filthy priest."[30] In close touch with Peyrat, for whom he felt "friendship, esteem, and admiration," Michelet published in 1866 in his *Louis XV, 1724–1757* an adulatory portrait of Voltaire as *"le rieur plein de larmes,"* as a man whose mocking wit was not a testimony to his incorrigible frivolity, as Catholics believed, but to his will to act and react in the face of overwhelming stupidity and suffering.[31] Commenting on this work, the editors of *Le Siècle's* edition of Voltaire saluted Michelet as "the first man . . . who sought to demonstrate the present political relevance of almost all Voltaire's works."[32]

In their writings, Michelet, Peyrat, the journalists of *Le Siècle*, and others propagated a Voltairean language and imagery that appealed especially to the instinctive republican distrust of priestly intentions and episcopal pretensions. After 1870, the Voltairean current in republican opinion was transmitted by militant anticlericals like Georges Clémenceau, who sat with the Extreme Left in the Chamber of Deputies, and by Arthur Ranc, one of the more radical followers of Gambetta. With their low estimate of the Church's doctrinal integrity, Voltaireans generally regarded questions of Church, State, and School as questions of political rather than religious liberty. Where the Roman Catholic Church was concerned, such republicans believed, public safety rather than freedom of conscience was the real issue. Inclined to view Catholic belief and practice as interested hypocrisy or unthinking routine, they assumed that firm action against Catholic interests would provoke an initial protest but no sustained, widespread resistance from French Catholics.

II

The Voltairean imagination, peopled with sly and wily clericals preaching not only unconditional acceptance of the dogma

---

30. Edmond de Goncourt and Jules de Goncourt, *Journal*, 1:904.
31. Jules Michelet, *Histoire de France*, 12:183. On Peyrat and Michelet, see Gabriel Monod, "Les Débuts d'Alphonse Peyrat dans la critique historique," *Revue historique*, p. 30. See also Michelet's praise for Peyrat's *Histoire élémentaire* in his *La Bible de l'Humanité*, p. 439.
32. Voltaire, *Oeuvres complètes de Voltaire*, 1:32.

of the Church but also moral surrender to spiritual directors, inspired many republican activists who called for an uncompromising program of laic legislation including separation of Church and State. Their demands encountered opposition, however, not only from the anti-republican Right but also from three republican currents of opinion that maintained a firm distinction between clericalism and a Catholicism perceived as doctrinally authoritarian, but not morally totalitarian. For republicans of this persuasion, Catholicism was first and foremost an unchangeable revealed dogma, defined and preserved by a powerful ecclesiastical hierarchy. They were sometimes apprehensive about the cultural impact of an intellectual authority that, because it did not develop a person's capacity for rational judgment, might, in some cases at least, sap the capacity for individual moral choice; and they worried about the Church's marked predilection for authoritarian forms of government. Yet despite these reservations, they viewed the priest less as a director than as a teacher, and the Church, with its emphasis on free will and personal responsibility, as an imperfect but rudimentary school of moral development. Such men were firmly anticlerical, but they were moderate in temperament and consciously un-Voltairean in their view of Catholicism. The first and perhaps the most important of these currents of opinion was the "positivist republicanism" represented in the press by Littré and his équipe at the semi-monthly journal *La Philosophie positive* (1867–1883), by André Lavertujon, the editor of the prominent liberal newspaper *La Gironde*, and, in parliamentary politics, by the distinguished Ferry.[33] A second republican source of anticlerical moderation was the liberal newspaper *Le Temps,* which was founded in 1861 by the liberal Protestant Auguste Nefftzer and later edited by Adrien Hébrard. A third liberal and republican current, cooling anticlerical enthusiasm, flowed from the upper reaches of the French University, where Victor Cousin had convinced a generation of philosophers like Ernest Bersot, a future direc-

33. The term *positivist republicans* designates nineteenth-century French republicans who, while rejecting the orthodox positivism of the Positivist Society, were nonetheless especially influenced not only by Comte's epistemology, but by his historical and social theories. See Philip A. Bertocci, "Positivism, French Republicanism and the Politics of Religion, 1848–1883," *Third Republic/Troisième République.*

tor of the *École normale*, Paul Janet, a future Professor of the History of Philosophy at the Sorbonne, and Jules Simon that free thought was not incompatible with respect for Catholicism and that there were ample grounds for peaceful coexistence of School and Church in a liberal nineteenth-century society.

"Positivist republicanism" was especially important in the history of republican anticlericalism because two representatives of this particular strain of Comtist thought, Ferry and Littré, occupied influential positions in the republican movement in the early Third Republic. Littré, the author of *Conservation, révolution et positivisme* (1852), the principal liberal popularization of Comte's views, became in the 1870s one of the foremost theoreticians of an empirical and gradualist republicanism, as hostile to the radicalism of the Extreme Left as to the conservatism of the clerico-monarchist Right. Ferry was not only an important leader of the Republican Left, one of the two most important republican parliamentary groups, but also the minister of public instruction who, between 1879 and 1883, shaped the various republican proposals for educational reform into that laic program that bears both his name and the mark of his positivist spirit.

For Littré, Ferry, and other positivist republicans, positivism meant not only a scientistic theory of knowledge but also a philosophy of history that combined a theory of cultural development with a particular set of historical preferences. Despite Comte's interest in the sociology of knowledge, he and his school always insisted on the ultimate priority of ideas in the historical process. Thus Comte's theory of progress, the famous Law of the Three Stages, a description of the development of human consciousness through three "states [or stages] of intelligence"—the theological, the metaphysical, and the positive—constitutes the motor force in his explanation of political, economic, and social evolution.

In this view, each of the three stages represents a "particular understanding of the world."[34] Feeling dominates the theological mentality, which takes into account only a small portion of the data about the external world suggested through the operations of the intellect or the will. The theological outlook, best exemplified by Roman Catholicism, interprets nature and

34. Frank Manuel, *The Prophets of Paris*, pp. 276–77.

society in terms of "spontaneous fictions admitting of no proof." In politics, the logical corollary of this state of mind is monarchy in which the king acts as a representative of divine power. The metaphysical mentality, ideally suited to exposing the limitations of the theological, regulates the transition to the positive. Intellect rather than feeling dominates this outlook, best represented by Voltaire and eighteenth-century philosophy. In this stage, men no longer explain the world in terms of the arbitrary behavior of supernatural power but in terms of the regular movement of "personified abstractions or entities"—through a divine first principle, or through abstract entities like matter, spirit, or nature. In politics, the logical corollary of this outlook is the revolutionary republic and the "Declaration of the Rights of Man and of Citizen." The positive mentality rejects the "unverifiable entities" of both theology and metaphysics. It knows only phenomena as they impinge upon consciousness and the laws that describe the relations between phenomena. In the positive stage, Comte anticipated that man might achieve, on the basis of thought and feeling, the kind of intellectual and moral consensus that was, in its time, the glory of medieval Catholicism. On the basis of this emerging consensus, positivist republicans believed it was possible to construct a new liberal republicanism that, while eschewing revolutionary change, would combine progress and order.

Comte and positivist republicans viewed the chronic oscillation between revolution and reaction that had plagued French society since 1789 with impatience. Eager to inaugurate a new positive and organic period in history, they often viewed the metaphysical mentality as a more serious enemy than the nineteenth-century remains of the theological mentality. France had reached the point, they believed, where a metaphysical, revolutionary republicanism had outlived its usefulness and had become counterproductive, for it frightened a society in need of order as well as liberty, and thereby strengthened the fading forces of theological monarchism. This attitude had important ramifications for the approach that positivist republicans took toward the Church. The Enlightenment and its prodigy, the French Revolution, had proven, they argued, that reason was irrepressible and that the days of the theological spirit were numbered. Voltaire's "écrasez l'infâme" was a war cry that had served humanity well when reason was fighting for its life; in the nineteenth century, however, the cause of reason would be better served by a tolerant indifference that avoided even the semblance of that persecution alone capable of rekindling Catholic fervor.

One of the great weaknesses of the metaphysical outlook, positivist republicans believed, was its fundamental lack of understanding of religion. As the Law of the Three Stages implied, religions reflected the efforts of the human mind, at a particular stage of intellectual development, to construct a general view of man and his world. Roman Catholicism, they conceded, represented a relatively advanced effort to explain the physical and moral worlds and had endowed humanity with a moral code that, while not perfect, was nonetheless admirable. The Voltairean view of religion as the invention of power hungry rulers and scheming priests was superficial and naïve. Only a man of Voltaire's "essential superficiality" could have portrayed a cynical Mohammed in the lines, "*Il faut un nouveau culte, il faut de nouveaux fers, / Il faut un nouveau Dieu pour l'aveugle univers.*"[35]

From this point of view, positivist republicans opposed the Voltairean current in republican ranks. As Littré protested in 1878, positivists and Voltaireans were not to be confused: although Catholics might seem ignorant and backward, positivists did not question their integrity, and avoided "injurious, angry and scornful remarks."[36] In 1867, Littré, who was a member of the commission established by *Le Siècle* to oversee the erection of a statue for Voltaire, published an article that acclaimed the philosophe as a "champion of free thought and human reason" but expressed reserves about the wisdom of choosing, as the Voltaire of nineteenth-century subscribers, Houdon's eighteenth-century Voltaire with its eyes and lips depicting deep and irrepressible laughter. In Bordeaux, Lavertujon, the positivist editor of *La Gironde*, refused to support *Le Siècle*'s subscription on the grounds that the action was religious in character, without any immediate political objec-

---

35. Émile Littré, *Conservation, révolution et positivisme*, p. 124. See also François Pillon, "Voltaire et Rousseau jugés par Auguste Comte," *La Critique philosophique* 8 (25 April, 2 May 1878): 202–8, 209–17.

36. Émile Littré, "Le Centenaire de Voltaire," *La Philosophie positive* 21 (July–August 1878): 93–94, 97.

tive and therefore inappropriate.[37] Ferry avoided anything but
cursory references to Voltaire in his discussions of questions
involving Church and public education and considered the
"frivolous attacks, insults and hatreds," "the sarcastic and
mocking spirit" of eighteenth-century historians of religion
to be superannuated and unscientific.[38]

The reservations of positivist republicans toward Voltairean criticism both set the tone for their discussion of religious
questions and underscored the importance that they attached
to the distinction between Catholicism and clericalism, "religious Catholicism," and "political Catholicism." This discrimi-
nation, coming from a Voltairean, always seemed rhetorical,
since it ran against the Voltairean tendency to reduce the religious to the political. For positivist republicans, however,
political or theocratic Catholicism was a rather late development
in the Church; only toward the end of the Middle Ages,
Comte had written, did the Church succumb to the temptation
to resort to the temporal power in order to retain its hold over
an increasingly restless flock. The symbol of this "theocratic
degeneration" was the Society of Jesus, the Church's militia,
created to use political force to repress Protestant spirituality.
In the nineteenth century, the Jesuits, with their allies among
the secular and regular clergy, and among Catholic laymen,
were the soul of the Catholic or Clerical party, a party devoid
of all moral scruples and intent upon bending the whole human race to its will. Religious Catholicism, on the other hand,
was the creed of the great mass of French Catholics, many of
them anticlerical, who wanted both the Republic and a chance
to practice their religion in private. These "universal suffrage
Catholics," as Littré called them, were less enemies to oppose
than brothers to convert and posed no threat to the republican
form of government. As for the secular clergy, the country
curé—the true French clergy—they were for the most part
admirable moral magistrates, working with an ethical doctrine that taught brotherly love, if not civic awareness. When

37. Ch. d'Henriet, "La Statue de Voltaire," *La Philosophie positive*
1 (May–June 1867): 371, 376, 380–83; André Lavertujon, "Bordeaux, 26
janvier. . . ," *La Gironde*, 27 January 1867; André Lavertujon, "Bordeaux,
27 janvier. . . ," *La Gironde*, 28 January 1867.
38. Jules Ferry, Senate, 11 December 1879, Ferry, *Discours et opinions
de Jules Ferry*, 3:237, 240.

the theocratic influences in the Church were brought under control, the weight of the priests would fall on the side of the established republican order.

Le Temps, destined to become a bastion of republican moderation under the Third Republic, was founded in 1861 by Auguste Nefftzer, a veteran journalist who had served as Émile de Girardin's right-hand man at La Presse. Liberal rather than democratic, Nefftzer's newspaper appealed especially to the Protestant element in the haute bourgeoisie, and in its strong defense of the principle of liberty of conscience it expressed the spiritual concerns of a Protestant minority in a country where Catholicism was all but an official State religion.[39] The Alsatian Nefftzer was a former student at the Protestant Theological Faculty of Strasbourg, and a life-long admirer and student of the new German biblical criticism, especially that of the Young Hegelian Ferdinand Christian Baur and of the Tübingen School. In its efforts to familiarize the general reader with a Christianity that denied the divinity of Jesus, La Temps reflected his liberal Protestant concerns.

In certain respects, liberal Protestantism and positivist republicanism were natural allies, and it is no surprise that Nefftzer should have appreciated the talent and political acumen of the young Ferry, who wrote regularly for Le Temps from 1865 to 1869. Both schools interpreted the theological, metaphysical, and scientific outlooks as historical forms of human consciousness. For Nefftzer, there was no conflict between science and Christianity; every effort to know the truth about the world, "every sincere expression of the human spirit has a deeply religious and Christian character."[40] Christianity itself, until the establishment of a hierarchy aimed at fixing an unchangeable orthodoxy, had been the work of the spirit— of an open-ended debate about the significance of Jesus. Catholicism had succeeded for a time in erecting a spiritual dictatorship, in imposing the authority of the priest between man and his God, but the Reformation had reopened the way for man's progressive enlightenment. Thus Nefftzer joined his historically minded positivist friends in their confidence that the scientific spirit was irrepressible. Since free inquiry was its

39. Jacques Chastenet, Cent ans de République, 1:369–70; Auguste Nefftzer, "Programme," Le Temps, 25 April 1861.
40. Auguste Nefftzer, Le Temps, 3 December 1861.

principle, freethinkers were bound to guarantee freedom to opposing views; but such a position was also practical, for in an atmosphere of free discussion the scientific outlook would prevail.

Nefftzer also shared with positivist republicans marked reticences toward eighteenth-century religious criticism. In an essay entitled "Christianisme" (1863), and in the pages of *Le Temps*, Nefftzer scrupulously avoided the questions of fraud and material interest that characterized Voltairean treatments of religious subjects.[41] Just as Littré translated Strauss's first *Life of Jesus*, so Nefftzer and a friend translated the second; for both, the work of the great German scholar represented a modern scientific alternative to eighteenth-century biblical criticism.[42] Like Littré, Nefftzer served on the commission established by *Le Siècle* to oversee the erection of Voltaire's statue; but although *Le Temps* endorsed the subscription through its feuilletonist Auguste Villemot, the newspaper buried the issue and did not participate in the polemic developed by *Le Siècle* and *L'Avenir national*.[43] This respect for the integrity of the religious conscience drew also, perhaps, on a Protestant horror of those who would presume to pass judgment on the personal relations of a man with his God.[44]

Like the positivist republicans, then, Nefftzer and *Le Temps* clearly distinguished between clericalism and Catholicism. They directed their political action not against Catholicism but against the "government of priests," the tendency of the Church to attempt to use the secular arm for its religious purposes. During the 1860s, *Le Temps*, in contrast with *L'Avenir national* and *Le Siècle*, was a consistent supporter of the Liberal Union, an electoral alliance of Catholic liberals and republicans in support of "necessary liberties." Voltaireans like

41. Auguste Nefftzer, "Christianisme," *Dictionnaire général de la politique*, ed. Maurice Block, 1:338–45.

42. David Friedrich Strauss, *Vie de Jésus*, trans. Émile Littré, 2 vols. (Paris, 1839); David Friedrich Strauss, *Nouvelle vie de Jésus*, trans. Auguste Nefftzer, 2 vols. (Paris, 1864).

43. Auguste Villemot, "La Comédie contemporaine," *Le Temps*, 3 February 1867.

44. For a sense of Nefftzer's individualism in the relations of man to God, see Auguste Nefftzer to Delphine Nefftzer, 1864, in René Martin, *La Vie d'un grand journaliste, Auguste Nefftzer, fondateur de la "Revue germanique" et du "Temps,"* 1:56–57.

Peyrat opposed such an alliance on grounds of both principle and tactics. Catholics, they argued, had no real commitment to liberty for anyone but themselves, and such an alliance would serve to perpetuate the naiveté about Christian democracy that had so damaged the republican cause under the Second Republic. Still Nefftzer persisted, for he believed that republicans should not underestimate the "elasticity" of the Church; Catholics might well adapt to liberal institutions that respected their rights.[45]

The French University, the lay-teaching corporation created by Napoleon to educate the sons of the middle class, was, as Antoine Prost has noted, a nineteenth-century bulwark of that cautious liberalism associated with the Left Center.[46] In questions involving Church and State, most professors and administrators generally adopted the attitude of studied moderation that Victor Cousin, a philosopher, teacher, and educational politician had first formulated during the July Monarchy in his successful efforts to found French academic philosophy. Cousin's establishment of a strong secondary-school philosophy curriculum for all *baccalauréat* candidates involved the assertion of the rights of the secular reason against forces pressing for an ecclesiastical tutelage. His enterprise had far-reaching implications, for to defend the rights of philosophy was to defend the very principle of the lay University. Cousin, shrewdly assessing the balance of forces in his society, believed that if this program was to succeed, it was imperative not to confuse the defense of the intellectual and corporative autonomy of the University with an aggressive attack upon the Catholic religion. In efforts to reassure Catholic apprehensions, he insisted not only on the University's commitment to freedom of conscience but also sought to inculcate in his philosophy teachers a set of attitudes to guide them in their efforts to distinguish the fine line between defense of the rights of philosophy and disrespect for the Catholic religion. Although all *universitaires* did not adopt these attitudes, it was difficult for most to refuse assent to views that were so well suited to their social and political situation in French society.

45. Martin, *La Vie d'un grand journaliste, Auguste Nefftzer*, 2:192–216, 298–304; Auguste Nefftzer, *Le Temps*, 19 August 1862.

46. Antoine Prost, *Histoire de l'enseignement en France, 1800–1967*, pp. 80–92.

Cousin's conception of the relations between free thought and Catholicism rested on his own "philosophic spiritualism." Few today would agree with Cousin's conviction that he had constructed, on the basis of psychological introspection, a firmer theism and a more solid ethics than the empiricist Locke or the critical Kant thought possible. Yet in his time, Cousin was able to convince a generation of earnest young philosophers, who lacked only intellectual greatness, that his "philosophy of common sense" was the scientific validation of the most basic Christian verities: the existence of God, his providence, the freedom of the will, the immortality of the soul and the existence of a moral law. Although classical philosophy had discovered the various components of this spiritualism, only Christian revelation had, up to now, successfully combined these disparate elements in a single doctrine. With Cousin's "philosophy of the nineteenth century," which pointed to the history of philosophy for confirmation of the findings of the psychological method, philosophic spiritualism had come of age.[47] As far as the fundamental spiritualist verities were concerned, philosophy and Catholicism were, according to Cousin, two different ways of believing a basic set of truths. Philosophy represented the principle of reason and drew its conclusions by deduction from indubitable natural premises; Catholicism represented the principle of authority and arrived at its basic doctrines by acceptance of the revelation handed down by the Church.

From this point of view, Cousin argued that philosophy and religion were not enemies but natural allies. Philosophy was not the servant of religion, yet it was not the master either; both should enjoy a proper independence. Theology needed the habits of intellectual rigor that philosophy cultivated, and a philosophy "which recognized its true nature, its purpose, its scope, and its limits, would never be tempted to impose its methods on theology. It is always bad philosophy and bad theology which quarrel with one another."[48] Reason,

47. Hester Eisenstein, "Victor Cousin and the War on the University of France" (Ph.D. diss.), pp. 21–52; see also "Spiritualisme," *Dictionnaire des sciences philosophiques*, ed. Adolphe Franck, 6:763–64.

48. Victor Cousin, "Préface de la deuxième édition" (1833), *Fragments philosophiques*, 1:37–38.

Cousin believed, could not verify every "truth" that Catholics knew through religion. Cousin urged his philosophers to avoid doctrines like the Trinity, which he considered "beyond" rational justification and to concentrate, in their writing and teaching, on the "irreproachable" spiritualist verities. In effect, such advice amounted to the establishment of a reserved terrain for the Church. As for the respective rights of religion and philosophy in case of a dispute over boundaries, the diplomatic Cousin, with the suavity of a Roman prelate, maintained a discreet silence.

Thus Cousin established the basis for an academic defense of the rights of reason, and the grounds in principle and policy for a respectful stance vis à vis the Catholic religion. Respect, in these circumstances, was a difficult word to define; there were always differences within his philosophic "regiment" on the point at which such discretion became an official hypocrisy. But, as the debate over Voltaire suggests, these disagreements revolved on questions of degree rather than of basic policy.

In Catholic minds, the person of Voltaire linked the principle of free thought not only with irreligious persiflage but also with outrage, according to the nineteenth-century legal definition of the term. Thus, for Cousin, Voltaire was *persona non grata*, who despite his role in the Enlightenment, must be dissociated at all costs from the "philosophy of the nineteenth century." Voltaire, he insisted, was not really a philosopher at all but merely a "rebellious bel esprit," who combined a "slightly superficial common sense" with a dose of Lockean empiricism. Although his intentions were generally good and although he had defended God and liberty, his wit and his "deplorable habit of making fun of everything" did him great disservice.[49]

The younger members of Cousin's school, while adopting a much more favorable attitude, nevertheless dissociated themselves from Voltaire's attacks on Christian revelation. Ernest Bersot, with Cousin's portrait in mind, described Voltaire as an apostle of reason and a "fanatic for evidence" who deserved

49. Victor Cousin, "Voltaire philosophe," *Le Constitutionnel*, 16 February 1846. This article reproduced, for the most part, the first two lectures of Cousin's course of 1818–1819 which he republished in *Cours de l'histoire de la philosophie moderne*, vol. 3.

well of philosophy for his "incomparable common sense" and for his defense of the ideas of God, free will, and duty. But Bersot declined to admire Voltaire, the "blind opponent of all revelations," for contemporary philosophers had learned to respect philosophic and religious differences, and especially the religious sentiment.[50] Simon, for his part, steadfastly maintained that the philosophe's defense of the principle of free thought had assured his place in the history of philosophy but readily conceded that Voltaire's attacks on Christianity were not above reproach.[51] And Simon's friend and fellow *normalien*, the philosopher Émile Saisset attacked Michelet's "Voltairean renaissance" that, he feared, would compromise philosophy teachers and the University. Like Bersot, these *universitaires*, given the choice between exposing Tartuffe and enlightening Orgon, would always prefer the latter.[52]

Like other kinds of moderate anticlericals, such *universitaires* clearly distinguished the Church from clericalism. When they thought of the Church, they thought of the Sacred Congregation of the Index that had obliged Galileo and so many others to abjure the findings of intellect; churchmen could be expected to oppose free inquiry and its fruits, the advancement of knowledge. But clericalism, they believed, was not inherent in Catholicism nor in the Church, with the possible exception of the Society of Jesus. When a Catholic layman or priest resorted to political action to impose his religious views on French society, he acted not according to the logic of his faith or of his Church but according to his own misguided passions. In the realm of ethics, moreover, such progressive *universitaires* were especially inclined to view charitably a Catholicism that, with its emphasis on free will, the moral law, the immortal soul, and a remunerative God, would complement secular efforts to lay a foundation in the conscience for republican virtue.

50. Ernest Bersot, "Introduction," *La Philosophie de Voltaire*, pp. viii, xxxii–xxxiii, xl–xliv. See also his *Études sur le XVIIIᵉ siècle*, 2:70. The Voltaire of Bersot, rather than that of Cousin, appears in Franck's semi-official academic reference, *Dictionnaire des sciences philosophiques*, 6:973–86.

51. JS, *La Liberté*, 2:397–98.

52. Eisenstein, "Victor Cousin," pp. 238–47; Ernest Bersot, *La Correspondance de Voltaire*, p. 20.

In a strategy that combined opposition to clerical encroachment with respect for Catholicism, *universitaires* hoped for support from Catholic liberals committed to liberty of conscience.

*   *   *   *   *

Although Simon left teaching in 1851, the politician never superseded the *universitaire*. Throughout his career, Simon's approach to problems of Church, School, and State bore the mark of Cousin, the philosophic mentor who had initiated a generation of *normaliens* in the intricacies of this sort of cultural politics. In the 1860s and 1870s, the republican movement, rebuilt from the ruins of December 1851, sought to reach out toward the center of the French political spectrum, and Simon was well situated, by general culture, temperament, and diplomatic skills to play an important role in this effort. With other anticlerical moderates like Ferry and Nefftzer, who unlike Voltaireans, were particularly sensitive to the rights of Catholic consciences, he sought to construct a republican movement around a strong commitment to the twin principles of philosophic and religious freedom.

Simon ultimately broke with Ferry in 1879 and in subsequent years opposed important aspects of the latter's laic laws. In Simon's view, these laws represented both a personal defeat and a republican rejection of a scrupulous liberalism in the realm of the philosophic and religious conscience. The famous Article 7 sought to nullify the Society of Jesus as a force in French secondary education, to the profit of State-run *lycées*. Moreover, the language of Ferry's legal definition of laicity contained an implicit attack on all representatives of theism, Catholic and philosophical. This definition held that in place of the catechism, French public primary-school children should receive "moral and civic instruction." Although Simon accepted the elimination of the catechism from the curriculum, he wanted French children to be taught their "duties toward God and country." Ferry's refusal to put God in the law, even though he recognized that the vast majority of Frenchmen were spiritualists, convinced Simon that laicity had become a stalking horse for the irreligion of a republican minority. In his opposition to key elements of the laic laws, Simon, consistent with the politics of his whole political career, registered his protest against what he viewed as concessions to the Voltairean elements in the republican movement, who could not or would not distinguish between clericalism and Catholicism.

This chapter, which locates Simon in the nineteenth-century republican anticlerical landscape, has drawn special attention to his sense of the need to apply the principle of liberty of conscience in an even-handed way to freethinkers and believers alike. This liberalism, however, was not so broad and straightforward as Simon would have us believe.[53] Marxist historiography, in its treatment of nineteenth-century liberalism, has amply demonstrated how natural rights philosophy, with its universalistic statement of the rights of private property, served in actual practice the narrower political and social interests of the bourgeoisie. But in the French case at least, historians have given less attention to the way in which the abstract liberal commitment to intellectual and religious liberty was qualified and limited by certain religious and moral presuppositions. In this respect, the example of Simon, a nineteenth-century republican less immediately concerned with economic liberty than with natural religion, social ethics, and liberty of conscience, can be instructive. In this conscientious theist, a narrow professorial high-mindedness, allied with a particular ideal of civilization, worked to shape and limit the abstract commitment to liberty of conscience. For the man who opposed the Ferry Laws in the name of "God, Country, Liberty," duty to a higher being, a self-assured sense of social differentiation, and a strenuous economic liberalism were inextricably intertwined in a single cultural vision. To describe the development of this complex of attitudes, in the context of the republican debates over the politics of culture, is the object of this book.

53. For a semi-official portrait, see Léon Séché's apologetic *Jules Simon; sa vie et son oeuvre.*

CHAPTER III

THE MAKING OF A PHILOSOPHER:
A QUIET CRISE DE CONSCIENCE

François-Jules Simon-Suisse was born at Lorient (Morbihan) on 27 December 1814 into a middle-class family that was Catholic and Breton on the mother's side. But for his father's liberal predilections, the intellectually precocious Jules, with an unusual interest in spiritual problems, might easily have followed the example of his sister Hermione-Françoise and entered the service of the Church.[1] Unlike many of the peasant youths who were his classmates at the Royal College of Vannes, Simon would put his secondary education to secular not priestly ends.[2] The *baccalauréat* would open the way to the

1. Léon Séché, *Jules Simon; sa vie et son oeuvre*, pp. 3–4.
   Simon's father, Alexandre Simon-Suisse (1775–1843), a cloth merchant, was born in Loudrefin (Meurthe) and settled in Lorient after the Revolution. When he married Marguerite-Vincente Fontaine (1787?–1845) in 1802, he gave up his Protestant affiliation and converted to Catholicism. Many of Jules Simon's contemporaries, including, of course, Édouard Drumont, believed that Alexandre Simon-Suisse was Jewish. This opinion has until recently rested mainly on various appreciations of Jules Simon's physiognomy. New research has indicated that Alexandre Simon-Suisse had close relations with Jewish merchants in Morbihan, but has not proven that he was himself Jewish. Jules Simon never wrote anything about his father's religious or racial origins. But in a review of Drumont's *La France juive*, published in *Le Temps* on 17 April 1890, he did reveal that he did not consider himself Jewish. Sources: Jean-Louis Debauve, "Les Origines de Jules Simon," *Bulletin mensuel de la Société polymathique du Morbihan, 1957*, pp. 111–18; Maxime Du Camp, "Les Académiciens de mon temps," Maxime Du Camp Papers, 30, folio #388; Léon Séché, "Les 'Premières années' de Jules Simon. Souvenirs personnels," *Revue politique et littéraire*, pp. 616–17; JS, "Mon Petit Journal," *Le Temps*, 17 April 1890. On the Christian piety of Simon's mother, see JS, "Le Pelotin de fil," *Les Derniers mémoires des autres*, pp. 120–21; JS, *Premières années*, pp. 115–16.
   2. Claude Langlois, *Un Diocèse breton au début du XIXe siècle*, pp. 308–13.

elite Parisian *École normale supérieure* and to a career as a professor of philosophy. For this particular young man of Catholic background, such a vocational choice would require a profound intellectual and social transformation, which was not really completed until he had passed his thirtieth year. In this process, which is the subject of this chapter, the Catholic became a freethinker, the *normalien* and *universitaire* became the rival of the priest, the provincial Breton became a cosmopolitan Parisian, and François-Jules Simon-Suisse became Jules Simon.

Although the Catholic ambience of Simon's childhood can probably never be adequately reconstructed, the evidence suggests that the young Jules's religious interests were unusually strong. His later, fragmentary reflections on his youth suggest that he spent much of his boyhood in the company of priests whom he regarded not merely as confessors and teachers but as friends. Although he later came to regret the ignorance and to fear the political passions of the clergy, such reservations never overcame his instinctive willingness to believe in the fundamental religious sincerity and basic kindness of French clergymen.[3] At the Royal College of Vannes where, after a family financial disaster, he became a scholarship student in 1829, he resided in a student boarding house, the "pensionnat Daudé," run by a Lazarist father. The faculty of the college included several clerics, including Abbé Ropert, who taught Simon French and Latin. One of his closest friends at the school was Fortuné Frélaut, who later became a priest in the Church of Saint Patern (Vannes) during the Second Empire.[4] In this period, he was on especially close terms with Abbé Moizan, a former member of the refractory clergy, closely involved, if Simon is to be believed, with the Chouans after 1830.[5]

3. See, for example, Simon's remarkable unpublished literary portrait of Félix Dupanloup, bishop of Orleans, written in the spring of 1877, 87 AP 14 VII (see Abbreviations, p. viii).

4. JS, *Premières années*, pp. 86–87; Jean Allanic, "Histoire du Collège de Vannes (suite et fin)," *Annales de Bretagne*. On Fortuné Frélaut, see A.N. F^{19} 3056. Simon wrote a fictionalized account of his relationship with Frélaut in "Le Prêtre," *Revue de famille* (April–June 1892), pp. 1–13, 96–107, 172–200, 289–338.

5. Simon drew several different portraits of his childhood friend Abbé Moisan [sic] — one as curé of Auray in *La Peine de mort* (1869)

The most remarkable evidence of the impact of Catholicism on Simon's imagination is a little handwritten prayer book, entitled *Le Bonheur*, which the young man composed, for the most part, between 1831 and the fall of 1833, his last two years in Brittany. This collection of prayers contained the basic elements of his Catholic faith and expressed his particular interest in the Catholic promise of redemption and his feeling for religious experience. Throughout these writings, the Roman Catholic Church appears as the sacred interpreter of God's will on earth. Indeed, God speaks "through the voice of the priest"; the sacrament of the Eucharist is the most august, sacred, and "terrifying of all the gifts God bestowed on man, because of the prodigious love which is its source."[6] At some moments, only the belief in Christ the Redeemer can give the awe-stricken Simon the courage to contemplate God's fearsome omnipotence. "Here stands the dread altar where the mystery will take place . . . Almighty Lord! How terrified I would be of Your immensity if I were not aware of Your love."[7] At other moments, the young Simon mystically sings of a God who descends into the soul to fortify and purify.[8] When Simon left Brittany for Paris in the fall of 1833, his faith consisted not merely of a simple Catholic piety but of a rich complex of emotions associated with ecclesiastical ritual and the actions of archangels, seraphim, saints, and martyrs.[9]

At the *École normale*, Simon began an intellectual and religious evolution that led to his break with Catholicism, and some time later, to his publication of *La Religion naturelle* (1856). The written record does not enable one to delineate the progressive stages of this evolution with any great precision

---

and another as the *desservant* of Saint-Jean Brévélay in *Premières années*. I find no evidence that Moizan held either of these posts, but in 1828, he held a succursal at nearby Plumelec (Morbihan). See *Étrennes morbihanaises pour l'an 1828* (Vannes: Lamarzelle, 1828), p. 40; JS, Montpellier, to Mme. Jules Simon, 4 October [1869], 87 AP 8.

6. JS, "Le Chant d'amour," p. 189, "Prière que l'on peut faire le matin pour demander à Dieu de profiter dignement des grâces de l'eucharistie," *Le Bonheur*, p. 196, 87 AP 21.

7. JS, "Prières de la messe pour le jour de la communion," *Le Bonheur*, p. 197, 87 AP 21.

8. JS, "Le Chant d'amour," pp. 181–82, 192, "Prières de la messe pour le jour de la communion," pp. 199, 202, *Le Bonheur*, 87 AP 21.

9. JS, "Le Chant d'amour," *Le Bonheur*, p. 187, 87 AP 21.

or certainty, nor does it reflect the hesitations, the retraced steps, the ambivalences, and the outright contradictions that most men experience when they are working out their most difficult personal problems. In the analysis of this process, it is difficult to separate the logic of ideas from the other, nonintellectual factors under the pressure of which Simon moved almost imperceptibly away from his childhood faith. It is clear, however, that the final break, when it came, in the mid-1840s, did not involve the kind of uncontrollable inner turmoil that an abrupt and sensational rupture would have almost certainly provoked. And the training that Cousin offered to his prospective professors of philosophy at the *École normale* provided an institutional framework that offered both sure guidance and professional incentives for conscientious, talented, and ambitious young men detaching themselves from a tenacious Catholic past. Simon, it seems, ceased to practice his childhood faith when he perceived that Catholicism had become merely a form through which he expressed his adherence to the basic elements of a natural religion that philosophic spiritualism, he believed, had definitively established. He broke with the faith at a time when Catholic attacks on the University were calling into question not only the legitimacy of free thought but also the raison d'être of his chosen profession—academic philosophy.

In contrast with the experience of many republicans, the feeling of an opposition between a political and religious principle does not seem to have been paramount in Simon's loss of that faith. Indeed, in the months after the revolution of 1830, Simon combated friends who sympathized with the Chouan resistance to the government of July. As he wrote to his companion Frélaut, they were mistaken in their belief that the Christian religion required them to reject principles of moderation and peace, in favor of civil war.[10] In Simon's home, an orthodox Catholicism coexisted with a liberal antipathy to the divine right politics of Charles X. As a result, the ideas of the philosopher Cousin, who was a dominant influence at the *École normale*, naturally appealed to Simon. From the time of the Restoration, Cousin had been arguing that representative government, while incompatible with systematic repression of

10. JS, Vannes, to Fortuné Frélaut, 28 December 1831, 87 AP 8 VI.

free inquiry, relied, more than other political regimes, on the moral stature of the governed. Philosophy and Catholicism, he believed, were called to collaborate in upholding the great moral truths necessary to the foundation of a free society.[11] For Simon, liberty should never become a license to violate the moral law. So long as the Church's ethical system was based on the fraternal "love thy neighbor as thyself," there could be no acute antinomy between Catholicism and republican politics.[12]

The real inner conflict, for him, was not between two political principles, a Catholicism viewed as inherently monarchical and a free thought deemed essentially republican, but between two competing cognitive principles—revelation and natural reason. Although a philosopher might, for philosophic reasons be a faithful Catholic, philosophy and religion did recognize different authorities—and the Church required the philosopher to accept on faith mysteries that reason could not verify. To choose between the two authorities was for Simon, above all, to commit himself to a particular mode of life. From 1833, when he began studying philosophy in earnest, until the mid-1840s, when he had established himself both as a scholar and professor of philosophy at the Sorbonne, Simon was gradually finding his identity as a philosopher—as one who derived his moral and material sustenance from what reason rather than religious authority might tell men of human destiny.

I

The process by which Simon gave up his Catholic faith divides into two related but distinguishable periods. In the first, which extends from the time of his entrance to the *École normale* in 1833, through his first years as Cousin's *suppléant* in the Chair of the History of Philosophy at the Sorbonne in 1839–1841, Simon served a kind of philosophic novitiate. In

11. Victor Cousin, *Cours, 1819–20*, 2:381–82, cited in Hester Eisenstein, "Victor Cousin and the War on the University of France" (Ph.D. diss.), p. 23.

12. In his writings of the 1840s, Simon frequently expressed his admiration for Christian ethics. See his praise of this "pure and totally divine ethics" in "Introduction," *Oeuvres de Malebranche*, 1:xx–xxi. See also "*Essai d'un traité complet de philosophie du point de vue du Catholicisme et du progrès*, par M. Buchez," *RDM* 26 (15 May 1841): 602.

this time of trial, the young phliosophy student, at Cousin's urging, concentrated on acquiring a mastery of fundamental spiritualist concepts and avoided direct confrontation with those points of Catholic doctrine that posed the most difficult problems for an advocate of Cousin's philosophy. In this period, Simon was not a Catholic philosopher but rather a philosophy student and a Catholic. In the second period, which extends from the beginning of the Catholic war on the University in the spring of 1841 through the remaining years of the July Monarchy, Simon, supported by a new-found sense of philosophic mission, marked his distance from Catholicism, its doctrines, and its clergy.

Simon's initial exposure to the *École normale* was profoundly unsettling, although the young man somehow found the resources to maintain a high level of academic achievement. The third of fifteen students admitted to the *École* in 1833, he ended the year second in the general ranking for his class. "A man whose mind and character are already very much formed," noted the director of the *École*, Joseph-Daniel Guigniaut. "Moreover, he has a mind which is perhaps more agile than strong. His work and his conduct have been exemplary." In the following two years, the young *normalien* was ranked first in the section of philosophy, ahead of Émile Saisset and Alfred Lorquet.[13] Yet Simon's letters, written to his Breton friends, acutely expressed his bewilderment and anguish in an *École normale* leagues, and perhaps even a century removed from his native Brittany. "Never was St. John more alone in the desert than I am in Paris," the lonely *normalien* wrote back to his friend Gabriel Gallerand.[14]

In this desert, however, Simon was to find little reinforcement for the religious vision of his adolescence. This is not to say that all of the young man's problems may be traced to religious turmoil. Some of his problems were quite mundane. The young Breton suddenly thrown into competition with students from the famous Parisian *Lycée Louis-le-Grand* naturally suffered from academic anxieties.[15] Sickness and a light case of

13. Director's Reports (1833/1834–1835/1836), Archives de I,École normale supérieure.
14. JS, Paris, to Gabriel Gallerand, 27 November 1833, 87 AP 8 VII.
15. JS, Paris, to Gallerand, 13 October 1833, 3 August 1834, 87 AP 8 VII.

smallpox forced him to bed on at least two occasions.[16] The provincial had to become more worldly; moral scruples followed in the wake of operas and balls.[17] And there was Simon's temperament, readily inclined to melancholia, sensitive to the slightest innuendo—all too ready to believe that his teachers bore a grudge against him and that his classmates were plotting his imminent downfall.[18]

A primary factor in this loneliness, however, was the difficulty Simon experienced in acclimating himself to the sophisticated, secular atmosphere of an *École normale* dominated by the energy, the eloquence, and the insights of Cousin. Although Simon was not to study formally with him until later, his teachers were all disciples of Cousin, and the master himself enjoyed frequent informal contacts with the students, especially during their recreation hour. Even after relations between Simon and Cousin had cooled, Simon could never deny Cousin's gifts as a teacher:

> To appreciate Cousin, one must envisage him in his study, *tête-à-tête* with a bright *normalien* . . . at one moment amusing, at another grave, . . . passing in review the living and the dead, men and women, men of letters and statesmen, disseminating ideas, improvising outlines or systems, spilling out the treasures of his imagination, and finding instinctively those turns of phrase which make the fortune of a writer. One departed transformed. An hour with him was worth a whole year of study. . . . Cousin was a *maître*.[19]

Although Cousin vaunted the religious "orthodoxy" of his philosophic spiritualism, a young believer like Simon was startled by how much of the Catholic doctrine the master did not even pretend to explain. Nor was he reassured by the philosophic confidence of Cousin, who, especially in conversations with his students, urbanely talked as if there really could be no alternative to free thought for members of the

16. JS, Paris, to Gallerand, 7 December 1833, 24 July 1834, 87 AP 8 VII.
17. JS, Paris, to Gallerand, 8–12 February 1834, 87 AP 8 VII.
18. JS, Paris, to Gallerand, 8–12 February, 24 July, 3 August 1834, 87 AP 8 VII.
19. JS, "Variétés. Victor Cousin et son régiment," *Le Journal des débats*, 23 November 1886.

French intellectual and cultural elite. Cousin was a living example, both compelling and disconcerting, of the way of philosophy.[20]

As a response to a growing sense of religious and social insecurity, Simon sought in vain for friends who could take the place of his Breton companions, Frélaut and Gallerand. A simple Catholicism was not enough in such a liaison; as he wrote Gallerand of Madol, the student with whom he seems to have been closest:

> Madol is an exception, no doubt, but I cannot rest my head upon that breast, and yet God knows he has a very good heart; but he goes in too much for the sciences, for a thousand things. I should like someone who wanted to live with God and remained distant from everything else; I know well that only the two of us will do that together.[21]

At the same time, Simon began to experience intermittent attacks of uncontrollable religious anxiety. As he recalled a few months later:

> I had some moments which frighten me when I think of them. Here is what I did. I went to the little prayer space which is at the furthermost part of the dormitory, down below. I went there without being able either to pray or to cry, to do anything. I sat myself down there, and then, since it was peaceful, since there was no one there, since there was a crucifix and a tabernacle, at the end of one hour I found myself praying, Gallerand. Yes, I assure you that not one time did I go away from there as unhappy as I had been when I came.[22]

The struggle to secure his faith and to maintain a close human tie with Gallerand were soon intertwined in Simon's mind. In late November, he wrote his friend:

> You should write to me. . . . I shall read your letters as I leave Notre Dame de Paris. For it is there that I find the only being

20. Victor Cousin, "Préface de la deuxième édition," *Fragments philosophiques*, 2:37.
21. JS, Paris, to Gallerand, 8–12 February 1834, 87 AP 8 VII.
22. JS, Paris, to Gallerand, 20 March 1834, 87 AP 8 VII.

with whom I have any conversations. I mean . . . only there
do I find something which is in harmony with the vague, great
and sweet thoughts which fill my heart.[23]

For the remainder of the academic year, Simon continued to
complain of a religious malaise punctuated by crises; in early
February, efforts to encourage Gallerand by advising him to
trust in God and to find solace in their mutual friendship soon
turned to melancholic visions of life as a prolonged death
agony. "I would like to be able to pray for you, my dear friend,"
he said and added:

It is still the best thing to do, and God knows that I do
it when I pray for myself; but exhort me to live a little with
God, for the truth is that no matter how great a desire I have
had for the last few months to belong to God, all kinds of
bad tendencies, sloth, shame, I no longer know what, have
restrained me as they would a true coward. . . . I have been
very unhappy off and on, for a long time. Just think that at
Rennes I slept away a whole year, my mind, my heart, all of
me; as soon as I found myself absolutely alone, I woke up
suddenly and since that day, whenever I think I am not yet
perfectly established in a faith, I experience anxiety and the
flutter of the most inexpressible hope. The poor friend that I
have here found me once in a kind of delirium which ended
only when I was able to cry; and I believe that it is a good
many years since I have shed a single tear. My Lord, my Lord!
I can no longer understand how we can forget that we must
come from, and go somewhere; I well believe that this thought
will never leave me again. . . . At least if we were together,
and if you had a full confidence in me, we would tell each
other all that we had in our hearts, we would go to pray
to the good Lord together, and I would not have these
redoubtable crises like the one the other day. . . . For me,
it is solitude which is the cause, for you know that I would
feel less alone with no one than with sixty indifferent
people. . . . You see, we shall have nothing more to reproach
ourselves for, we shall have lived as good men, and God shall
be a third friend who will wait for us on the other side of the

23. JS, Paris, to Gallerand, 27 November 1833, 87 AP 8 VII.

42/Jules Simon

tomb. It is now ten o'clock; I go to bed thinking of God, of virtue and of you. These are three ideas which do not leave me.[24]

Afflicted by this strange barrenness,[25] uncertain at moments whether the world makes any sense,[26] barely believing in God,[27] a mournful Simon concluded the academic year on a low note: "This Paris is killing me."[28]

Simon's encounter with the world of Cousin, a world in which understanding is believing, inaugurated a debate in Simon's mind between his will to believe and his flagging sense of the possibility of believing. It left him unhappy and uncertain, neither unbelieving nor Catholic, yet with an ardent desire to believe.[29] He was torn between the desire to embrace the Catholic religion and the philosophic need to limit himself to the truths of Rousseau's "Savoyard Vicar."[30]

For the time being, at least, the will to believe overshadowed philosophic reservations. In his search for spiritual guidance, Simon found the believers of proven modernity more suitable than moderns of doubtful faith; his models were not philosophers like Cousin, Jean-Philibert Damiron, or Adolphe Garnier, but Catholics like Henri Lacordaire, Lamennais, and Chateaubriand.[31] After consulting the Lazarist Aladel, the director of his sister's order, the Daughters of Charity, Simon made his first contacts with Lacordaire in January 1834.[32] A former lawyer and unbeliever, who had left the bar to become a Dominican and collaborator of Lamennais, Lacordaire had

24. JS, Paris, to Gallerand, 8–12 February 1834, 87 AP 8 VII.
25. JS to Gallerand, 24 July 1834, 87 AP 8 VII.
26. JS to Gallerand, 18–20 March 1834, 87 AP 8 VII.
27. JS to Gallerand, 3 August 1834, 87 AP 8 VII.
28. JS, Paris, to Gallerand, 5 August 1834, 87 AP 8 VII.
29. In his *conte* "Un Normalien en 1832," *Revue internationale de l'enseignement*, Simon used these words to describe the effects of philosophic study upon him and a fictitious "Jean Lebris" between 1829 and 1835 (pp. 378, 388–89).
30. JS, "Un Normalien en 1832," p. 383.
31. Ibid., pp. 388–89.
32. In "Un Normalien en 1832," Simon said that a certain Anadèle, a Lazarist *procureur général* known as a "fisher of souls," had referred him to Henri Lacordaire. He meant Aladel, director of the *Compagnie des Filles de la Charité*. See JS, "Un Normalien en 1832," p. 389; *Almanach du clergé de France, pour l'année 1834* (Besançon: Gauthier, 1834), p. 371; JS, Paris, to Fortuné Frélaut, 31 December 1833, 87 AP 8 VI.

inaugurated a series of Sunday lectures at the *Collège Stanislas* on 19 January 1834; years later, Simon recalled how he had eagerly listened to these early lectures "in a state of high emotion and even momentary inspiration."[33] Lacordaire was well suited for

> ardent youths who were easily moved, questioning but incredulous, and who wanted to see in Christianity only the poetic side that romanticism had brought to light. Lacordaire himself was a romantic; he possessed, with the exception of incredulity, all the passions of that youth which sat around him. He poured into the cup of Christianity the new wine of modern ideas and feelings. His youthfulness, his sacrifice, made a forceful impression upon his audience. They respected his conviction and admired his artistry, but they felt only vaguely the force of his argument. Indeed, as a person he was more inspirational than imposing. He exhorted rather than demonstrated; he was not a theologian but an apostle.[34]

After the third lecture, Simon wrote to Gallerand: "I am attending Lacordaire's lectures which rather interest me and do not remove my doubts; so I still have no other religion than the Gospel, which means I am Protestant, but that does not fill my heart enough."[35] Yet Lacordaire's example was not without importance in Simon's search for religious reassurance.[36] For a young man in search of religious certainty, Lacordaire would symbolize for several years to come those possibilities for faith that were open even to the modern man; in the fall of 1835, Simon wrote an occasional article for the Catholic *L'Univers religieux*, a newspaper that twice sought Lacordaire as its director.[37] The same promise contained in the person of Lacordaire also attracted him to Lamennais; when Simon, still a nominal Catholic in 1837, saluted Lamennais as "the man who has exerted the most influence upon my ideas and to whom all my sympathies have belonged for a long time,"

33. JS, "Un Normalien en 1832," p. 391.
34. Fontaine [JS], "Célébrités contemporaines: Le R. P. Lacordaire," *Le Journal pour tous*, 11 January 1862.
35. JS, Paris, to Gallerand, 4 February 1834, 87 AP 8 VII.
36. JS, "Un Normalien en 1832," p. 302.
37. JS, Paris, to Frélaut, 20 October 1835, 87 AP 8 VI; Théophile Foisset, *Vie du R. P. Lacordaire*, 1:86.

he was acclaiming not the unbeliever but the liberal Catholic author of *Paroles d'un croyant*.[38] For the same reasons, the author of *Le Génie du Christianisme* captured Simon's admiration; here was a Catholic who in the name of democracy could call the July Monarchy a "gouvernement-sophisme."[39]

Together with the examples of Lacordaire, Lamennais, and Chateaubriand, Simon's family ties and his identification with a Catholic Brittany offered him the material to calm his incessantly vacillating spirit. Throughout his first year at the *École normale*, he paid regular Sunday visits to his sister Hermione at her convent on the rue du Bac, and he maintained an assiduous correspondence with friends in Brittany.[40] An effort to explain Breton customs to his fellow *normaliens* helped him believe in the validity of his feelings, because unexpectedly, they were shared by others. As he wrote to Gallerand, after a lecture that he had given on the customs of rural Brittany:

> I was expecting to be derided because I spoke about religion; to the contrary, three or four came to shake my hand after the lecture, and there was one who was weeping! . . . The applause was not for talent but in sympathy for a thought; ah well, you would not believe how much I was moved by it; and how keenly I realized that I had been mistaken about many people. More than one who had not spoken to me before have since given me occasion to recognize that the future of education is not lost, although, assuredly, I am speaking here of a small number.[41]

Despite his religious crises, the Cathedral of Notre Dame remained a preferred place of meditation and prayer, and continued efforts to trust in God were his intuitive response to his own adversities and to those of his friend.[42] "Write me a letter like your last one," he wrote Gallerand in the aftermath of the insurrection of 1834,

38. JS, Caen, to Félicité R. de Lamennais, 27 April 1837, Dom Henri Quentin, "Autour de Lamennais. Lettres inédites de Béranger, de Jules Simon et de l'abbé Desgenettes," *Revue des sciences religieuses*, p. 5.

39. JS, "Chateaubriand," *Figures et croquis*, pp. 159–61; JS, "*Esquisse d'une philosophie* par M. F. Lamennais," *RDM* 25 (1 February 1841): 564.

40. JS, Paris, to Gallerand, 8–12 February 1834, 87 AP 8 VII.

41. JS, Paris, to Gallerand, 18–20 March 1834, 87 AP 8 VII.

42. JS, Paris, to Gallerand, 4 February, 21 April, 5 August 1834, 87 AP 8 VII.

... filled with your morning views of the Ocean, of the fields, the hay, the straw, the peasants, all that is Breton. . . we others here, what a difference! We have only Greek inside and shouting, bullets, and the "Marseillaise" outside . . . but I have also my good old cathedral that I love always and as much as Quasimodo.[43]

In the course of the following academic year, Simon achieved greater religious tranquility with some aid from his philosophy teacher, Damiron. In June 1835, he wrote to Abbé Frélaut that he was a Catholic.[44] Studying Aristotle night and day with Cousin, writing articles for L'Univers religieux Simon was able to renew this assurance at the beginning of 1836.[45] This combination of Catholic orthodoxy, philosophic predilection, and religious journalism must have been particularly pleasing to Cousin who, at that time, offered the chair of theology at the Sorbonne to Lacordaire.[46]

How had Simon managed to find this new religious equilibrium? Cousin always maintained officially that religion and philosophy were not enemies but natural allies. Like two immortal sisters, both deserved a proper independence. Philosophy, different in nature, purpose, and limits, was neither the servant of religion nor its master. With his constant concern for philosophic public relations, Cousin tirelessly reminded his students that only "bad philosophy" and "bad theology" quarrel and suggested that the two represented different forms of the truth. And he urged the philosophy students and teachers under his direction to concentrate, in their teaching and research, on the irreproachable spiritualist verities and on the history of philosophy. They should leave alone those Catholic mysteries that beyond reason, defied rational understanding. A model student, Simon dutifully followed this advice that aided him immeasurably to both shelter his Catholic orthodoxy and to develop a companionate philosophic spiritualism.[47]

Assigned to the Royal College of Caen after his graduation from the École normale in the summer of 1836, Simon per-

43. JS, Paris, to Gallerand, 6 August 1834, 3 a.m., 87 AP 8 VII.
44. JS, Paris, to Frélaut, 1 June 1835, 87 AP 8 VI.
45. JS, Paris, to Frélaut, 13 January 1836, 87 AP 8 VI.
46. Eisenstein, "Victor Cousin," pp. 101–2.
47. Cousin, "Préface de la deuxième édition," Fragments philosophiques, 1:37–38.

formed his duties in a manner that suggests that he found this modus vivendi between religion and philosophy quite suitable. The situation in Caen was delicate, for Simon's predecessor, Étienne Vacherot, had been involved in a conflict with the moderate headmaster of the school, Abbé Daniel, with the bishop of Caen, and with numerous Catholic families. Simon anticipated that the local seminarians who were obliged to attend his course might cause trouble. As he wrote his friend Frélaut, Simon hoped his Catholicism would stand him in good stead:

> In all the schools where similar things take place, my colleagues are caught between the Catholic leanings of their students and the opposite leanings of their academic superiors. I assure you that I've made my choice; I still believe that it is my reputed Catholicism which has won me this chair in a town known for its orthodoxy.[48]

Despite the new professor's Catholic reputation, the clergy of Caen was taking no chances. Obliged to defend each of his opinions one by one against the "very great ignorance" and "truly inconceivable presumption" of wary priests who even organized a counter teach-in, Simon weathered his first month in the intellectual capital of Normandy. Eventually, his orthodoxy was vindicated. "I have won," the amused young professor wrote to Damiron, "the flattery of the clergy." Before the academic year ended, Simon received accolades from the Catholic newspaper *Le Mémorial du Calvados* and became the first layman ever named to the committee to award the Prize for Religious Instruction. Simon believed that he had been successful because he had been both discreet and Catholic. Mindful of Cousin's dictum about "bad philosophy" and "bad theology," and not yet capable of developing a mature critique of Cousin's philosophy, he gave his students the same instruction he had received at the *École normale*, "without allowing . . . [himself] to change a thing."[49] He had avoided all of the "tick-

48. JS, Uzel, to Frélaut, 26 September 1836, 87 AP 8 VI; see also JS, Caen, to Frélaut, 6 November 1836, 87 AP 8 VI; Charles Pouthas, "Le Collège Royal de Caen sous l'administration de l'abbé Daniel," *Mémoires de l'Académie nationale des sciences, arts et belles-lettres de Caen.*

49. JS, Caen, to Jean-Philibert Damiron, 2 November 1836, Jean-Philibert Damiron Papers.

lish" questions he could and had appealed to "common sense" to settle the unavoidable ones.[50] Thus Simon won his reputation for orthodoxy by teaching what in good conscience he thought philosophically true and by leaving aside possible conflicts not yet sharp enough in his own mind to raise doubts capable of overthrowing his Catholic faith. Such a position was too ambiguous for Antoine Charma, the darling of freethinking Caen and a professor of philosophy at the Faculty of Letters; he interpreted Simon's philosophic uncertainties as mere subservience to the clergy and declared that the young teacher was no philosopher.[51]

Simon seems to have maintained this balance between philosophic prudence, uncertainty, and Catholicism at least until 1839, when Cousin made him his *suppléant* in the Chair of the History of Philosophy at the Sorbonne. In his opening lecture, full of deference for Cousin, Simon announced that through electicism, "experience, reason and [religious] authority" are reconciled—"and the cult of the past and respect for tradition cease to be incompatible with philosophic independence."[52] He dearly hoped that his course on Plato would expand the benefits of a liberal constitution by contributing to the triumph of the religious and philosophic spirit over "indifference and skepticism."[53] He would consider Plato's strengths and weaknesses from a contemporary point of view, "that is, bearing in mind that we are Christians and that we belong to the nineteenth century."[54] Still sympathetic toward Lacordaire's ideas, he spent the Easter holidays of 1840 at a retreat at the Juilly seminary.[55] With his nomination, a few months later, as *professeur agrégé de la faculté* at the Sorbonne, he had arrived at the threshold of a brilliant academic career.[56]

The public professions of Catholic faith that Simon made during the academic year 1839–1840 were the last of which

50. JS, Caen, to Damiron, 26 April, 4 July 1837, Damiron Papers; *Le Mémorial du Calvados*, 27 May 1837.
51. JS, *Premières années*, p. 225.
52. JS, "Discours . . . pour l'ouverture du cours d'histoire de la philosophie, décembre, 1839," *Études sur la théodicée de Platon et d'Aristote*, p. 183.
53. Ibid., p. 185.
54. Ibid., p. 223.
55. JS, "Le P. Captier," *Le Correspondant* 182 (1896): 585.
56. JS, Paris, to Frélaut, 13 June 1840, 87 AP 8 VI.

there is a written record. Up to this point in his career, his studies had probably accentuated his sense of the gravity of the problems that the Catholic doctrines of the Trinity, original sin, and creation ex nihilo posed for spiritualist philosophy. But concentration on the "orthodox" or irreproachable corpus of spiritualist philosophy rather than these difficult questions had deflected his gaze from areas of possible conflict between philosophy and the doctrines of the Church. What was true for the philosophy student was only slightly less true for the professional academic. Despite Cousin's assurances of the compatibility of philosophy and religion, the clergy lost no love on his regiment. Simon's orthodoxy had sheltered him from their attacks in these early years, but the hostility of the clergy to philosophy in general did not fail to shock him. "The clergy of Caen," he wrote Frélaut shortly after his arrival there, "include many honorable people; but although it has received me very well, I cannot help condemning its conduct towards my predecessor. Not only have they denounced him, but they have . . . slandered him without one shadow of reason."[57]

II

If it had not been for the Catholic campaign for liberty of education which began in the spring of 1841, this delicate balance of professional prudence, philosophic restraint, and religious commitment might have endured a few more years. But for the long run, this intellectual equilibrium was inherently unstable. On the personal side, Simon's research on Neoplatonism and the Alexandrian School was already obliging him to face more squarely the "ticklish" kinds of problems that he had been able to avoid during his philosophic novitiate.[58] On the political side, he found it more difficult to shelter himself from Catholic attacks. Catholic demands for the liberty of education promised in the Charter of 1830 sought, among other things, to bring an end to the University's requirement that all

57. JS, Caen, to Frélaut, 6 November 1836, 87 AP 8 VI.
58. Simon wrote his doctoral dissertations on the theodicies of Plato and Aristotle: *Du Commentaire du Proclus sur le Timée de Platon* (Paris: Moquet, 1839); *De Deo Aristotelis, diatribe philosophica* (Paris: Moquet, 1839). In the early 1840s, he pursued certain aspects of this research in a broader *Histoire de l'École d'Alexandrie*.

students who were candidates for the *baccalauréat* attend a public school for the last two years of their secondary education. This campaign, initially directed against the University monopoly, was soon expanded to encompass an attack on the very principle of lay education. Inevitably the philosophy and teaching personnel of Cousin bore the brunt of this onslaught. Not only did philosophy constitute one of the primary subjects taught during this two-year period but also the justification of the lay University rested on the defense of the legitimacy of the natural reason, the philosophic principle par excellence. These criticisms directly affected Simon who, as a close associate of Cousin, was singled out for special denunciation in *L'Univers*.[59] In response to these attacks on the University and upon himself, Simon adopted a sharper tone with the clergy. In February 1843, the man who in 1841 had declined to impugn the probity and the virtues of the Jesuits, despite his distaste for their objectives, was publicly accusing unspecified members of the clergy of willful slander.[60] Reproached by the Catholic friends of his youth, attacked by Nicolas Deschamps in *Le Monopole universitaire destructeur des lois, ou la Charte et la liberté de l'enseignement* (1843), Simon was by April detecting the hand of the clergy everywhere, even in certain difficulties connected with his approaching marriage.[61]

Even before the Catholic campaigns against the University and its official philosophy had reached a significant level, Simon had already achieved in his personal philosophic speculation a greater confidence in the adequacy of the metaphysical and ethical answers that natural reason gave for problems of everyday life. This growing philosophic self-assurance shows in Simon's efforts to sharpen his conception of the respective realms of philosophy and religion. This distinction, which had initially served to protect Simon's faith, now began to turn to the advantage of philosophy. Simon was moving away from that relatively close association of reason and faith suggested

59. *L'Univers*, 31 March 1842.
60. JS, "Philosophes et publicistes contemporains; M. de Bonald," *RDM* 27 (15 August 1841): 525; JS, "État de la philosophie en France," *RDM*, n.s., 1 (1 February 1843): 379.
61. JS, Paris, to Frélaut, 22 June 1846, 87 AP 8 VI; Nicolas Deschamps, *Le Monopole universitaire*, p. 126. For his suspicions of the clergy, see JS to Victor Cousin, 1843, Bib. VC 36/4762.

in Lacordaire's reasonable Christianity; reason, he concluded, should not run the risk of compromising both its freedom and power by allowing Christian orthodoxy to set the parameters of its inquiries. At the *École normale* and in the early years of his career as a teacher, Simon had been content to leave such Catholic doctrines as the Trinity, original sin, and creation ex nihilo, which posed special problems for the understanding, in the half-light of philosophic (although not religious) uncertainty. More recently, however, he began to treat such matters not merely as unresolved problems but as inaccessible to reason. In its spiritualist core, he continued to believe, Catholicism was rationally justifiable. But he increasingly emphasized that the Catholic faith was not answerable before the bar of reason either for the spiritualist verities or for other more debatable matters of doctrine. Ultimately, Catholicism rested on the "absolute submission of reason to authority." Philosophy, by contrast, challenged its devotees to find the courage to live independently, that is, by reason alone.[62]

In the most dramatic example of this new mood, an article written in early 1841 on Lamennais's *Esquisse d'une philosophie*, Simon expresses a growing conviction that the philosopher must distinguish clearly between the conceivable and the inconceivable. Up to now, Simon had limited his own observations on the nature of God to an affirmation of his existence, perfection, and general incomprehensibility. Probably the assertion of God's incomprehensibility had served to shelter Simon's philosophic uncertainties, as well as to express God's incommensurability. Now, however, he broke silence on the doctrine of the Trinity, which Lamennais had tried to translate into a philosophic doctrine in which God was both unity and three "persons"—power, intelligence, and love. The difficulty was the obvious one: how can God be three and one simultaneously? "I am able to conceive of the attributes as three separate entities; I am able to conceive of them as three integral aspects of a single being; to seek an intermediary position between the two conceptions is to depart from the facts of psychology." The Catholic doctrine of the Trinity was clearly a mystery—to defend it philosophically entailed dissolving a formal contradiction: Simon therefore concluded that philoso-

62. JS, "Histoire de l'École d'Alexandrie, par M. Matter," RDM 24 (1 October 1840): 97, 99.

phers could only demonstrate the limitations of reason through vain efforts to "fashion a philosophic truth from what is and must remain a mystery." Without explicitly denying the validity of the Trinity as a religious truth, Simon insisted that the philosopher per se was obliged to reject such an "inconceivable" doctrine.[63] And in the same article, he applied similar reasoning to the doctrine of original sin. As for creation ex nihilo, he suggested, neither theologians nor philosophers had ever shed much light on the problem of creation in general or on the Catholic doctrine in particular; the problem was "insoluble."[64] The escalation of the Catholic attack on the University in 1842, if anything, only hardened Simon's resolve to mark the distance between philosophic findings and revealed doctrine. In an article on Malebranche, Simon suggested that Catholic notions of the Incarnation and the Sacrifice of the Mass did not lend themselves to rational explanation.[65] As long as reason was not, in Simon's eyes, the only judge of truth, such findings did not provide sufficient grounds for breaking with the Church. But they did mark yet another step along the road to honest doubt. As Simon moved toward the view that he could accept only what reason could comprehend, the "inconceivable" would eventually become the "false."

*   *   *   *   *

Simon arrived at this sharp distinction between the findings of natural reason and such Catholic doctrines as the Trinity, original sin, and creation ex nihilo before the outbreak of the Catholic war on the University. In this respect, the heated polemics of the Catholic party did not substantially influence his growth in philosophic self-assurance. At this time, in the spring of 1841, he had probably not yet formally broken in his own mind with the Church. A philosophy teacher by profession, he was still not quite a freethinker. In the next few years, his philosophic confidence continued to grow, stimulated perhaps by a young scholar's indignation at the apparent presumption and ignorance of Catholics who were questioning the validity of the whole philosophy program that Cousin had

63. JS, "Esquisse d'une philosophie par M. F. Lamennais," RDM 25 (1 February 1841): 545–46.

64. Ibid., pp. 554–62.

65. JS, "Introduction," Oeuvres de Malebranche, 1:xviii.

established in the University. Forced to choose between his profession and his Catholic critics, between the University and the Church, Simon soon expanded his claims for the power and scope of philosophy. Without ever completely abandoning the image of philosophy and religion as two immortal sisters, he increasingly treated Catholicism as a relatively unsophisticated and slightly dated, pre-philosophic form of spiritualism. His personal identity as a freethinker was in the making.

Simon's statements between 1841 and 1846 about the relations between philosophy and religion show the signs of this evolution. Until the second half of 1842, Simon did not deviate from the philosophic "good manners" that Cousin had drummed into his students: in method, philosophy and religion were different; the former rested on the principle of free inquiry; the latter on the principle of absolute submission to revealed authority; in results, true philosophy and true religion were harmonious on the fundamental spiritualist verities and were generally complementary rather than antithetical.[66] Cousin's formulas about the prearranged harmony of true philosophy and true religion were of little practical help, however, for men who, presented with a conflict between their philosophic views and Catholic theology, felt compelled to give priority to one method or another. In actual practice, Cousin's young philosophers, confronted with the contrast between well-defined Catholic views and their own tentative philosophic probings, and mindful also of the master's wrath, either took refuge in a discreet silence or settled such questions in favor of the Church. As a result, despite his assertions that philosophy and religion were equally deserving of respect, philosophy was treated in his discussions as the indispensable auxiliary of a mature faith—a faith based on a reasoned decision to accept revelation; a faith that alone could give peace of mind.[67] In his "Introduction" to the edition of Descartes, however, Simon introduced a new distinction between philosophy and religion that amounted to a bolder assertion of the

66. JS, "Essai d'un traité complet de philosophie au point de vue du Catholicisme et du progrès, par M. Buchez," RDM 26 (15 May 1841): 603–4.
67. JS, "Philosophes modernes, Maine de Biran," RDM 28 (15 November 1841): 653; see also JS, "Philosophes et publicistes contemporains, M. de Bonald," RDM 27 (15 August 1841): 542.

rights of philosophy. While stressing that religion "neglects no mind, and puts its doctrines on the lips of small children," he pointed out that philosophy addressed itself exclusively to "cultivated minds." Thus, to some extent at least, philosophy and religion were likely to have a different clientele: religion, which "rests on man's psychological need to submit," suited one type of mind; philosophy, which expressed "the need to judge for oneself, to see with one's own eyes, to depend only upon oneself," suited another.[68] In its context, this distinction between two styles of intellectual life expressed Simon's growing certitude that the way of philosophy was more fitting for a man of the nineteenth century.

Certain nuances in subsequent writings suggest that the distinction between the clientele of philosophy and religion was part of a more general pattern. In his *Histoire de l'École d'Alexandrie*, Simon boldly asserted that "the truth is one or not at all; there is not a philosophical truth and a religious truth; there is a form of the truth which constitutes religion and a form of the truth which constitutes philosophy."[69] The insinuation that the Christian mysteries were more metaphorical than literal, coupled with the distinction between the respective clientele of philosophy and religion, implies that Simon had abandoned his belief that philosophy was a natural auxiliary of religion. Without denying that philosophy could serve the Catholic as it served Aquinas, he now suggested that religion could also serve as an auxiliary of philosophy. Did not Christianity, which presented spiritualist truths in a form suited to the unsophisticated minds of the people, represent a kind of popularized philosophy? Finally, Simon's critical treatment of Peter Abélard, published in early 1846, sums up Simon's discovery of a philosophic identity not only professional but also personal. "Emancipated and triumphant, philosophy no longer wishes to put up with a master," Simon wrote. Abélard, despite the dialectical predilections that have always appealed to philosophers, never thought of claiming for Minerva anything more than a "humble place as servant of theology."[70]

68. JS, "Introduction," *Oeuvres de Descartes*, p. iv; JS, "État de la philosophie en France," *RDM*, n.s., 1 (1 February 1843): 391–93.

69. JS, *Histoire de l'École d'Alexandrie*, 2:687.

70. JS, "Abélard et la philosophie au XIIième siècle," *RDM*, n.s., 13 (1 January 1846): 80.

The exigencies of Simon's situation as a member of Cousin's regiment, as well as his own ambivalent attitudes toward Catholicism, explain why the written record should reveal Simon's loss of faith more through a series of quiet affirmations and pregnant silences than through startling negations. Evidence to establish the precise date when Simon ceased to practice the Catholic religion is unavailable. His writings suggest that the critical period was between mid-1842 and the end of 1845, when the Catholic campaign against the University was at its height. Lingering doubts, political considerations, and perhaps the desire not to disappoint his pious mother, who died in 1845, deterred Simon from the sharp break with the Church that a formal adhesion to natural religion would have entailed. But philosophy, with its proofs of the basic spiritualist verities, was now providing the orientation in life that he had previously drawn from his Catholicism.[71] The specifically "Catholic" became the "inconceivable," the personally irrelevant, and, by indirection, the "false." Simon's reflections of 1846 on the efforts of another Breton to rationalize the corpus of Catholic doctrine might very well sum up his own personal experience:

> These mysteries, these religious dogmas, when attenuated
> and made accessible to reason . . . become nothing other
> than philosophy. . . . What does it matter if you keep the
> poetic envelope, the myth, after explaining the truth it con-
> tains? What importance can this poetic element really have if
> philosophy makes your system live, while religion becomes a
> dead letter?[72]

71. JS, *Premières années*, p. 326.
72. JS, "Abélard et la philosophie au XIIième siècle," *RDM*, n.s., 13 (1 January 1846): 73.

CHAPTER IV

THE MAKING OF A REPUBLICAN: EARLY ENCOUNTERS WITH DEMOCRACY, VOLTAIRIANISM, AND REACTION

Jules Simon was not quite a *républicain de la veille*, a man who belonged to the republican movement before 1848, but he applauded the fall of the July Monarchy and unhesitatingly rallied to the new regime. *La Liberté de penser*, a philosophic journal that Simon had just founded with a number of young philosophers boldly welcomed the advent of the Republic. In the elections of April 1848, Simon was elected to the Constituent Assembly from the Breton department of Côtes-du-Nord; in the Assembly, where he supported the moderate republicanism of the newspaper *Le National*, he distinguished himself as the *rapporteur* of the parliamentary commission that examined the proposed Carnot Law on primary education. Defeated in his attempt to secure election to the Legislative Assembly in 1849, he continued to support the cause of a moderate, un-Voltairean republicanism as a journalist at *Le National*, political analyst at *La Liberté de penser*, and philosophy professor at the *École normale* and the Sorbonne.[1] In reaction to the Bonapartist coup d'etat of 2 December 1851, Simon converted his course at the Sorbonne into a political demonstration. He castigated Louis Napoleon's violation of his oath to protect the Constitution of the Second Republic and declared that in the upcoming plebiscite he would vote no in the name of eternal justice, even though alone—sentiments to be immortalized by his friend Victor Hugo in *Les Châtiments*: "*Et s'il n'en reste qu'un, je serai celui-là.*"[2] Forced from the Uni-

1. Simon never signed his articles for *Le National*. See JS, "Mon Petit Journal," *Le Temps*, 31 December 1890; Alexandre Rey to JS, 21 July 1890, 87 AP 6.
2. The fullest account of this episode is Hippolyte Monin, "La Dernière leçon de Jules Simon en Sorbonne (décembre, 1851)," *La Révolu-*

versity because of his refusal to take the *serment* or oath of allegiance to the Bonapartist government, Simon wrote *Le Devoir* (1854) as a protest against the civic lethargy that, he thought, had led the French middle classes to let their liberties slip into the hands of Caesar.

By family background, Simon sided with the great Revolution and against the "white" Chouans. But his republicanism drew its distinctive character from his philosophic convictions and sense of professional vocation.[3] The Orleanist *juste milieu*, he increasingly came to believe in the 1840s, would not stand firm in the defense of reason or of the lay University. The doctrine of political capacity that underlay the regime's defense of limited suffrage seemed, in effect, to deny the latent rationality of the vast majority of Frenchmen.[4] Despite Cousin's best efforts to work out a modus vivendi with the Church, neither philosophy nor the University had achieved any real autonomy or security. The Republic, on the other hand, Simon and his friends at *La Liberté de penser* believed, would abandon the sterile attempts to find inexistent "middle ways" between divine right and parliamentary democracy, between revelation and reason.[5] In its legislation concerning the relations of Church, State, and School, the Republic would vigorously uphold those fundamental spiritualist verities that would ground republican virtue. *Le Devoir*, with its emphasis on the parallel between Christian and philosophic ethics, expressed Simon's conviction that to defend spiritualist principle was to uphold those qualities of independence of mind, civic awareness, and self-control on which the development of political liberty depended.

---

tion de 1848; see also Léon Séché, *Jules Simon; sa vie et son oeuvre*, pp. 57–59; E. Audray [Lucien-Anatole Prévost-Paradol], "Rentrée des Facultés. Faculté des lettres de Paris," *RIP*, 5 February 1852; Arthur Ranc, *Souvenirs-correspondance, 1831–1908*, pp. 72–77; Victor Hugo, "Ultima verba," *Les Châtiments*, pp. 283–85 (see Abbreviations, p. viii).

3. On the political views of Simon's father, see JS, "Le Pelotin du fil," *Mémoires des autres*, p. 117; JS, *Premières années*, pp. 93, 313–14; JS, "Le Serment," *Nouveaux mémoires des autres*, p. 270.

4. Amédée Jacques [JS], "La Liberté de penser," *LP* 1 (15 December 1847): 3.

5. JS, "De la réforme électorale," *LP* 1 (15 December 1847): 80.

I

Simon was never particularly enamored with the July Monarchy. Between 1833 and 1839, he evolved from a youthful, sentimental republicanism to a reformist acceptance of the regime, only to grow increasingly critical in succeeding years of a Guizot government that seemed insufficiently committed to the defense of the University.

As a young *normalien*, Simon favored that combination of attachment to legal means of political reform, devotion to natural rights, resentment of the political privileges of the *pays légal*, and vague trust in the people that characterized the republicanism of *Le National* and its editor Armand Carrel.[6] He also admired the popular songwriter Béranger, whose republicanism consisted of a constant anticipation of that moment, admittedly far off, when the French people would have matured sufficiently in the exercise of their rights and the performance of their duties to be worthy of the Republic.[7] Within the *École normale* itself, the general oppositional atmosphere and the democratically flavored classes of Jules Michelet, and of Philippe Lebas, the son of a *conventionnel*, reinforced but did not radicalize Simon's republican sympathies. Discouraged by the revolutionary rhetoric of the Society of the Rights of Man and the farcical trial of the "April conspirators" (1834), Simon broke off relations with his republican friends shortly after the passage of the repressive laws of September 1835.[8] Yet his disenchantment was not definitive. Even in 1837, he agreed to approach Lamennais, on behalf of a group of republicans from Loudéac (Côtes-du-Nord) and to offer him a political candidacy.[9]

6. JS, Paris, to Fortuné Frélaut, 1 June 1835, JS, Paris, to Frélaut, 13 January 1836, 87 AP 8 VI; see also JS to Félicité R. de Lamennais, 27 April 1837, Dom Henri Quentin, "Autour de Lamennais. Lettres inédites de Béranger, de Jules Simon et de l'abbé Desgenettes," *Revue des sciences religieuses*, p. 4.

7. JS to Ernest Bersot, n.d., Ernest Bersot Papers, Bibliothèque municipale de Versailles; Ernest Bersot, "Béranger," *Essais de philosophie et de morale*, 2: 315–52.

8. JS, Paris, to Frélaut, 13 January 1836, 87 AP 8 VI.

9. JS to Lamennais, 27 April 1837, Quentin, "Autour de Lamennais," p. 5.

By 1839, however, when his first writings began to appear, Simon was no longer in the republican camp. The Charter of 1830, he publicly declared, provided an adequate framework for the development of French liberties, which would flow, not from the convention-like single assembly desired by republicans but from the existing bicameral system.[10] At the same time, Simon was marking his distance from the socialistically oriented segment of the Extreme Left. Once the campaign against the University had begun in the spring of 1841, Simon became the regular defender of the University in the pages of the *Revue des Deux Mondes*. He directed these articles against both the Catholic and republican critics of the University, or as Cousin called them, the "carlo-demagogic" coalition.[11] Such an alliance, which joined the Clerical party to socialistically inclined republicans like Leroux, Buchez, and Lamennais, was unnatural to the core. Like their jesuitical allies on the Right, Simon believed, these "radicals," a new variety of *"bande noire,"* had sacrificed all doctrinal integrity to the desire to dominate.[12]

In his first encounter with electoral politics in 1846 and 1847, Simon's relations with republicans of all nuances were no warmer.[13] In fact, prior to his decision to run for a seat in the *arrondissement* of Lannion (Côtes-du-Nord) vacated by General Thiard, a deputy of the Extreme Left, few outside of Simon's immediate entourage were sure of where his political

10. JS, "Discours . . . pour l'ouverture du cours d'histoire de la philosophie, décembre, 1839," *Études sur la théodicée de Platon et d'Aristote*, pp. 185, 219–20.

11. Hester Eisenstein, "Victor Cousin and the War on the University of France" (Ph.D. diss.), pp. 139–49.

12. JS, "Du mouvement philosophique en province," *RDM* 30 (1 April 1842): 76, 83; JS, "État de la philosophie en France. Les Radicaux, les éclectiques, et le clergé," *RDM*, n.s., 1 (1 February 1843): 358, 391, 394. For the evolution of the republican *Le National* from support of freedom of education to defense of the "University monopoly" as clerical pressure increased, see Georges Weill, "Les Républicains et l'enseignement sous Louis-Philippe," *Revue internationale de l'enseignement*.

13. For information, but little critical analysis, on Simon's first political campaign, see Charles Le Goffic, "Les Débuts politiques de Jules Simon," *Revue encyclopédique*; Félix Chambon, "Les Correspondants de Victor Cousin. Une Élection en Bretagne en 1847," *L'Amateur d'autographes*; JS, "Le Prêtre," *Revue de famille*, 15 May 1892, pp. 289–98; JS, *Premières années*, pp. 293–338; Auguste Vermorel, *Biographies contemporaines. M. Jules Simon, avec un portrait*, pp. 8–9.

sympathies really lay. Guizot's minister of public instruction, Abel Villemain, had even offered Simon a ministerial candidacy.[14] When he entered the electoral contest, Simon declared clearly that he was "liberal" and "dynastic" and counted upon the support of Charles de Rémusat and Adolphe Thiers for the Left Center, of Odilon Barrot for the Dynastic Left, of Glais-Bizoin of nearby Loudéac for the Extreme Left, and of the retiring incumbent Thiard to rally the whole Left behind his program of electoral and parliamentary reform. His only fears were that the democratic Extreme Left and the Legitimist Right might join forces behind a Catholic democrat like Cormenin, or that the Committee of the Left might choose to "parachute" one of its veteran candidates, Eugène Bethmont, a recently defeated Parisian deputy, into the *arrondissement*.[15]

Simon did not, however, receive the support he had expected. Despite his initial optimism, the Parisian electoral committee of the Left Center withheld its support from him, perhaps out of reluctance to endorse a public employee at a time when the Left was united in its opposition to the influence of *députés fonctionnaires* in the chamber. Moreover, Simon's liberalism was either so suspect or so unknown on the Left that *Le National* labeled Simon a stalking horse for Guizot, and Odilon Barrot and the Committee of the Extreme Left supported the last-minute candidacy of Cormenin, in order to avoid sending a governmental employee to the chamber.[16]

In the absence of solid support from Paris, a dismayed Simon was obliged to deal with three other candidates, "a drunkard, an imbecile [and] a mediocrity," who were challenging his claim to the suffrages of the Left.[17] Despite the efforts of his local electoral committee, and of friends like Rémusat, Prosper

14. JS to Charles de Rémusat [February 1847], JS, *Premières années*, p. 44.

15. JS to Victor Cousin [1847], Bib. VC 36/4769; JS to René Robert, 11 August 1846, 87 AP 18; Goffic, "Les Débuts politiques de Jules Simon," pp. 422–24; for Simon's electoral program, see JS, "A MM. les électeurs de l'arrondissement de Lannion, 20 janvier 1847."

16. JS to Cousin [September 1846], Bib. VC 36/5769; JS to Cousin [February 1847], Bib. VC 36/4770; "Élections de Lannion. Pas de fonctionnaires à la Chambre" (Paris, 1847); Odilon Barrot, Dupont de l'Eure, et al," "Lettres des comités de l'opposition (31 janvier–4 février 1847)" (Paris, 1847); Louis de Cormenin, "A MM. les électeurs de l'arrondissement de Lannion, 14 février 1847" (Paris, 1847).

17. JS to Cousin [September 1846], Bib. VC 36/4769.

Duvergier de Hauranne, and Cousin, Simon failed to achieve a majority on the first ballot. His chances of election on the second ballot evaporated when Yves Tassel, the candidate of the Extreme Left, who had fewer votes than Simon on the first ballot, broke his promise to desist in Simon's favor. Instead, Tassel, profiting from the clergy's bitter hostility to Simon, gained so much support from the "Legitimist and neo-Catholic party," eager to defeat a philosopher and perhaps even a "ministerial," that he won the election.[18]

Judging from his choice of Parisian allies, who were predominantly men of the Left Center, this first campaign had no marked republican character. But in his electoral program, Simon treated electoral reform in a way which suggested that, in the long run, he was probably willing to go much further toward the realization of universal suffrage than his patrons. In his eyes, the reforms should "make a revolution by the people, profitable to the people."[19] Eleven months later, perhaps spurred by his defeat, Simon openly declared his adherence to the principle of popular sovereignty.[20] In a critical article on Duvergier de Hauranne's *De la réforme parlementaire et de la réforme électorale* (1847), he rejected the doctrinaire notion of *capacité* that underlay the political thought of both the premier Guizot and his principal rival Thiers. According to this doctrine, the vote was not a fundamental political right but rather a function performed by the qualified. Duvergier de Hauranne had used the doctrine to argue against Guizot for a limited expansion of the suffrage to include more of the talented and knowledgeable members of the liberal professions. In contrast, Simon insisted that *capacité* was not an appropriate basis for electoral reform. To employ it was to cater to the conservatives' wish to deny the principle of popular sovereignty "and by implication, the revolution of 1830."[21] Scornful of the Liberal political theory of men like Benjamin Constant or Royer-Collard, he believed that the doctrine of *capacité* merely camouflaged the moral poverty of men unable

18. JS to Cousin, 26 February 1847, Bib. VC 36/4771.
19. JS, "A MM. les électeurs de l'arrondissement de Lannion, 20 janvier 1847."
20. JS, *Premières années*, p. 296.
21. JS, "De la réforme électorale," LP 1 (15 December 1847): 83.

or unwilling to accept one of the two possible bases for a political theory—popular sovereignty or divine right. To interpret *capacité* in a sense contrary to the principle of popular sovereignty was to make a travesty of 1830; in this case, "this heroic and terrible revolutionary drama . . . [would appear as] a quarrel between masters in which the nation intervened only to shed its blood."[22] This advocacy of popular sovereignty distinguished Simon from the Left Center, but not so sharply as might appear at first glance. For unlike the Extreme Left, Simon defined popular sovereignty in an especially narrow way. For one thing there was no opposition between the charter and this principle: "The Charter," he wrote, "is the history of the Revolution in a single page."[23] For another, Simon maintained that even under a regime of universal suffrage, the ballot would be withheld from those few deemed unworthy or incapable of exercising their rights.[24] Finally, anticipating the spread of popular education, he accepted progressive rather than immediate realization of this "universal" suffrage.[25] Thus, for Simon, popular sovereignty never implied full and immediate universal manhood suffrage, let alone direct democracy.

These attitudes facilitated Simon's easy transfer of allegiance from the July Monarchy to the Second Republic in February 1848. With minimal embarrassment, Simon justified his shift of political loyalty by asserting that the Republic would defend the same principles for which he had always fought: liberty and the sovereignty of the people. Even under the July Monarchy, he smoothy assured his readers, he had favored popular sovereignty, but "hostile to bloody struggles" and "trusting in the resources offered by the constitution," he had identified himself with the Left Center.[26] The revolution of 1848, however, had demonstrated what he had not previously realized: a Republic capable of respecting the natural rights of the individual was possible in France, and he no longer needed to devote his efforts to reconciling the principle of popular sovereignty with a perpetual and hereditary executive. The moderation of the people during the February Revo-

22. Ibid., p. 84.   23. Ibid., p. 83.
24. Ibid., pp. 85, 87.   25. Ibid., p. 89.
26. JS, "Révolution de 1848. Le Gouvernement provisoire. Les élections. L'Assemblée nationale," *LP* 1 (15 March 1848): 313.

lution had done great service to the republican cause. This conduct had won over men who had considered the Republic unattainable without great bloodshed, and even many who had opposed it on principle. Amidst the general euphoria of late February, Simon concluded that "the Republic itself had no enemies. People hated only the bloody memories associated with its name and which will not return. Everyone has spontaneously understood that liberty no longer needed to disguise and burden itself with the name of monarchy in order to preserve itself."[27]

II

In December 1847, Simon and Jacques, a republican philosophy teacher at the *lycée* of Versailles, founded the monthly *La Liberté de penser, Revue philosophique et littéraire* to defend philosophy and the University against the Church and the Guizot government. This publication, which wits quickly labeled "the journal of the little *cousins*" (gnats), expressed a long-felt conviction, widespread among the younger philosophy teachers, that Cousin's manner of defending philosophy all too frequently ended in the sort of impossible compromises so characteristic of *juste-milieu* government. Yet Simon and some of his collaborators did not reject Cousin's overall goals —an alliance of Church and University in defense of liberty of conscience for freethinkers and Catholics alike and for the defense of the fundamental spiritualist verities. Consequently, Simon was obliged to combat his coeditor Jacques, who with other associates, sought to steer the *Revue* in a Voltairean direction. In this conflict, Simon publicly formulated, for the first time, his own distinctive anti-Voltairean anticlericalism.

"Philosophy has been slandered," Simon announced in the lead article of the new journal, "it must defend itself, its principle has been attacked, it must prove its legitimacy and power." The journal's title, *La Liberté de penser*, he insisted, was not a provocation directed at Catholics but rather a calm assertion of the fundamental rights of philosophy. Expressing the determination of philosophy professors to "fight under their own flag," Simon and his friends were implicitly rejecting some of the restraints that Cousin had imposed upon the regi-

27. Ibid., pp. 314, 325, 334.

ment.[28] In the face of Catholic attacks, Cousin had habitually defended the philosophy and teachings of his professors as irreproachably "orthodox." Such a policy, by seeming to place professional philosophy under the supervision of the bishops, came dangerously close to converting philosophy into mere theology. Simon and other younger philosophers always preferred a prouder and more self-confident defense stressing the legitimacy of philosophic inquiry and rights of the lay University.[29] In accordance with this sense of the needs of philosophy, the editors included in this first number a full article by Ernest Bersot on Voltaire. While Cousin, always eager to disarm the Church, habitually dismissed Voltaire's so-called philosophy as "slightly superficial common sense" and deplored his "habit of making fun of everything," Bersot accorded the philosophe measured praise as an apostle of reason, an accomplished philosopher, and a brilliant polemicist who, despite his excesses, was without peer in his ability to turn ridicule against "fools, hypocrites and fanatics."[30]

To Simon's mind, this firmer line did not imply the abandonment of Cousin's conciliatory policy toward the Church. As his discriminating treatment of French Catholicism suggests, Simon believed that there were ample grounds for a modus vivendi between the University and the Church, philosophers and priests, liberals and Catholics. Catholics, he conceded, were required by doctrine and history to renounce the right of free thought for themselves, but they were not bound to oppose the principle of self-government. Catholic Christianity was based on a "spirit of gentleness and persuasion, not of domination and violence"; the faith did not oblige Catholics to seek an alliance between throne and altar in order to impose their views on unbelievers.[31] In one of his first articles for *La Revue*

28. Jacques [JS], "La Liberté de penser," *LP* 1 (15 December 1847): 1–4; JS, "Une Révolution dans un verre d'eau," *Nouveaux mémoires des autres*, p. 160; Paul Janet, *Victor Cousin et son oeuvre*, pp. 338–39; Georges Weill, *Histoire de l'idée laïque au XIXe siècle*, pp. 107–8.

29. JS, *Victor Cousin*, pp. 182–83.

30. Ernest Bersot, "La Philosophie de Voltaire," *LP* 1 (15 December 1847): 32, 49; Victor Cousin, "Voltaire philosophe," *Le Constitutionnel*, 16 February 1846.

31. [JS], "Bulletin. Vicissitudes de l'Église catholique des deux rites en Pologne et en Russie, traduit de l'allemand par M. de Montalembert," *LP* 1 (15 February 1848): 303. I attribute this article to Simon because

des Deux Mondes, Simon had combated the efforts of the celebrated Legitimist apologist Louis G.-A. de Bonald, to show that Catholicism implied political authoritarianism. He accused Bonald of mistakenly attributing to Catholicism political attitudes that, in fact, were only a personal expression of his own response to a revolution that had overturned his world. Only the trauma of the Revolution, Simon argued, could have driven a man personally so charitable to turn his faith against reason and liberty in politics.[32] Thus Simon extended a welcoming hand to the many Catholics who, he believed, would accept, as part of modern civil life, the principle of liberty of conscience. And he supported Catholic demands for liberty of education, which was promised in the Charter of 1830, with the stipulation that the State regulate that liberty.[33] The clergy should not be either oppressor or oppressed.[34] The natural enemies of *La Liberté de penser,* he thought, were not Catholics nor even the clergy in toto but the Clerical party, that coalition of misguided priests, the Society of Jesus, and laymen like Louis Veuillot and Charles de Montalembert, who hypocritically sought in the name of liberty to restore theocracy in France. Even Catholics, he insinuated, should support this struggle against clericalism, for "without [Veuillot's] *L'Univers religieux,* we would have in France a respected and peaceful Church; we would not have a Clerical party."[35]

Simon's attachment to a firm but respectful attitude toward

in the 1840s he had written an extensive unpublished review of this work, and because he contributed not only signed, but also anonymous and pseudonymous, articles in the hectic early months of *La Liberté de penser.* See JS, "Une Révolution," *Nouveaux mémoires,* pp. 185–186 and also 87 AP 20 II.

32. JS, "Philosophes et publicistes contemporaines, M. de Bonald," *RDM* 27 (15 August 1841): 541.

33. JS, "A MM. les électeurs de l'arrondissement de Lannion, 20 janvier 1847"; Jacques [JS], "La Liberté de penser," *LP* 1 (15 December 1847): 3.

34. JS, "A MM. les électeurs de l'arrondissement de Lannion, 20 janvier 1847."

35. Sarpi [JS], "Cas de conscience d'un philosophe à propos des *Cas de Conscience* de Monseigneur l'évêque de Langres," *LP* 1 (15 January 1848): 124. For evidence of Simon's authorship, see JS, "Une Révolution," *Nouveaux mémoires,* p. 186. For composition of the Clerical party, see [JS], "L'Assemblée nationale," *LP* 4 (15 November 1849): 453; [JS] "L'Assemblée nationale," *LP* 5 (15 March 1850): 310; JS, "L'Université," *LP* 4 (15 November 1849): 536.

the Church was the primary source of tension among the principal collaborators of *La Liberté de penser,* especially after the revolution of 1848 and the clerical reaction drew them more deeply into politics than they had originally anticipated.[36] When the journal was in the planning stages, Simon had asked the militantly anticlerical Edgar Quinet for support, and to dramatize the philosophic vigor of the new publication he dissociated himself from Saisset's attack on Michelet's Voltairean *Du Prêtre, de la femme et de la famille.*[37] But once the *Liberté de penser* was launched, it became apparent that Simon, unlike Jacques, did not share Michelet's uncompromising hostility to the Church. Differences of tone and substance in articles dealing with the relations of Church and State suggest that the two friends had agreed not to allow their differences to interfere with their desire to defend philosophy.[38]

Both Jacques and Simon had their own allies among the collaborators of the *Revue.* Jacques, Émile Deschanel, and Eugène Despois (both young teachers at the *Lycée Louis-le-Grand*), the as yet unknown Ernest Renan and other contributors treated Catholicism with marked disdain and did not hesitate to play, albeit cautiously, on the Voltairean theme of religious hypocrisy. Thus, in an attack on "clerical liberalism," Renan suggested that the recent transformations of priests into democrats were modern miracles—like earlier religious miracles, he implied, these changes were fraudulent. Jacques, in an article on the Catholic revival, called into question the sincerity of modern Catholics: not including the "idlers, hypocrites, and dolts," he asked rhetorically, how many true and honorable Catholics are left? For another writer, the term *jesuitism,* with its connotations of political and religious hypocrisy, epitomized Roman Catholicism. "Neo-Catholics," men who asserted that they were both Catholics and political liberals, were either heretics of liars. Convinced that Catholicism had lost much of its vitality and had become largely a matter of convention, Jacques

36 .This view contradicts Regina Pozzi's Marxist study, "Un Episodio della lotta ideologica in Francia sotto la Seconda Repubblica. *La Liberté de penser* (1847–1850)," *Critica storica,* which argues that the principal cleavage was over the social question.

37. Edgar Quinet to Jules Michelet, 17 August 1847, Mme. Edgar Quinet, *Cinquante ans d'amitié. Michelet-Quinet, 1825–1875,* p. 132.

38. JS, "Amédée Jacques," *Mémorial de l'association amicale des anciens élèves de l'École normale* (Versailles: Cerf & fils, 1877), p. 200.

openly declared the incredulity of the *Revue*, and Deschanel made fun of the Catholic dogma of creation ex nihilo.[39] And irritated by Simon's scruples about his bold biblical criticism, Renan confided to his sister in early 1849, "The further I go, the more I am discovering that this Jules Simon is a shabby man who believes and loves nothing."[40]

On the other side, Simon, Cousin's former secretary Paul Janet, Ernest Bersot, the young Prévost-Paradol, and possibly Gustave Vapereau, a professor at Tours, sought to counterbalance the "exaggerations" of their friends. In one of his monthly political commentaries, in the form of a letter to Jacques, the director of the *Revue*, Simon summed up the differences between them:

> You are a Voltairean, I'm afraid. You will agree that I am not, and never have been. My profound hatred of hypocrisy and intolerance, as well as my love of philosophy and liberty give me the right not to hide my feelings in my discussions with you. For months, I have maintained that one does not have to be a Voltairean to be a passionate defender of philosophy. I am not a Voltairean, and this fact will help you find less strange a proposition which I hazard only while trembling, a proposition which will revolt many of your readers and which you will tolerate only out of deference and friendship for me.[41]

This was nothing new for Jacques; in the early months of the Republic, when they were discussing whether to print Renan's "Du libéralisme clérical," Simon had "so insisted on modera-

39. Ernest Renan, "Du libéralisme clérical," *LP* 1 (15 May 1848): 510–13; Amédée Jacques, "Le Christianisme et le cartésianisme au XVIIIe siècle et la renaissance catholique au XIXe siècle," *LP* 1 (15 February 1848): 249–50; Serrigny, "Du projet de loi sur l'instruction publique," *LP* 4 (15 July 1849): 150; Amédée Jacques, "Lettre à M. Michelet de Berlin, sur le panthéisme et la démocratie," *LP* 5 (15 January 1850): 149; Émile Deschanel, "Les Parents de Tartufe," *LP* 5 (15 December 1849): 15.

40. Ernest Renan, Paris, to Henriette Renan, 24 February 1849, Ernest Renan, *Oeuvres complètes*, 9:1174.

41. [JS], "L'Assemblée nationale," *LP* 4 (15 August 1849): 196–97. These political commentaries, unsigned and entitled "L'Assemblée nationale," could be attributed to Simon on the basis of internal evidence alone. Simon later admitted his authorship, "Une Révolution," *Nouveaux mémoires*, p. 185.

tion in theological questions that their . . . friendship had become strained."[42]

Seen in this context, then, Bersot's article on Voltaire, and an early contribution by Saisset, with their sharp remarks about that philosophe's lack of understanding of religious phenomena, were part of Simon's efforts to moderate Jacques's Voltairean anticlericalism. Another example of the same tendency was the clever Prévost-Paradol's treatment of Michelet's *Du Prêtre, de la femme et de la famille*. Better to praise the work as a classic protest against false religion, Prévost-Paradol passed over the radical critique of modern Catholicism implicit in Michelet's book and clearly distinguished it from Voltairean religious criticism. *Du Prêtre*, the work of a man full of a new faith in liberty and country, he insinuated, exuded the sort of religious sincerity that had marked the lives of Jesus and Mohammed and that had been so misunderstood by the "pitiless skepticism of the eighteenth century."[43] Although hostile to the political hypocrisy of the Clerical party, and especially of the Society of Jesus, Simon and his allies insisted that modern Catholics could support the cause of political liberalism with the same sincerity that marked their religious lives.[44] Thus, while sharing Jacques's distrust of specific "neo-Catholics" like Cormenin and Montalembert, Simon also called his readers' attention to the services of Catholic democrats like Philippe-J.-B. Buchez and Hyacinthe Corne to the Republic.[45] In addition, Simon expressed the faith that the majority of the clergy would serve the Republic faithfully. When Alfred de

42. [JS], "L'Assemblée nationale," LP 1 (15 August 1848): 212.

43. Bersot, "Voltaire," LP 1 (15 December 1847): 62; Émile Saisset, "De l'origine et de la formation du christianisme à l'occasion du livre de M. Newman. . . ," LP 1 (15 March 1848): 337–38; [Prévost-Paradol], "Bulletin," LP 3 (15 May 1849): 588–89. On Prévost-Paradol's authorship, see Pierre Guiral, *Prévost-Paradol; pensée et action d'un libéral sous le Second Empire*, pp. 68–73.

44. In his "M. de Lamartine: Trois mois au pouvoir," LP 3 (15 September 1848) and his "Rapport de la morale et de la politique," LP 3 (15 May 1849), Paul Janet repeated these themes.

45. On Montalembert, see [JS], "L'Assemblée nationale," LP 2 (15 January 1849): 10. On Louis de Cormenin, see [JS], "L'Assemblée nationale," LP 1 (15 June 1848): 8. On Philippe-J.-B. Buchez, see [JS], "L'Assemblée nationale," LP 1 (15 June 1848): 3, and [JS], "L'Assemblée nationale," LP 2 (15 January 1849): 102, note 1. On Hyacinthe Corne, see [JS], "L'Assemblée nationale," LP 2 (15 January 1849): 102, note 1.

Falloux, a declared enemy of the University, became minister of public instruction and worship, Simon attempted to reassure his fellow academics: "We believe that if M. Michelet or M. Edgar Quinet had been named Minister of Worship, the clergy would have served the Republic nonetheless; the University will do likewise."[46] When the Falloux Law of 15 March 1850 gave the Church a dominant position in French public education, Simon treated it more as a threat to the University, than to the Republic itself.[47]

This agreement to differ, resting on the mutual respect of old friends, common identification with the University, and shared ideals, proved to be a viable modus vivendi for a collaboration that survived the turmoil of two and a half years of civil strife in France. The reservoir of tact and self-restraint that sustained this understanding in an atmosphere of increasing religious and social tension was depleted, however, by the spring of 1850. In February, after Montalembert's assertion that "There is no middle ground . . . between socialism and the catechism," Deschanel gave his friend Jacques an article that systematically espoused all of the Voltairean themes that Jacques and his friends had previously been content to insinuate.[48] "Amen," replied the fiery young professor of rhetoric, "we also think that from now on the struggle is between these two principles, and that it can end only in the annihilation of one of them.[49]

Deschanel went further still and argued that Catholicism as a faith was already dead. The Catholicism of most French Catholics was anything but a matter of faith. Some were Catholic because they were too apathetic to protest when the Church counted them as such. Others were Catholics because they loved stained glass, Gothic cathedrals and/or Raphael's virgins, because they were born in certain parts of France like Brittany, or because, like Thiers, they were social conservatives. Others still, as in the case of government employees, were Catholics because they thought that an official religion

46. [JS], "L'Assemblée nationale," LP 2 (15 December 1848): 3.

47. JS, "L'Université," LP 4 (15 November 1849): 534; [JS], "L'Assemblée nationale," LP 4 (15 August 1849): 196.

48. Charles de Montalembert, Assemblée législative, 17 January 1850, Le Moniteur universel, 18 January 1850.

49. Émile Deschanel, "Le Catholicisme et le socialisme," LP 5 (15 February 1850): 214.

went well with an official uniform. As for the Catholic clergy, regular and secular, it was only a political party intent on domination. The "unfaithful trustee of the Catholic religion" that it had "falsified, corrupted, for reasons of ambition and self-interest," this clergy "had long ago lost, more perhaps than other Catholics, the spirit of that Faith which it was supposed to teach." For the clergy, "Catholic religious ceremony" was "a livelihood and an instrument." A few genuine Catholics, high-minded, and "delicate and charitable of heart" did exist, but they owed the purity of their faith to a naiveté that had prevented them from really trying to understand such doctrines as original sin, eternal punishments, redemption, and the divinity of Jesus. Since spiritualist philosophy had established the fundamental verities on an unassailable basis, the faith had become obsolete; Catholicism had become an anachronistic monument, and France was "socialist" without knowing it.[50]

In the controversy that this article provoked, Simon broke with Jacques and *La Liberté de penser*. Although he alluded to social motivations in later explanations of his actions, the context and content of Deschanel's articles suggest that, at the time, Simon felt the issue was as much religious as social.[51] When Deschanel had submitted his essay, Simon had opposed its publication and had induced Jacques to accept a substitute article that he planned to write overnight. The next day, Simon, as promised, produced an essay entitled "L'Éducation," which defended his own theses on the religious question.[52] Jacques, caught between two friends, published both articles without informing Simon, who, when he learned of this fait accompli, accepted it as, after all, a compromise. A few days after these two articles appeared, the minister of public instruction and worship, Marie de Parieu, suspended Deschanel from his functions at *Lycée Louis-le-Grand* for his espousal of socialism and for various attacks on the Catholic religion and clergy.[53]

50. Ibid., pp. 214–18, 223.
51. JS, "Note," *LP* 5 (15 May 1850): 633; Eugène Despois, "La Liberté de penser (1)," *La Libre conscience*, 29 December 1866; JS, "Une Révolution," *Nouveaux mémoires*, pp. 190–96; JS, "Mon Petit Journal," *Le Temps*, 2 March 1890.
52. JS, "Une Révolution," *Nouveaux mémoires*, pp. 190–96.
53. Amédée Jacques, "La République et le suffrage universel," *LP* 5 (15 March 1850): 358. See also in the same issue Émile Deschanel, "Con-

The next month, Jacques, with Simon's acquiescence, came to the support of his friend and published Deschanel's defense against Parieu's charges. But when Jacques and Deschanel insisted on publishing the promised second article, which explained Deschanel's adherence to socialism, Simon withdrew from the journal. In this article, Deschanel argued that socialism by definition involved militant anticlerical policies.

Deschanel associated a religious policy with the negative side of the socialist program. "Negative socialism" involved destroying the "social institutions of the past," the "coalition of the altar, the throne, and the strongbox," which he equated with "Catholicism, the source of all illegitimate authority."[54] In his discussion of "positive socialism," on the other hand, he developed for the most part ideas that he had published as a self-proclaimed socialist in the *Revue* in August 1848.[55] Deschanel's socialism was a typical example of that moderate social interventionism prevalent in 1848 among the republicans of *Le National*.[56] While professing his respect for the family, private property, and private enterprise, Deschanel argued that the State should guarantee work of some kind to every man of good will (*Droit au travail*). It should provide for obligatory, free, and lay education for all French children. It should encourage the establishment of producers' cooperatives by interest-free public loans. Finally, in a new and striking proposal, designed to combat the "feudality of capital," Deschanel advocated an inheritance tax (10 percent in the first year and increasing to 50 percent over an unspecified period).[57] Simon, an early republican critic of the National Workshops and an opponent of the *Droit au travail*, had been willing to tolerate Deschanel's use of the word *socialist* and his defense

---

sidérations exposées devant le conseil académique," p. 320. For an account of Deschanel's problems with the University, see Paul Raphael, "L'Affaire Émile Deschanel," *La Revue*.

54. Émile Deschanel, "Le Catholicisme et le socialisme (2)," LP 5 (15 April 1850): 428, 430.

55. Émile Deschanel, "Droit au travail," LP 2 (15 August 1848): 267.

56. Frederick A. DeLuna, *The French Republic under Cavaignac, 1848*, pp. 248–70.

57. Deschanel, "Le Catholicisme et le socialisme (2)," LP 5 (15 April 1850): 428–34, 438–43.

of the *Droit au travail* in 1848.[58] In 1850, when proponents of the "social and democratic republic" were gaining ground within the republican movement, Simon took a harder line toward a socialism that was not only more explicit but also intimately linked with a militant Voltairianism.

III

Le Devoir expresses the burning indignation of an unrepentant republican of 1848 against both the perpetrators of the coup d'etat of 2 December 1851 and against the general apathy with which the French middle classes had acquiesced to the destruction of the Second Republic. However imperfect, the Republic that Simon had served as representative, professor, and journalist had promised the progressive development of political and civil liberty in France and deserved, he thought, a vigorous defense against a president who had violated his pledge to "perform all the duties required by the constitution." To his amazement, many of his associates and friends of the past eighteen years proved themselves unable or unwilling to distinguish between the new regime of crime and casuistry and the preceding regime. Convinced that only leadership based on sound ethical principles could offer any guarantee of political stability, Simon refused all collaboration with a regime he thought doomed by its own moral bankruptcy. He expressed this indignation in his public protest on 17 December 1851 and in his refusal to take the *serment*, an act that meant some economic hardship and the sacrifice of a brilliant academic career.[59]

58. For Simon's views on social questions, see JS, "Publications relatives à l'organisation du travail," *LP* 1 (15 May 1848): 588. In his electoral program for the elections of May 1849, Simon said he was one of the first to attack the National Workshops, "A MM. les électeurs des Côtes-du-Nord," [1849]; [JS], "L'Assemblée nationale," *LP* 2 (15 September 1848): 291. For his hostility to the alliance of moderate republicans with any form of socialism, see "L'Assemblée nationale," *LP* 4 (15 July 1849): 102.

59. On 3 August 1843, Simon married Louise Marie Émilie Boissonnet, the daughter of a prosperous Rennes *négociant*. Her dowry enabled Simon to purchase enough land to meet the property qualification for a candidate for the Chamber of Deputies in 1846. Subsequent inheritances from her mother and uncle in the 1860s assured the financial security of

As the results of the referendum of 20 December showed, few in France shared Simon's interpretation of events. Apologies that former Liberals and republicans made for the new regime were like salt on his wounds. Editorials explaining the conversion of Le Pays, a newspaper edited by the conservative republican Arthur de La Guéronnière, contained many of the principal themes of these apologies. The coup d'etat, it was alleged, had saved French society from the unspeakable and inhuman cannibalism that socialists were planning to unleash on France at the time of the May elections. "Tears" provoked by Louis Napoleon's repressive measures were preferable to the "blushes" that socialist excesses would have caused.[60] When society was at stake, the ends justified the means.

There was also an appeal to the political realism of republicans. In an article directed at those intent on abstaining in the forthcoming referendum, La Guéronnière asked: "What good would it do to insist on an invalidated constitution and a defunct assembly. . . . We are citizens and practical men and we believe, with M. de Chateaubriand . . . that in politics as in physics, facts have dominion over theories."[61] Despite the protests of Littré, Simon's colleague at Le National under the Second Republic, Auguste Comte urged his positivist disciples to accept the coup d'etat and the new regime as a historical verdict on the political sterility of a metaphysical republicanism that had proven once again both its capacity to destroy and its incapacity to govern. In a similar vein, the liberal critic Charles Sainte-Beuve appealed to former Orleanists in August 1852: men who had claimed the right to rule, not on the basis of divine right, but because of the fact of the revolutions of 1789 and 1830, should be able to recognize a new fact. How could they deny support to a power that had been ratified by "the true bases of contemporary society"? Had they for-

the Simon household. See "Suisse dit Jules Simon (François Jules). Déclaration des mutations par décès, 5 août 1896," Archives de la Mairie du 8ième arrondissement," Paris, fo. 31, ce. 11, #1253.

60. Arthur de La Guéronnière, "La Guerre sociale," Le Pays, 11 December 1851; Arthur de La Guéronnière, "Un Nouveau quatre mai," Le Pays, 17 December 1851.

61. Arthur de La Guéronnière, "Suffrage universel et République," Le Pays, 12 December 1851; Arthur de La Guéronnière, "Pourquoi nous écrivons," Le Pays, 14 December 1851.

gotten the words of Madame de Staël: "Anger is of no use against facts"?[62]

Another characteristic of such apologetics was a tendency to link necessity with right, to argue like the Bonapartist Auguste Romieu in his *L'Ère des césars* (1850) that the will of the "providential man" was the law of human affairs, or like La Guéronnière, that the weight of numbers carried moral significance. Before the referendum, La Guéronnière had urged voters to vote yes, not as a sign of moral approval of Louis Napoleon's coup d'etat, but to signify that the consequences of a no vote were unthinkable. After the vote, he followed Louis Napoleon's lead and informed his readers that 20 December had "absolved and erased the revolution." Vox populi had become *vox dei.*[63]

Le Devoir was a broadly conceived attack on such imperial apologists. In it, Simon sought to stimulate his compatriots' sense of the dimensions of liberty by celebrating the moral capabilities of the individual conscience. Rational men, he argued, possessed the power to formulate and to live in accordance with the laws of the rational conscience. In both the individual and in society, Simon believed, freedom and self-control, liberty and order must be understood as mutually reinforcing correlatives. The empire, despite its pretensions, was in fact a flight from liberty and order; it was the product of a loss of nerve on the part of the French bourgeoisie. Terrified by the socialist threat, the middle classes had lost faith in the power of liberty to guarantee and to develop social cohesion and harmony. Half a century of chronic political instability and the legacy of the materialistic philosophers of the eighteenth and early nineteenth centuries had taught men to seek security in the practical and to distrust philosophy's efforts to uncover the universal and the absolute in ethics, or, for that matter, in political theory. Even French education, which had been steadily descending from the theoretical to the practical for over half a century, reflected this opinion. As a result, French society had sunk into an egoistic materialism oriented around place-

---

62. Charles-A. Sainte-Beuve, "Littérature. Les Regrets," *Le Constitutionnel,* 23 August 1852.

63. Robert Flint, *Historical Philosophy in France,* pp. 563–65; Arthur de La Guéronnière, "La Mission de L.-M. Bonaparte," *Le Pays,* 29 December 1851.

seeking and mindless routine and based on an utter confusion of justice and expediency.

Against these historical developments, Simon asserted that the rule of justice, which all rational men could understand, is the only real savior of society. This book is not a systematic treatment of an ethical theory but a "simple and clear résumé of the most important ethical notions" with supporting arguments.[64] The argument rests on the assumption, never defended in the text, that a perfect and omnipotent God willed the world and its inhabitants. Since God created with a purpose, every part of the creation has its place in the whole, its role or "law." Man, as a creature of God, also has a law, but God created him free to reject or accept this law.[65] On the basis of this assumption, Simon expounds an ethics based on psychological introspection with full assurance that the intellectual guides and sentimental inclinations that he uncovers reflect not merely subjective preferences but the divine intent.

The idea of the good or justice, Simon maintained, is one of those "impersonal" conceptions, like the notions of the true and the beautiful that are implicit in every man's sense of the infinite and the absolute.[66] The idea of justice, which we conceive as absolute, contains a universal imperative within it. "We need only to conceive of justice to gain the conviction that all men have rights and that each right implies a corresponding duty."[67] Justice for Simon is "this thing which I call not *my* Right, but Right, and not only Right, but Right and Duty."[68]

Simon sums up this concept of justice in two formulas taken from biblical sources. To the negative strictures of Tobias 4:15 ("Do not do unto others what you would not have done unto you"), he adds the more generous words of Matthew 8:12 ("Do unto others what you would have others do unto you"). While giving priority to the individual's right to life, liberty, and estate, he insists that man is duty bound to aid his fellow men in the preservation of their rights.[69] In Simon, this sense of duty, which rested on a religious respect for a God-given moral universe, combined with the habits of Christian

64. JS, "Préface de la première édition," *Le Devoir*, p. i.
65. Ibid., p. 101.   66. Ibid., p. 85.
67. Ibid., p. 264.   68. Ibid., p. 254.
69. Ibid., p. 317.

charity learned in his youth to sustain a conscientious and per-
severing commitment to political and social improvement.[70]

The idea of justice in Simon's ethics is more of a constrain-
ing force than an instrument of self-assertion. Implicitly rejecting any notion of original sin, he accepts the Cartesian
view that "all passions are by nature good, and we have only
to guard against their bad usage or their excesses."[71] But
justice appears in the thought of this admirer of Plato as a
règle, a rule, a bridle whose role it is to "tame," "master,"
"discipline," "utilize," and "purify" the passions, those "phenomena of the soul which well up in us without our cooperation, or at least without the necessary cooperation of our
will."[72] Although man's love of self, love of his fellow man,
and love of God correspond to his basic natural needs to preserve himself, to belong to a society, and to relate to the Absolute, these passions are constantly on the verge of degenerating
into blind and violent self-assertion.[73] "A soul which does not
know how to bridle (*régler*) its passions and to establish a just
hierarchy among them, is a disordered soul that does not belong to itself."[74] The passions require not a light rein but a
heavy "yoke."[75]

In the pages of *Le Devoir*, Simon measures the arguments
in support of the coup d'etat and the plebiscite of 20 December
against his notion of justice as an absolute and universal imperative existing independently of the mind that knows it and
of the physical universe. All arguments from utility, or the
interest of society are inadequate; like Epicurus and Hobbes,
proponents of such views conceive of ethical judgment more
as a calculation of the results of particular actions than as a
sounding of the rational conscience. The historical approach
to ethics, prevalent among Saint-Simonians and Comtists, also
gives primacy to facts over ideals. This outlook, which Simon
views as a sophisticated version of the claims of Sainte-Beuve
and La Guéronnière in favor of the ethical value of political
faits accomplis, rests on a confusion in the use of the term
law. The law of progress, like the law of gravity, is a law in
the descriptive sense. It is a generalization from particular
known facts. To base the moral law on a historical law is to

70. Ibid., p. 378.
71. Ibid., p. 148.
72. Ibid., pp. 27, 84–85, 229, 346.
73. Ibid., pp. 101, 346.
74. Ibid., pp. 413–14.
75. Ibid., p. 405.

place ethics in the realm of the hypothetical, for all knowledge based on historical experience is fallible. Besides, Simon argues, the argument is circular. For if one admits that history is a mixture of all human phenomena, the just and the unjust, then one must admit that it is necessary to understand the moral law before one can identify it in history. To solve this problem, proponents of the historical school can do no better than "to proclaim just all deeds which the majority approves or which success seems to justify."[76] Arguments based on the alleged existence of "two moralities"—one for providential men and another for the common man—do not meet Simon's standard either. In an unmistakable reference to an 1853 incident at the Sorbonne involving the critic Désiré Nisard and the dean Joseph-Victor Leclerc, he insists that "if there are two moralities, there is no morality." The theory of "two moralities" is nothing but an expression of untrammeled ambition that, not content with sacrificing all for the vanity of power and wealth, has the audacity to idealize itself.[77]

Beneath this discussion of ethical principle, with its thinly veiled attack on the apologists of the coup d'etat, Le Devoir contains a deeper critique of the empire. This regime, not the Church, Simon suggests, is the mortal enemy of political and civil liberty. Louis Napoleon and his men sought to silence all those whose consciences motivated them to denounce the coup d'etat and then converted the referendum of 20 December into a vindication of the moral rectitude of their actions. "It is a strange folly which begins by destroying the authority of each intelligence, and which then wishes to make something healthy and valid from the union of all these enervated minds."[78] All apologies for Louis Napoleon, in their appeals to historical laws, providence, or special circumstances, reflect these efforts to bypass the inner voice of conscience. In its economic policies, the new regime, so distrustful of liberty, would inaugurate a kind of state socialism, the nineteenth-century equivalent of the "bread and circuses" that corrupted the population of Imperial Rome. In his efforts to extinguish

76. Ibid., p. 304.

77. Ibid., pp. 136, 381. See also Gabriel Vauthier, "Troubles à la Sorbonne en 1856," La Revolution de 1848, pp. 388–90; and Jules Barni, "Les Deux morales," L'Avenir, 28 October 1855.

78. JS, Le Devoir, p. 305.

poverty, Napoleon III, the author of *L'Extinction du paupé-risme* (1844), would only extinguish liberty. With these predilections, the regime would naturally turn toward those who shared a similar distrust of the individual conscience—the Jesuits and the Clerical party of Veuillot. After all, is not the detestable theory that "the ends justify the means," employed so often by Bonapartist apologists, the same doctrine that discredited the Jesuits?[79] This new direction has already found expression in the revised philosophy curriculum, which stresses logic at the expense of the history of philosophy and smacks of a new "scholasticism." Like Scholasticism, this new preoccupation with formal logic, rather than with underlying assumptions, would stifle free inquiry.[80] The counterpart of this new emphasis on logic is a spate of books on practical ethics or casuistry, which falsely appear to make the conscience obsolete. Police power, by its very logic, would create a privileged position for the clerical obscurantism of Veuillot and his friends in their struggle with the healthy forces in French Catholicism.

*   *   *   *   *

The political experiences of the later years of the July Monarchy, of the Second Republic, and of the early Second Empire convinced Simon that only republicans were true conservatives. France would achieve political stability when its citizens accepted the philosophic and political legacy of the Enlightenment: tolerance of believer and freethinker alike, and a conception of sovereignty which recognized that political authority resided, ultimately, in the people. In the development of a disciplined liberty, both the lay University and the Church were to play important educative roles. Philosophic spiritualism, allied not to clericalism but to traditional Catholic civility, would give France a dutiful citizenry at last capable of realizing not only political liberty and civil equality but also that third promise of the Revolution—fraternity.[81] The days of the Second Empire were numbered, for like the July Monarchy, it gave only lip service to this legacy.

79. Ibid., pp. 344–45.
81. Ibid., pp. 383–84.

80. Ibid., pp. 325, 385.

CHAPTER V

LA RELIGION NATURELLE:
SIMON'S RELIGIOUS CONSCIOUSNESS

In *Le Devoir*, and in his previous philosophic writings, Jules Simon hardly discussed the deistic premises that lay at the root of most of his theories on ethics and politics. As its title implies, *La Religion naturelle*, which appeared in May 1856, marked the end of Simon's reluctance to discuss first principles. No longer restrained by philosophic, religious, or political scruples, he finally felt prepared to give mature expression to views that he had spent years solidifying and clarifying. On both the philosophic and the literary level, his task was difficult. The problem was to formulate a rational religious perspective that, in contrast with the "chilly deisms" associated with the eighteenth century, might come close to satisfying a Christian structure of sentiment. Simon's deism would combine the freethinker's commitment to natural reason with the Christian's sense of God's ineffable perfection and pervasive presence in day-to-day life. Such a position, in a society where the lines between philosophy and religion were clearly drawn, almost invited misunderstanding. For the ultramontane Veuillot, Simon could only be adopting the language of the Christian in order to lure unsuspecting children of God into the wastelands of philosophy.[1] For the liberal Catholic Albert de Broglie, Simon was an "unconscious and involuntary Christian," only temporarily seduced by a philosophy whose inadequacy he virtually admitted.[2] To varying degrees, the press of the freethinking democratic opposition, always on the alert for potential relapsed Catholics, interpreted these overtones as indica-

1. Abbé P. Roux-Lavergne, "*La Religion naturelle* par Jules Simon," *L'Univers*, 28 July, 1, 10 August 1856; see also Jules Barbey d'Aurevilly, "Jules Simon," *XIXe siècle. Les Oeuvres et les hommes*, pp. 75–76.
2. Albert de Broglie, "De *La Religion naturelle* par Jules Simon (Deuxième Article)," *Le Correspondant* 39, no. 1 (1 October 1856): 35.

tions that Simon was too timid to accept the dictates of his reason and to break cleanly with Church.[3] But there were some who were able to place the Christian overtones in Simon's work in proper perspective, and the most important of these men was the republican journalist, Frédéric Morin.

As a personal friend with a similar background and vocation, Morin was well situated to appreciate the subtleties of Simon's particular cast of mind. A *lyonnais* of staunch Catholic and republican upbringing, Morin was a former *normalien* and philosophy teacher who, in the tradition of Buchez, continued to search until the last years of the 1850s for a way to reconcile Catholicism with the needs of free thought and self-government.[4] With his own direct experience of the conflicting pressures that contemporary society was exerting on republicans of Catholic background, Morin repeatedly insisted that rigorous free thought and religious feeling were not incompatible.[5] He urged republicans to view both the philosophic seriousness and the Christian overtones in Simon's work not as a union contrary to nature, and thus inherently instable, but as a stable duality. In *La Religion naturelle*, Simon combined an uncompromising philosophic manner with an acute Christian sensibility. In Morin's eyes, Simon was the contemporary "thinker who was both most free of prejudice, uncontrolled passion and fanaticism" and who "stood the closest to the most illustrious masters of the Christian tradition in his manner of feeling and of conceiving things." Morin viewed this duality as a strength rather than a weakness, for it allowed Simon, like Rousseau, to sound depths of human life that other philosophers could not reach.[6]

La Religion naturelle confirms Morin's view of Simon as a

3. Alphonse Peyrat, "*La Religion naturelle* par Jules Simon," *La Presse*, 19 May 1856; Louis Jourdan, "*La Religion naturelle* par Jules Simon," *Le Siècle*, 6 July 1856.

4. "Frédéric Morin," *Dictionnaire biographique du mouvement ouvrier français*, ed. Jean Maîtron, 3:124–25. See also Frédéric Morin, *Politique et philosophie*, Introduction by Jules Simon.

5. Frédéric Morin, "*Almanach de J.-J. Rousseau*, par Marc Viridet," *Les Idées du temps présent*, pp. 102–3.

6. Frédéric Morin, "*Essai critique sur 'La Religion naturelle'* de M. Jules Simon par Michel de Castelnau," *RIP*, 4 November 1858, p. 502 (see Abbreviations, p. viii). See also Frédéric Morin, "Le Livre de *La Religion naturelle* et la faculté de théologie," *RIP*, 19 February 1857, pp. 682–85.

man fundamentally at peace with himself, secure in a philosophic faith that expressed both his qualities of open-mindedness and of Christian sensibility. From a modest but firm defender of the rights of philosophy, Simon had become, in the 1850s, an apostle of reason. In their reliance on revelation, he had concluded, both Catholicism and Protestantism failed to give reason its due. "Inundate men's souls with light," he enjoined an audience in Liège, Belgium, in 1856: *"hors de là, point de salut."*[7] He had offered his previous writings as useful complements to Catholic teachings; now, he presented *La Religion naturelle* to the "elite minds" of the mid-nineteenth century as a real alternative to Christianity. From our knowledge that God is perfect and a creator, he wrote, "philosophy, humanity can deduce all that really matters for the direction and solace of life."[8]

If Simon's defense of reason is firm, it is no less restrained. Philosophers, he insists, must practice humility. Invoking his earlier distinction between divine incomprehensibility and mystery, he urges fellow freethinkers to recognize their inability to comprehend how creation took place, or how free will might be reconciled with divine omnipotence.[9] It is enough to know that God is the omnipotent creator of the world and that man has free will. In certain moods, he acknowledges that philosophy can be a frustrating endeavor, for the God "who makes known his perfection without allowing us to glimpse his perfections remains too remote from us." And he seems almost to protest against the limitations of reason: "An unknown God above our heads, an unknown bliss beyond the grave. . . . Such cold knowledge does not protect us enough."[10] But these are passing moods, perhaps articulated to encourage former Catholics who yearned for a rational creed as explicit in all its details as Catholicism. As a man who had known their philosophic anxieties and conquered them, Simon might well calm their philosophic nerves.

Simon's deism, like the spiritualism of Cousin, rests on the

7. Ed. Robinet, "Jules Simon à Liège," *RIP*, 28 February 1856; although Simon always maintained good relations with Protestants, he seems never to have been seriously tempted to join a reformed church. See JS, *R.N.*, p. 404.

8. JS, *R.N.*, pp. 164–65, 244.

9. Ibid., pp. 134, 236, 238, 243, 257, 278.

10. Ibid., p. 246.

psychological method. By introspection alone, even without examination of the physical world, man knows that a God exists who is infinite and perfect. Since he is infinite and perfect, he must therefore be also eternal and necessary. Since the world exists, but is neither eternal nor necessary, God must have created it. In his infinite wisdom, power, and goodness, he created a world in which all things, while necessarily imperfect, are arranged "for the best." Hence for Simon, the creation was an act of divine love.[11] In this deism, Simon is particularly eager to defend God's perfection. Pantheists, in a vain effort to solve the eternal riddle of creation, he writes, degrade God by making him consubstantial with an imperfect world.

Simon's choice of title, *La Religion naturelle*, was itself an implicit challenge to Catholicism and reflected the freethinker's desire to establish that reason alone is capable of satisfying men's essential religious and moral needs. What give Simon's deism its distinctive character, however, are the Christian elements in his thoughts and feelings. As Peter Gay has aptly demonstrated, historians who attempt to call attention to the Christian elements in the thought of declared freethinkers always run the risk of falling into the error of "spurious persistence." The philosophes, he has reminded us, drew heavily on the inspiration of pagan antiquity in their struggle to free themselves from Catholicism; judging from the intentions of the philosophes, the eighteenth-century "heavenly city" was urban renewal with a vengeance, not a mere reconstruction with new materials, on a medieval blueprint.[12] In the case of Simon, however, Catholicism was never the absolute enemy; the role of philosophy was to purify, not to annihilate a Christianity that had rendered unparalleled services to the spiritualist cause. Simon passed through the school of Cousin without radically disturbing his Christian structure of sentiment, and he may even have found some new support for this structure in the writings of thinkers like Locke and Rousseau. The remainder of this chapter seeks further to describe these fundamentally Christian overtones, as they manifest themselves in Simon's views on how man can know that God exists; how man and God interact in the moral realm; and how man should worship God.

11. Ibid., pp. 36–37.
12. Peter Gay, *The Party of Humanity*, p. 191.

With their constant invocation of the sense of divine presence, Simon's discussions of the proofs for the existence
of God seem to draw heavily on this Christian structure of
sentiment. Formal philosophic proofs, it is argued, are both
superfluous and inadequate. For the man who has an idea of
the infinite that contrasts sharply with knowledge derived
from the senses, such proofs are usually superfluous. In the
final analysis, Simon believes, Descartes's first three proofs for
the existence of God are reducible to the proposition that
it "is evident that the infinite exists; it is absurd that it not
exist; nothing disproves the existence of the infinite; if the
infinite does not exist, nothing is possible, and, to the contrary,
all is possible if the infinite exists." Simon argues that this
is hardly proof, for it does not introduce the idea of the infinite
to our minds; it only gives formal recognition to our belief in
the existence of the infinite. It is not an "argument, it is a
principle, a kind of intuition, a self-evident truth."[13] Descartes
should have simply said, as Bossuet did later, that "our mind,
when it contemplates perfection, understands that perfection
must by its very nature exist; on the other hand, when it con-
siders imperfection, it recognizes that the imperfect being can
exist only on the condition that some foreign cause produces
it."[14] For Simon, the truth hardly needs proof; it is readily
apparent. The testimony of the heart, which strives for the
good and the beautiful, and of the will, which accepts the guidance of the moral law, only confirm God's existence. Descartes's so-called proofs only belabor the obvious: "After all,
God is not proven, but is everywhere visible."[15]

Although Simon finds his own psychological makeup so full
of God as to render Descartes's proofs superfluous, he readily
acknowledges that they would be virtually useless for others.
What sense could the religious skeptic, unable to uncover any
innate idea of perfection within himself, make of such proofs?
Indeed, Simon doubts that the most scientifically rigorous proofs
are possible in philosophy. Despite his defense of the suffi-
ciency of philosophy to answer man's most important questions,
he concedes that philosophic proofs will never "force agreement from the most rebellious minds" in the manner of a

13. JS, *R.N.*, p. 19.   14. Ibid., p. 20.
15. JS, *La Religion naturelle*, 3d ed. (Paris: Hachette, 1856), p. 31.

geometrical proof.[16] To illustrate this point, Simon repeatedly evokes the one-hour apostolate of Denis Diderot, who lost a reasoned faith as quickly as he had gained it.[17] Unbelievers especially should avoid "giving themselves to debatable formulas, which, besides . . . will never seem a sufficient base for such a belief."[18] Philosophy should consist more of meditation than of ratiocination.[19] If one cannot move from a certainty of God's existence and of Providence to such other fundamental parts of the spiritualist edifice as free will, immortality of the soul, and duty, then perhaps one can arrive at God by the opposite route. "God is the cornerstone, which cannot be disturbed without peril to the building; God's unshakeable and supreme solidity is proven consequently by the stability of the building."[20]

For the man who has learned to look and listen, Simon believes, "nature, society, our conscience speak of God at every instant."[21] God is always present, in moments of both suffering and joy.[22] Such a man has come to "live with God in heart and mind, to find him at the end of all his research, to place him in all his hopes."[23] A "secret instinct working like a natural force" directs both his mind and his heart toward God.[24] "The religious man is a lover of Providence; he never wearies of studying and celebrating the beauty of his love."[25] Life derives its meaning from men's efforts to find appropriate means of responding to the divine; God is both the source of metaphysical certainty and of man's sense that he has a role to play on what might otherwise appear to be a naked rock under an abstract heaven.[26] Simon's sense of God's proximity is so immediate and so incontestable that he does not believe that many men can ever sustain either atheism or agnosticism. Even the most hard-bitten "positivistic types" cannot prevent the name of God from coming to their lips in moments of misfortune or of great import.[27]

To transform man's "instinctive belief in the existence of God" into a set of descriptive statements about God was the

16. JS, R.N., p. 294.

17. Ibid., pp. 33–35.

18. Ibid., pp. 26–27.

19. Ibid., p. 27; see also La Religion naturelle, 3d ed., p. 31.

20. JS, R.N., pp. 33–34.

21. JS, "Préface," R.N., p. i.

22. Ibid., p. ii.

23. JS, R.N., p. 35.

24. Ibid., p. 4.

25. Ibid., p. 185.

26. Ibid., p. 141.

27. Ibid., p. 369; see also pp. 4–5.

goal of Simon's philosophic meditations.[28] Yet unlike many contemporary pantheists and spiritualists who described the divine nature in great detail, he felt obliged to admit that for the most part, God is "incomprehensible, largely inaccessible to man's reason."[29] In this respect, Simon was more like William James's religious man whose profound sense of the divine presence "polarizes" his life through and through, yet for the purpose of "definite description, can hardly be said to be present to [his] mind at all."[30] For the infinite, the eternal, and the divine are different in essence from the finite, the temporal, and the worldly.[31] Yet to say that God is incomprehensible does not mean that man knows nothing at all about God except that He exists. Man can know something of God by analogy, even though Simon believes that God also possesses an infinite number of attributes that have no analogy with what man knows and that will always remain fathomless.[32]

In Simon's thought, this pervasive sense of the divine presence is complemented by, and perhaps sustained by, a vivid religious imagination. As a young Catholic *lycéen*, Simon had composed a prayer that, in the language of Christian mysticism, expressed a yearning for a "holy ecstasy" in which the soul, "filled with celestial languor," receives a direct, even personal, communication from God.[33] At the *École normale*, this interest in direct experience of God took, under Cousin's tutelage, a more philosophic turn: in Plato's *Timaeus* and Aristotle's *Metaphysics* (Book 12), which he translated, Simon learned of the wondrous experiences of the philosophic mind, drawn by its love of God, to the very summit of the dialectic.[34] In subsequent writings, Simon maintained an attitude toward

28. Ibid., pp. 6–7.
29. JS, "Préface," *R.N.*, p. iii; see also p. 37.
30. William James, *The Varieties of Religious Experience* (New York: Macmillan, 1961), pp. 60–61.
31. JS, *R.N.*, p. 278.   32. Ibid., pp. 37, 40.
33. JS, "Le Chant d'amour," *Le Bonheur*, p. 182, 87 AP 21; see also "Prières de la messe pour le jour de la communion," *Le Bonheur*, pp. 198–99, 87 AP 21.
34. JS, Paris, to Fortuné Frélaut, 13 January 1836, 87 AP 8 VI; JS, Caen, to Victor Cousin, 10 December 1837, Bib. VC 36/4761; JS, Caen, to Jean-Philibert Damiron, 4 July 1837, Jean-Philibert Damiron Papers; JS, *Premières années*, pp. 177, 237–45; Thomas Aquinas, *Commentary on the Metaphysics of Aristotle*, trans. John P. Rowan (Chicago: Henry Regnery, 1961), 2:891.

mystical experience that differed significantly from eclectic orthodoxy. Although he agreed with Cousin that such experiences did not prima facie yield new philosophic knowledge, Simon went out of his way to insist on the value of such direct, ecstatic visions of God for all who seek a truth they love.[35] In *La Religion naturelle,* his most explicit passage on mystical experience relates how the philosopher arrives at a conception of God and then takes off: One

> glimpses the eternal and immutable essence, the source of all being and all truth amidst the dazzling images which conceal it. After laboriously reaching the summit of knowledge, one's mind grasps, in a fleeting instant, all the verities of which it has dreamt; it forgets its infirmities and its miseries in the full possession of him who is the object of thought par excellence; time and space seem to recede, and the eternal seems to unfold in full splendor. Then everything becomes troubled, everything fades out, one's heart grows quiet again, the mind reasserts itself, this great dream leaves only a memory, and one begins again to seek and to work in the hope of a new ecstasy. This moment, which passes like lightning, is a foretaste of celestial bliss.[36]

Although Simon rejects philosophic or religious views that center upon mystical experience, his own Christian structure of sentiment does not permit him to reject ecstasy as mere hallucination.

For Simon, religious ecstasy originates in the most noble and pure aspirations of the soul—in the yearning of the human heart and mind for God, the ultimate object of love and knowledge.[37] In his *Histoire de l'École d'Alexandrie* (1845), Simon applauds the Alexandrians who "place [ecstasy] at the summit of the dialectic, as the final term and the reward of our efforts to reach the truth." They recognize that the ecstatic soul, "inflamed, ardent, no longer knowing fatigue and other obstacles," achieves new "insights into the nature of the infinite." "These glimpses enable us not only to perceive but also to feel God's perfection." Such insights, however, Simon

35. Victor Cousin, "Du mysticisme," *RDM,* n.s., 11 (1 August 1845): 469–78.
36. JS, *R.N.,* p. 354.
37. JS, "Introduction," *Oeuvres philosophiques de Bossuet,* pp. 30–32.

insists, must undergo critical examination. To gain acceptance
as new knowledge, a "truth" grasped or possessed in a moment
of ecstasy must lend itself to subsequent rational demonstration.[38] In Simon's eyes, the moral significance of these inspired
insights probably outweighs the scientific. As he later repeats
in *La Religion naturelle*, ecstasy is an encouragement to men
not to give up hope in God's goodness. It is "really that fore-
taste of future bliss which Plotinus spoke of, that interval
which God grants us to catch our breath amidst our miseries."[39]
And in *Le Devoir*, while questioning the strictly philosophic
value of these mystical insights, he suggests that they constitute the substance of religious devotion: "Every devout soul
is mystical at certain times, for without some mysticism, there
is only fidelity to doctrine and to precepts, but no real devotion."[40] These visions "enliven the intelligence" and "nourish
the heart"; they stimulate love of God and the search for truth
when they do not yield new knowledge.[41] They transform the
solitary thinker into a philosophic apostle.

Simon's conception of the interaction of man and God in
the moral realm also illustrates the Christian overtones in his
thought. His sense of the divine power and goodness compels
him to reject the kind of cold deism that would make God a
clock-maker deity, a "stranger to the world."[42] Without sacrificing human free will, Simon depicts a God who is a "Father,"
and who governs the world and man directly; the attributes
of Providence are "goodness, foresight, solicitude, incessant
activity."[43] Providence "loves the world, cares for it, governs
it; he answers our prayers with good deeds; Providence can
be reached; in our lowliness, we have some effect on this infinite grandeur." Simon's proof of God's Providence rests primarily upon his conception of the creation, and secondarily
upon the observation of nature. "Creation answers for Providence," for since God stands outside of time, he cannot turn
away from his work.[44] God is eternally a creator and the same

38. JS, *Histoire de l'École d'Alexandrie*, 2:680–85.
39. Ibid., p. 685; see also JS, *R.N.*, pp. 236–37, 273–74.
40. JS, *Le Devoir*, pp. 185–86.
41. JS, *Histoire de l'École d'Alexandrie*, 2:685.
42. JS, "Préface," *R.N.*, p. iii.   43. JS, *R.N.*, p. 142.
44. Ibid., pp. 224–27.

will encompasses the creation and the governing of the world. "That separation, which some would like to establish, between the act of creating the world and the act of governing it is derived from that persistent misconception which leads us to limit God to the conditions of our own existence."[45] Since the act of creation and all of world history, past and future, are one in the will of a perfect God, divine love, divine power, and divine intelligence infuse all forms of earthly existence.

To talk of such a God as a "Father," Catholic critics were quick to point out, was misleading for others and perhaps even self-deceiving. Simon acknowledges this criticism of his use of the anthropomorphic metaphor. Catholics, he rebuts, were vulnerable to the same criticism. Did not Augustine write in a discussion of the Trinity that "we say that God is one in three persons, less to clarify than to avoid falling into silence." And he takes care to include a cautionary note to warn his readers "never to forget that God is incomprehensible: and when we say that he is, that he thinks, that he wishes, let us remember that only means that he is the perfect and unknown cause of what we call being, thought, love and will."[46] Both the justification and the caveat were weak and inadequate, especially in the light of the fact that Simon makes no real effort to restrict the usage of the anthropomorphic metaphor. Indeed, he often writes as if a paternal God intervened in historical processes in response to particular prayers, even though elsewhere he explicitly rules out such a possibility.[47] This weakness in his thought and expression is important, because it suggests the depth of his conviction that God is not indifferent to human affairs. The anthropomorphic metaphor, while lacking philosophic rigor, seemed the best possible expression of his innermost sentiments.

Simon's discussions of the problem of evil and of man's "justification" dramatically illustrate the God-centered quality of his ethics. Since God is perfect, Simon argues, his creations are as perfect as creations may be, but they nevertheless share the imperfections inherent to all created things. In physical and human nature, good, "that is, order . . . prevails over disorder

45. JS, "Préface," R.N., pp. iii–iv.
46. JS, R.N., pp. 90–91.
47. Ibid., pp. 176, 185, 366–67, 381, 430.

and evil . . . and it prevails, not marginally, but overwhelmingly, almost infinitely."[48] Just as the physical universe, while largely beneficient, is not devoid of an irreducible amount of physical suffering, man, while "more inclined to virtue than to vice, intelligent enough to withstand the world's attractions and to aid his fellow men," is prone, because of his inherent limitations, to more or less frequent wrongdoing.[49] While rejecting the Christian notion of original sin, Simon feels such outrage at man's moral weakness that he sometimes appears to regret human liberty.[50]

Without a compensating system of divine rewards and punishments in the afterlife of the immortal soul, the painful and thankless sacrifices that the virtuous life requires are sufficient to refute all claims for the existence of a cosmic moral order, and more generally, for divine perfection. Because God is justice, and human life is unjust, there must be justice in the afterlife. In fact, Simon argues, the just man suffers so much in this world that evil alone could be sufficient proof of the soul's immortality for all who worship a perfect God.[51] Like the Christian, Simon thus rejects the efforts of Fourierists and others of similar persuasion to consider "this transitory life as an end in itself."[52] Both his and the Christian approaches to the problem of evil must be understood not as isolated doctrines but in their relationship to the immortality of the soul and to the powers of God.

Even Simon's treatment of "justification" still contains the echo of a Christian conception of God's goodness. Blessed with liberty, love, and intelligence, all men without exception possess the capability of doing God's will. Whatever uncertainties "shroud the wretched events of this life, we do know one thing —that we will have happiness in the next life if we are just in this one."[53] Yet although a man who performs good works may be certain of his reward, no man earns it in the strictest sense.[54] For while all men know the moral law (the will of God), no one obeys it perfectly. But since God is perfectly good as well as perfectly just, he neither punishes evildoers eternally

48. Ibid., pp. 149–51, 213.
49. Ibid., pp. 205, 209, 369–70.
50. Ibid., p. 120.
51. Ibid., pp. 320, 327.
52. Ibid., p. 174.
53. Ibid., pp. 191, 362.
54. Ibid., p. 343.

nor requires the living to perform that infinite expiation that alone could compensate for a single act of disobedience to his law.[55] Both good and bad men benefit from something that looks very much like divine grace.

Simon's discussions of evil and justification are especially important indicators of the strength of the Christian currents in his philosophic outlook. He defines man's freedom to determine his own destiny only within a frame of reference that includes both Creator and creature. This balance of countervailing forces, built into the very structure of his thought, was to guarantee that the author of *La Religion naturelle* would find it difficult in his later years to follow his republican deist friends very far along the road from natural religion to "independent morality"—an ethics independent of all deistic conceptions. To adopt such a position would have meant to reject that Christian manner of "accepting the universe" that Simon had carried over into his moral philosophy. In a discussion of specific "manners of acceptance of the universe," the psychologist William James distinguishes between the religious and the moralistic stance. James suggests that the religious man accepts the universe "heartily and all together," while the moralist accepts it "only in part and grudgingly." Compare Job's "Though He slay me, yet will I trust in Him!" with Marcus Aurelius's stoic submission, often with the "heaviest and coldest heart" to the law of the whole: "If the gods care not for me or my children, there must be a reason for it."[56] According to the psychologist, the religious man is characterized by "this added dimension of emotion, this enthusiastic temper of espousal, in regions where morality strictly so called can at best but bow its head and acquiesce." He consents to misfortune outwardly as a form of sacrifice while inwardly, with the "keynote of the universe sounding in . . . [his] ears, and everlasting possession spread before . . . [his] eyes," he knows that evil is permanently overcome.[57] In contrast, the nonreligious state of mind undergoes sacrifice, at best without complaint, but never in a spirit of joyful and helpless acceptance of externally imposed limitations.[58] Viewed in this context, Simon stands much closer to

55. Ibid., pp. 349, 447.
56. James, *Varieties of Religious Experience*, pp. 49–50.
57. Ibid., p. 55.   58. Ibid., p. 57.

Job than to Marcus Aurelius; courage, resignation, and consolation, all parts of what he terms a *tireless hope*, inure him against the hardships of life.[59]

Like the Stoic, Simon gains courage from the conviction that "a benevolent and omnipotent God" has placed him on the earth to subject him to the trials necessarily entailed in obedience to the divine will and has also given him the power to prevail over his misfortunes.[60] Yet unlike Marcus Aurelius, Simon accepts the test not grudgingly but with feelings that range from qualified pleasure to joy. Naturally, the consoling thought that this life is a preparation for the next often lies behind this attitude; Simon faces life's sorrows squarely because he knows that "my rest, my homeland, my God are elsewhere."[61] But sometimes, when the price of virtue in human suffering seems greater than distant rewards in another life, only the knowledge that the sacrifices men make to virtue coincide with the will of God himself (the moral law) makes life acceptable to Simon. At his most discouraged moments, this knowledge makes the struggles of life a "bitter pleasure."[62] At other moments, this knowledge "makes the law more sacred and sweet, and thereby gives virtue the character of love and eliminates most bitterness from sacrifice."[63] At still others, he finds God's will "a kind law, whatever sacrifices it demands, because love is in all its precepts."[64] Indeed, God's will sometimes is so attractive that one can do it for its own sake, without any certainty of a reward in the afterlife.[65]

Simon's attitudes toward worship, like his conception of the human condition, also reflect the Christian pattern of his thoughts and feelings. In his writings on Catholicism, Simon continually stresses the role of public worship; the elaborate and solemn ceremonies of the Church always fortified men's faith by providing an ideal opportunity to satisfy their need to honor God publicly and regularly.[66] Consequently, hesitation and uncertainty mark his discussion of how adherents of natural religion should worship.[67] And in the third edition, he

59. JS, *R.N.*, p. 118.   60. Ibid., pp. 361–62.
61. JS, "Préface," *R.N.*, p. v; see also p. 361.
62. JS, *R.N.*, p. 118.   63. Ibid., p. 244.
64. JS, "Préface," *R.N.*, p. v.   65. JS, *R.N.*, pp. 222, 345.
66. JS, *Histoire de l'École d'Alexandrie*, 1:169.
67. JS, *R.N.*, pp. 428–39.

frankly admits that "here, natural religion does not yield all which humanity asks of it."[68] Despite his emotional desires, reason, while demonstrating the necessity to honor God, does not require any specific prayers or rituals.[69] Unlike the Church, which offers everyone a formal rule of worship, Simon can only offer an informal method for the conscientious.[70] Outside of moral actions, worship consists of an "assiduous communion" with God through regular moments of private prayer, self-imposed expiation for bad actions, and public declarations of one's beliefs.

The conflict between Simon's sense of the religious needs that formal worship satisfies and his belief that natural religion cannot prescribe any single system of worship leads him to a rather surprising compromise. Might not his deists follow the example of those philosophers of classical antiquity who prayed in the temples without accepting religious orthodoxy in its entirety? Could one not, in good conscience, participate in public prayer, and perhaps even baptism, marriage, and extreme unction—actions that did not involve a formal adherence to Catholic dogma—while refraining from those actions that presupposed an "absolute faith," recitation of a credo, confession, and communion? In *Le Devoir* and in an early draft of *La Religion naturelle*, Simon rejected this compromise because of the false appearances it would create.[71] Prior to publication, however, his publisher, the former *normalien* Louis Hachette, induced Simon to soften his opposition for both philosophic and political reasons. In the end, Simon concludes that a believer in natural religion cannot participate in Catholic ceremonies that presuppose an "absolute faith" without criminal hypocrisy. While warning of the dangerous possibilities for abuse inherent in participation in other ceremonies, he concedes that he cannot severely condemn it "when it is motivated by no strictly worldly interest." For this, as for everything else, God will be the final judge.[72]

The publication of *La Religion naturelle* was a landmark in Simon's personal and social development. The process of

68. JS, *La Religion naturelle*, 3d ed., p. 429.

69. JS, *R.N.*, p. 429.   70. Ibid., p. 430.

71. JS, *Le Devoir*, pp. 392–93; Louis Hachette, Paris, to JS, 22 May 1856, 87 AP 4.

72. JS, *R.N.*, pp. 440–41.

political and intellectual assimilation that had begun with the crisis of late 1833 and early 1834 was completed. Without a brutal rupture with his Breton youth, Simon had successfully transmuted the powerful if inchoate emotions of a provincial Catholic republican into forms more suitable to the milieu of the University and of the French professional classes.

CHAPTER VI

The Politics of
La Religion naturelle

Jules Simon wrote *La Religion naturelle* for a reading public of liberal and democratic persuasion that was seeking answers to questions about human destiny not from the Church but from reason. The content of the religious columns of the democratic press of the 1850s suggests that his potential audience was large. Indeed, these columns expressed a wide variety of heterodox religious aspirations, both intense and inchoate. *Le Siècle*, the early empire's only important republican newspaper, offered its fifty thousand subscribers the religious commentaries of two former Saint-Simonians, the individualistic Louis Jourdan and the romantic Eugène Pelletan. The "independent Christians" of *Le Siècle* rejected all organized forms of Christianity and considered religious assertions that went beyond the existence of God, immortality of the soul, and the biblical ideals of charity and fraternity to be mindless dogmatism.[1] The republican personnel of officially nonpolitical publications like the *Revue de Paris* of Laurent-Pichat and Maxime Du Camp, *La Libre recherche* of Pascal Duprat, and *L'Avenir* of Eugène Pelletan opened their pages to many forms of religious heterodoxy but reserved a cool reception for positivistic and materialistic currents of thought. Such republican works as Pelletan's *La Profession de foi du XIXe siècle* (1854) and Jean Reynaud's *Terre et Ciel* (1854) stimulated interest and debate in rather wide circles. In her popular republican salon the strong-minded Comtesse d'Agoult (Daniel Stern) invited her guests to share her pantheistic enthusiasms. As a professional philosopher, Simon hoped to make "even speculative questions accessible to common sense," to fortify republican deists with a systematic spiritualistic framework capable of exposing the fallacies of cur-

1. Léonor Havin, Eugène Pelletan, "Profession de foi," *Le Siècle*, 25 January 1855.

rent pantheistic and materialistic philosophic views.[2] Such a contribution, he thought, would complement the ethics he had developed in Le Devoir; it might strengthen the moral fiber of republicans and galvanize a broad democratic opposition drawn from the ranks of both republican freethinkers and Catholic liberals.

As it turned out, La Religion naturelle was for Simon not simply a major declaration of philosophic and religious principle but the opening statement in a spirited discussion that he carried on throughout the second half of 1856, especially with his philosophic critics. This polemic is instructive for the light that it sheds on the fading fortunes of that republican deism generally associated with the republicans of 1848, and on the development of those scientistic, positivistic, and materialistic currents of opinion that younger republicans were to adopt. On the basis of this extended polemic and the more general reception of the work, this chapter will evaluate Simon's success in bringing about a rapprochement of freethinking republican theists and Catholic liberals.

I

Although La Religion naturelle combats both materialism and pantheism, Simon believed, at the time of writing, that pantheism, especially the Saint-Simonian variety, was the more threatening. His antipathy was both philosophic and political: the pantheistic identification of God with the world led either to oriental fatalism or amoral atheism, ethical attitudes more suited to an authoritarian empire than a liberal Republic.[3] On the other hand, he regarded materialism, the "sensualism" of

2. JS, "Avertissement," La Religion naturelle, 3d ed. (Paris: Hachette, 1856), pp. xxi–xxii.

3. For Simon's arguments against pantheism, see JS, R.N., pp. 125–35; JS, "État de la philosophie en France. Les Radicaux le clergé. les éclectiques," RDM, n.s., 1 (1 February 1843): 379–81. For a Saint-Simonian pantheist's view of La Religion naturelle, see Adolphe Guéroult, "Revue des livres.—La Religion naturelle de M. Jules Simon," Revue philosophique et religieuse, 1 July 1856, pp. 476–78. Prominent Saint-Simonians supported the Second Empire. See Georges Weill, L'École Saint-Simonienne, son histoire, son influence jusqu'à nos jours, pp. 255–59.

Condillac and Diderot, as virtually extinct, unable to compete with the ideas of the new French spiritualism.[4] All that was left of this philosophic school was an approach to knowledge that stressed an empirical method rooted in material evidence—the so-called positive spirit. Indeed, although he had a nodding acquaintance with Comte and must have been familiar with Littré's republican positivism, Simon had always treated positive philosophy with Olympian disdain. Since positivism eschewed metaphysics, he suggested, it was "nothing at all as a theory." As a state of mind, the stern moralist stigmatized it as a godless negation, the "implacable enemy of progress, science and civilization."[5] And in *La Religion naturelle*, there is only the slightest allusion to the doctrine. Simon was soon to learn, to his regret, that on the Left the intellectual tide had turned. Among freethinkers, the real opposition to Simon's views came not from pantheists but from the advocates of a more positivistic approach to philosophic questions.

Foremost among these critics was Hippolyte Taine, whose bitter attacks on Cousin and his "classical" or "text-book" philosophers directly touched his former philosophy professor Simon. When Taine had arrived at the *École normale* in the fall of 1848, his mind already bore the mark of the materialistic philosophic tradition. His maternal grandfather, an enthusiast of Condillac and Laromiguière, had carefully initiated the young Taine to the *Langue des calculs*.[6] At the same time, during his years at the *Lycée Bourbon*, he had reacted against the skepticism that his abandonment of both Catholicism and natural religion had entailed and placed his hopes in an extreme pantheism.[7] As a young adept of Spinoza, he wrote to his friend Prévost-Paradol of his vacation life at Poissy: "My philosophy is not irrelevant to my pleasures; I find nature one hundred

4. JS, "Maine de Biran," *RDM* 28 (15 November 1841): 641; JS, "Du mouvement philosophique en province," *RDM* 30 (1 April 1842): 79; JS, "*Essais de philosophie* par M. Charles de Rémusat," *RDM* 30 (1 May 1842): 433–34; JS, R.N., p. ii.

5. JS, *Le Devoir*, p. 144. On Simon's acquaintance with Auguste Comte, see André Lavertujon, *Gambetta inconnu: cinq mois de la vie intime de Gambetta*, p. 123, and JS, *Premières années*, p. 426.

6. André Chevrillon, *Taine: formation de sa pensée*, pp. 4, 25–30.

7. Hippolyte Taine, "Destinée de l'homme" (1847–1848), quoted by Chevrillon, *Taine*, pp. 35–36.

times more beautiful now that I have thought about what it is."[8] Driven by a tremendous curiosity about the particular, and an intense desire to grasp the whole, Taine spent his years at the *École normale* elaborating this synthesis. Disdainful of such spiritualist idols as Plato and Descartes, he sought intellectual inspiration in Aristotle, Spinoza, and Hegel.[9]

At the *École normale*, Simon worked hard with his extraordinary pupil to oblige Taine to come to terms with spiritualist philosophy.[10] Although Simon remained on good terms with him throughout his years there, Taine ran into official resistance to his efforts to secure an *agrégation* in philosophy, and ultimately, after the coup d'etat, was obliged to seek a degree in literature.[11] Such tribulations could not shake Taine's commitment to empirical science and idealistic philosophy. The educated public, reassured by Taine's almost religious admiration of nature, delighted in his bold and brilliant nonconformity. In the second half of 1855, Taine began to publish in the *Revue de l'Instruction Publique*, a stronghold of official philosophy, a series of articles defending the empiricistic Laromiguière, and criticizing Cousin's philosophic career. In the same period, he made his debut in the liberal *Revue des Deux Mondes* with a critical article on Jean Reynaud's *Terre et Ciel* and received a prize from the *Académie française* for his *Essai sur Tite Live.*

Only in Taine's fourth article on Cousin, entitled "Théorie de la raison, par M. Cousin," published on 6 December 1855, did a clear picture of his real intentions begin to emerge. The target was not simply the philosophic hero of a bygone day but spiritualistic philosophy itself and its current advocates, especially Simon. Taine focused on Cousin's theory of the reason because it was the cornerstone of the whole spiritualist edifice. Lest anyone should miss his point, he began with an elaborate apology for the cruel necessities of science:

> I begin my enterprise almost with regret. I involuntarily
> think of one of the leaders of this school [M. Jules Simon], who

8. Hippolyte Taine, Poissy, to Lucien-Anatole Prévost-Paradol, 20 August 1848, Hippolyte Taine, *H. Taine, sa vie et sa correspondance*, 1:28–29.

9. Chevrillon, *Taine*, pp. 90–92.

10. Ibid., p. 99, note 1; see also Gabriel Monod, *Renan, Taine, Michelet*, p. 66, note 1.

11. André Cresson, *Hippolyte Taine, sa vie, son oeuvre*, pp. 5–6.

was my teacher, whose tone entices and whose conversation seduces, who imposes his convictions through eloquence and erudition, and who wins hearts by the persuasive grace of his mind and of his goodness. He delineated and defended this doctrine, at least in part. I separate the defender from the cause, for if memory should carry me back to the words of the defender, I would no longer have the courage to attack the cause; I would let myself be charmed; I would think of nothing but to follow, with mind and ear, along that line of reasoning. . . . I would be silent, and I would be doing the right thing. Consider therefore only the theory, and see if it resists, without other supports, and without any other judge than the truth.[12]

As most Frenchmen with philosophic interests knew, the philosophy of Cousin rested on a theory of reason he had developed in opposition to Locke, Condillac, and to certain aspects of Kantian epistemology. Against the empiricists, Cousin had argued that man is born with certain innate ideas that serve as the rational basis for man's knowledge of an infinite God and an absolute moral law. In the most general terms, Cousin's argument was that one can never deduce the infinite from the finite or the universal from the particular, and that the scientistic approach to knowledge would yield only perpetual uncertainty, and ultimately a sterile skepticism. Taine rejected this line of reasoning, so damaging to the scientific outlook, in the name of a "reductive operation called abstraction." By such an operation, the mind, working like an analytic geometrician arrives by observation and analysis at certain necessary propositions.

Taine's rejection of Cousin's epistemology led him to attack the spiritualistic conception of God without even the pro forma expression of respect for the religious sentiment that had graced his recent sharp attack on Jean Reynaud. Cousin had argued that just as human perceptions require a human subject, so the absolute truths require an "absolute being like them, where they have their ultimate basis"; the ideas of Truth, Beauty, and Goodness are attributes of God. Taine, tak-

12. Hippolyte Taine, "Variétés. Études sur les principaux écrivains du XIXe siècle. Théorie de la raison, par M. Cousin," *RIP*, 6 December 1855, p. 470.

ing advantage of Cousin's vague use of language, concluded that by attributes here, Cousin meant knowledge of an absolute truth. Now, if absolute truths are really thoughts of the divine intelligence, he wrote:

> When I notice that four is the double of two . . . I see . . . another's idea, God's idea; it is God himself, because one does not see an idea without seeing an intelligence producing it. If I write algebraic formulae for an hour, I see God for an hour. My neighbor, the fat mathematician, who, chalk in hand, smokes merrily while he tranquilly makes his calculations, is all the while contemplating this immense intelligence which one can not conceive without falling into a stupor.[13]

In Taine's polemic, laughter was even more devastating than logic. He advised Cousin to choose between "ecstasy" and Condillac.

In 1856, Taine's attacks upon spiritualism moved into the realm of ethics. He opened his "Préface" to his *Essai sur Tite Live*, published in January, on a note of Spinozistic determinism: "Man, Spinoza says, is not in nature 'like an empire in an empire,' but like a part in a whole; and the movements of the spiritual automaton which is our being are as regulated as those of the material world of which it is a part."[14] In May, he depicted Cousin's teacher Royer-Collard searching desperately for a philosophy that would shore up Christian morality, and paying thirty sous to a *bouquiniste* for the "new French philosophy" contained in the Scottish Thomas Reid's *An Inquiry into the Human Mind: On the Principles of Common Sense!*[15] By late July, he was bringing his dialectical powers to bear on Maine de Biran, "the cornerstone of the [spiritualist] temple, the first real spiritualist, the apostle of the free force." For Taine, on the other hand, the operations of the ego were a function of the necessary laws that regulate its properties.[16]

For Simon, the favorable reception that republicans gave to Taine's ideas, even more than the articles themselves, must have been cause for consternation. Most republicans, Simon was

13. Ibid., p. 471.
14. Hippolyte Taine, *Essai sur Tite Live*, p. vii.
15. Hippolyte Taine, "Variétés. Études sur les principaux écrivains du XIXᵉ siècle. M. Royer-Collard," *RIP*, 8 May 1856, pp. 79–82.
16. Hippolyte Taine, "Variétés. M. Maine de Biran," *RIP*, 31 July 1856, pp. 249–53.

dismayed to discover, classed Taine's articles against Cousin and eclecticism with his critique of Jean Reynaud. In their eyes, these articles represented another more spectacular attack on those who were seeking some sort of compromise between Catholic tradition and modern thought. When Taine's articles reappeared in January 1857, under the title *Les Philosophes français du dix-neuvième siècle*, the democratic journalists of *La Presse* and *Le Siècle* applauded this act of intellectual independence without committing themselves to the new doctrines Taine wished to substitute for the old. Only the *Revue de Paris*, edited by Laurent-Pichat and Maxime Du Camp, was clearly hostile:

> So far it does not seem that M. Taine has fully developed the philosophical doctrines which he would substitute for the old ones. He fights spiritualism; now there is much of value in spiritualism. We do not dare treat him as an atheist; he is too intelligent for that; but nevertheless, his sarcastic humor carries him toward negation.[17]

The first major republican review of *La Religion naturelle*, by Alphonse Peyrat, suggested once more, in a more dramatic way, that Simon had underestimated the appeal of scientistic and anti-metaphysical thinking for members of the democratic opposition. Writing in *La Presse*, the newspaper of the democratic maverick Émile de Girardin, Peyrat suggested that by the standards of scientifically and materialistically oriented philosophers like Lucretius, Bacon, and Diderot, Simon's work was not very philosophic. The skeptical Peyrat ridiculed Simon's suggestion that the whole world testified to God's existence and found the work full of "the kind of level-headed notions, of supposed truths which circulate freely because no one today bothers to refute them." Real philosophers, he sternly suggested, should admit their own limitations and should avoid the temptation to have recourse to God to camouflage certain intellectual difficulties. Moreover, Simon's discussion of the future life, of that "Heaven"

17. "Chronique de la quinzaine. Bulletin bibliographique," *Revue de Paris*, 13 June 1857, pp. 633–34. See also: Taxile Delord, "Variétés. *Les Philosophes français du dix-neuvième siècle*, par H. Taine," *Le Siècle*, 16 February 1857; Auguste Nefftzer, "Variétés. La Jeune philosophie, *Les Philosophes français du dix-neuvième siècle*, par H. Taine," *La Presse*, 20 March 1857.

where men stand in the presence of a God who "knows each of us by name," was no more than a product of the philosopher's "ardent imagination, an unreliable guide which he does not sufficiently mistrust." Peyrat was astonished at Simon's complacency toward an ecstasy "equally rejected by philosophy and by serious religion" and horrified by his apology for the freethinker's participation in selected ceremonies of a positive religion. Simon, he believed, had done an "unforgivable" disservice to the cause of reason; for by failing to recognize reason's proper limits, he had humiliated it in a vain effort to understand what Peyrat regarded as unknowable and irrelevant. "If M. Simon had asserted a little less and doubted a little more, he would not have authenticated in two-hundred forty-two pages the future life and Providence, only to confess on the two-hundred forty-third page that he had only incomplete ideas on such subjects."[18]

This offensive review provoked Simon to reply in the hope of preventing republicans from prejudging the book before they gave it a fair reading. Particularly irritating were Peyrat's remarks about Simon's views on the freethinker's participation in the ceremonies of positive religions. With his Voltairean suspicion that most Catholics were religious hypocrites, Peyrat saw in Simon's work an apology for religious insincerity. According to Peyrat's reading, Simon had approved freethinkers' attendance at such services. In fact, however, Simon had expressed qualified disapproval of such practices. His friends, remembering his discussions in *Le Devoir* of the same subject, urged him to point out Peyrat's error and to show that his attitude on this point had not changed. Simon wrote Peyrat a note calling attention to the matter and asked the journalist to acknowledge his error in anyway he chose. To Simon's great consternation, Peyrat published his letter and raised the tone of the polemic. In his previous review, the journalist recalled, he had noted only a part of the "bizarre dreams, chimerical conjectures and insane imaginings which, in my opinion, deprive this book of almost all philosophic value." On the particular issue in question, he exposed Simon's full position, which seemed both to condemn and to condone freethinkers'

18. Alphonse Peyrat, "*La Religion naturelle*, par Jules Simon," *La Presse*, 19 May 1856.

participation in the services of positive religions. Here, as elsewhere, Peyrat argued, Simon's position was "two-faced" and contradictory, honoring free thought while revering the Catholic religion. And, in the Voltairean manner, always eager to find worldly interests behind the discussion of spiritual matters, Peyrat concluded maliciously that the contradictions were so abundant as to appear almost systematic. *La Religion naturelle* was, he implied, really more political than philosophic, a "legitimate daughter of M. Cousin" that, while pretending to represent a *juste milieu* in philosophy, really maneuvered for position in the competition for the praise of the liberal Catholic *Correspondant* and the prizes of the *Académie française.* For personal political advantage, Peyrat implied, Simon was putting "his flag in his pocket." "Moderation and good taste are nice things," Peyrat moralized, "but as always, and especially these days, sincerity is better."[19]

In reply to his critics, and particularly to Taine and Peyrat, Simon wrote a twenty-four page "Avertissement" in early August and attached it to the third edition of *La Religion naturelle.* Although he did not mention these protagonists by name, his meaning was clear for all who followed such polemics. These men, he believed, represented currents of opinion even more dangerous to the cause of reason and free thought than the ultramontanism of Veuillot. Although he did not define these categories with very much precision, he distinguished two sorts of attitude, the skeptical and the Voltairean, in the philosophic opposition. Simon used the term skeptical to refer to both atheists and agnostics, to materialists and to positivists, and "apostles of positive science," to all those who refused to affirm the existence of God. By Voltairean, he designated a person who refused to regard Catholic religious needs as genuine and who looked forward to the absolute extinction of Roman Catholicism.[20] The two attitudes might coexist in the same person as in the case of Peyrat. But one might be a skeptic and not a Voltairean, like Taine, or a Voltairean

19. Alphonse Peyrat, "Lettre de M. Jules Simon," *La Presse*, 24 May 1856; see also on this episode, JS to Marie d'Agoult, July 1856, Daniel Ollivier Papers, n.a.fr. 25189.

20. JS, "Avertissement" (10 August 1856), *La Religion naturelle*, 3d ed., pp. ii–iii, xi–xiii.

but not a skeptic, like the theistic *Le Siècle*. In his "Avertissement," he sought to offer a rebuttal to Taine and his supporters and a critique of Voltairean tactics and purposes.

Simon began, as Taine's former professor of philosophy, by angrily declaring that all Taine's study of the history of philosophy had been fruitless—"neither Plato, nor Zeno, nor Descartes, nor Leibnitz" had made any impression on his "cold heart" and "sterile intelligence." But his refutation of Taine rested more on a simple reassertion of the spiritualist point of view than on any effort to deal critically with Taine's notions. He argued that the logical consequence of Taine's espousal of positive science is Pyrrhonism. For if one begins with the assumption that there is nothing real outside of sense experience, "every principle based on experience would necessarily have the character of experience itself. It would have the same value as an induction." Even the moral law, even the idea of justice, would, under Taine's system assume the status of any scientific discovery, a provisional truth constantly at the mercy of further research. In such a context, reasoning loses all significance. By denying that we have ideas of the ideal "first truths, which are prior and superior to all experience," positivists imprison us in "day-to-day reality, so sad and so poor," forbidding us "hope while limiting our destiny to the life of a body whose end is anticipated and inevitable." The science of the positivists is "a negation in theory, a dissolvent [of society] in practice." One could understand fanaticism in the name of faith, Simon cried, but "these insults, sarcasms, betrayals are incomprehensible when placed in the service of a sterile reason and an intolerant liberty. What! You believe nothing and you are not humble?"[21]

In other times, Simon believed, it would have been possible to ignore such skeptical doctrines, which were so repugnant to the most elementary common sense. But in the contemporary political and religious climate, these attitudes had taken on new life, for they found new support in a resurgence of Voltairianism in French life. Simon explained this alliance in historical terms. During their struggle in the 1840s against the demands of a portion of the clergy for liberty of education, spiritualist philosophers, who really stood for the principle of

21. Ibid., pp. xi–xv, xxii–xxiii.

free thought, unfortunately became identified with "official philosophy" and the "University monopoly." In the highly charged atmosphere of polemic and counter-polemic, an honest disagreement about the precise meaning and implications of the principle of liberty of conscience was lost. The debate was transformed into a struggle between Catholic ultramontanes intent on combating reason and the very principle of free thought and Voltaireans who "after having attacked the Jesuits and gradually adopted the tone of the *Encyclopedia*, were dying to attack Christianity." Intent upon defending the philosophy curriculum of the University against the ultramontane onslaught, and fearful of being compromised by Voltairean defenders, Cousin and his philosophy professors, who were spiritualists to a man, accepted the "equivocations . . . half measures . . . embrassing situations" associated with self-censorship. Thereby, they drew the honest and legitimate criticism of Voltaireans. The coup d'etat of Louis Napoleon, and the new regime's alliance with the Church widened the gap between Voltaireans and the representatives of academic spiritualist philosophy. For exasperated Voltaireans, it seemed clearer than ever that compromise with Catholicism was tantamount to complicity in the new tyranny. Since they had become involved in philosophic disputes only through their polemic with the Clerical party and had no solid scientific and philosophic knowledge, they unscrupulously adopted agnostic, materialist, or atheistic doctrines as a means of combating spiritualists. They transformed a tactical difference with spiritualists into a philosophic dispute. Convinced that spiritualist philosophic attitudes merely reflected insincerity or self-interested compromises, they broadened their attacks to include not only Christianity but also "spiritualist philosophy, with its metaphysics so completely impregnated with Christianity." [22]

From the high ground of philosophic principle, Simon called on the Voltaireans of *La Presse* and *Le Siècle* to reexamine the motives underlying their suspicions about philosophic spiritualism and their permissive attitudes toward the kind of skepticism that Taine represented. He reminded his critics that free thought is not incompatible with reasoned acceptance of the spiritualist verities. It is wrong to confuse philosophy with

22. Ibid., pp. iv–xv.

politics. Republicans should not bandy about positivistic or materialistic theses simply because they are useful weapons against the Church or the University philosophy. Look to the truth of a doctrine and not its origins: "If spiritualism is true, we should be spiritualists, whatever the mistakes of particular spiritualists."[23] And he reminded his republican friends that spiritualism is closest to their innermost feelings, for it is the philosophy of reason and liberty.

II

Simon entertained hopes that his work would help provoke the kind of consolidation of republican deism that would moderate his friends' hostility to the Church and prepare the ground for increasing cooperation between the forces represented by *Le Siècle* and the rationalistic and liberal Catholics of *Le Correspondant*. Secure in their own religious beliefs, appreciative of the doctrines that natural religion shared with Christianity, fully aware of the liberalism of some elements in the Church, spiritualistic republicans might enlist the support of Catholic allies in their opposition to the political and religious authoritarianism of the Second Empire. Simon believed that such an alliance with liberal and republican Catholics would be possible if he could allay Catholic fears that natural religion would become a Voltairean weapon. The difficulties in such an undertaking were obvious: If natural religion had raised the fears of Catholics even when it was presented as an auxiliary of positive religion and roughly equated with sound ethics, what of a natural religion that posed as a substitute and/or rival to the Catholic faith?[24]

Anticipating these apprehensions, Simon sought first to define his audience. In his prefatory remarks, he explicitly stated that he was directing his remarks not to Catholics but to those "who cannot accept the principle of revelation, or who, unable to accept all the truths taught by the Church . . . feel

23. Ibid., pp. i, xv–xvi.

24. In the 1840s, Cousin and his followers seldom used the term *natural religion*. When they did, they seemed to follow Voltaire's practice of equating it with a set of commonly accepted ethical beliefs. Victor Cousin, "Sur le scepticisme de Pascal, I," *RDM*, n.s., 8 (15 December 1844): 1014. Simon used the term in the same sense in his "Préface" to *Le Devoir*, p. i.

obliged to give up positive religion and turn unreservedly to philosophy."[25] His principal aim in writing *La Religion naturelle*, he insisted, was to show "religious minds who, however, accept no other authority than reason," that there is an alternative to skepticism. He sought to

> stimulate the religious sentiment, without which there will never be a gentle law, a fraternal society or a solid virtue, in certain saddened and lonely souls. If I could revive one hope, fortify one will, reaffirm one shaken conscience, console and tranquilize one suffering heart, I would consider these humble pages to have served their purpose.[26]

In both his initial "Préface" and in the "Avertissement" to the third edition, his enemies were primarily pantheists, skeptics, and Voltaireans. And the arguments in the text itself were directed against the same groups and not against Catholic dogma.

His discussion of natural religion itself generally substantiates his declared intention to provide a home for the philosophically minded unbeliever and a basis for personal and public moral effort. Although he believed that the history of humanity showed a progressive process of enlightenment, as truths first grasped by the learned slowly filter into the common sense of the many, he insisted that natural religion is presently capable of satisfying the needs of only the few.[27] Catholics need not be unduly alarmed. In later editions, he made this point even more strongly, arguing that because the principles of natural religion rest only on the assent of the individual's reason, they can have no authority over "passive intelligences." "To be brief, its symbol, if it has one, cannot be separated from the proofs which establish it; this condition means that it will never be universal."[28] In general, Simon maintained that natural religion can satisfy the needs of contemporary "cultivated minds" and kept silent about the religious beliefs appropriate for the vast majority.[29]

Finally, Simon sought to associate natural religion with liberty of conscience in the minds of his potential Catholic

25. JS, "Préface," R.N., p. ii.   26. Ibid., pp. v–vi.
27. JS, R.N., pp. 460–61.
28. JS, *La Religion naturelle*, 3d ed., pp. 346–47; for the earlier version, see R.N., pp. 398–99.
29. JS, R.N., pp. 416–17.

allies. For freethinkers, he argued, liberty of conscience is a foregone conclusion, because it is simply a derivative of the philosophic principle. The right to think freely means, by definition, the right to free expression. Catholics or any adherents of positive religions can also accept the principle of liberty of conscience without compromising their faiths. Against the testimony of Rousseau's Savoyard Vicar, who officiated for a doctrine that he did not, strictly speaking, believe, Simon insisted that advocates of liberty of conscience need not be religiously indifferent. Indeed, the right to liberty of conscience requires civil toleration but does not preclude the ecclesiastical intolerance of positive religions. To reassure Catholics even further, Simon took care not to mix his defense of liberty of conscience with defense of religious sects like Enfantin's Saint-Simonian circle. He would oppose such sects when their practices proved incompatible with "pure" morals.

With these guarantees, Simon hoped, liberal and republican Catholics might accept the support of the proponents of natural religion in their struggle against the political and religious authoritarianism of Veuillot and his following. In the new "Préface" to the third edition of Le Devoir, Simon had applauded those within the Church who were defending the rights of philosophy and political liberty against ultramontane threats.[30] Now in La Religion naturelle, he alluded to Veuillot as the personification of all which is "necessarily human" and foreign to the essence of the Catholic faith. Because they refuse to accept liberty in the Church, they believe themselves justified in opposing liberty in the society as a whole.[31] In the "Avertissement" of August 1856, Simon replied to the Univers's review of his book by citing a number of Thomistic articles in defense of natural reason from the most recent code of the Sacred Congregation of the Index.[32]

To seal this alliance between republican deists and those Catholics whom he considered modern, Simon sought to induce republicans to adopt a respectful attitude toward Catholic religious beliefs. Republicans, he hoped, would focus their

30. JS, "Préface," Le Devoir, 3d ed. (Paris: Hachette, 1855), pp. v–vi.
31. JS, R.N., p. 415.
32. JS, "Avertissement," La Religion naturelle, 3d ed., pp. ix–x. See Abbé P. Roux-Lavergne, "La Religion Naturelle par Jules Simon," L'Univers, 28 July 1856.

attacks on those manifestations of the clerical spirit that often offended the liberal Catholic journal, *Le Correspondant*. In addition to civil toleration, a principle that could be given a legal form, the right to liberty of conscience imposed a moral obligation on the individual to respect the consciences of others.

> It is not enough to tolerate religions: one must respect them. After all, what is a religion, even a false one, if not a homage to Providence. . . . There is something sacred in every effort by which a human soul directs itself toward God. Is it appropriate for us to complain about particular formulations, to pose objections to this or that doctrine, when we know how many conceptions of God have been exposed and refuted by the greatest geniuses?[33]

Simon offered *La Religion naturelle* as an example of the kind of respect, both in tone and substance, which natural religion owed to Catholicism. Freely acknowledging spiritualist affinities with Christianity, he dealt even with such doctrines as the fall or the eternity of punishments in a balanced and sober manner.[34] Insults and calumnies, he reminded Voltairean readers of *La Religion naturelle*, convinced no one and discredited deism.[35]

Some Catholic liberals were favorably disposed to such overtures, although they had not given up hopes for a France that would be religiously united. Augustin Cochin, the editor of the Catholic *Journal des villes et des campagnes* and a contributor to *Le Correspondant*, was one of those working for such a rapprochement. How far such a Catholic was willing to go is evident in a letter that he wrote to Montalembert about Jean Reynaud's pantheistic *Terre et Ciel*. There were democrats of religious orientation with whom one might work:

> You probably have not read a book which I want to recommend; it is by a man who is more than strange, but certainly of uncommon vision: it is *Terre et Ciel* by M. Jean Reynaud. The [*Journal des*] *Débats* made fun of it, and the *Univers*, if anything, will only denounce it, and tear it up. In my

33. JS, *R.N.*, p. 443.
34. Ibid., pp. 191–92, 349–50; JS, "Avertissement," *La Religion naturelle*, 3d ed., p. xv, xviii.
35. JS, *R.N.*, p. 442.

opinion, that would be a mistake. This is a strange work, and the theory of the preexistence and transmigration of souls is laughable. But most of the book is Catholic; what is significant is that our faith, its solutions, its doctrines are treated with respect, and those with some taste for questions concerning the origin and destiny of our souls . . . will find in *Terre et Ciel* pages of incomparable eloquence, knowledge and fullness. I believe that this is the sort of effort which Catholicism should welcome; a bishop should write to the author; ten pages may be against us, but fifty are for us; if we shoot down the author and his friends, right away we make irreconcilable enemies; if we take him seriously as he deserves, then we have a reconciled adversary and perhaps a converted soul. Why not let him have *in dubiis libertas* the hypotheses which harm no one? We hold out only our fingertips instead of our hands to men who would like nothing better than to shake them. . . . By noting how democrats talk of Catholicism even while criticizing it, you will appreciate all the more the progress in attitudes toward this religion which fifty years ago was considered neither true, nor good, nor beautiful.[36]

Although Montalembert agreed to use his influence to secure a more favorable Catholic press for the work, he evidently was not able to sway Edmond de Fontette at *Le Correspondant*.[37]

Prior to the publication of *La Religion naturelle*, Catholic liberals and democrats had treated Simon with marked cordiality, although without any attempt to disguise their differing viewpoints.[38] By 1856, *Le Correspondant* had become even more favorably disposed to Simon. Its new editorial board, containing such men as Cochin and Falloux, was determined to combat the ultramontane Veuillot.[39] Albert de Broglie began his review in *Le Correspondant* with a veiled reference to *L'Univers*,

36. Augustin Cochin to Charles de Montalembert, 7 August 1854, quoted in Augustin Cochin, *Augustin Cochin, 1823–1872. Ses lettres et sa vie*, 1:119.

37. David Griffiths, *Jean Reynaud, encyclopédiste de l'époque romantique*, p. 358.

38. For two favorable Catholic views, see Edmond de Fontette, "Le Devoir," *Le Correspondant* 34, no. 3 (25 June 1854): 321–47; Jérôme Morin, "Philosophie des origines du devoir à propos du livre *Du Devoir* de M. Jules Simon," *Revue du lyonnais* 10 (March 1855): 212–18.

39. Albert de Broglie, *Mémoires du Duc de Broglie, 1821–1901*, 1:278, 287.

which had reiterated its uncompromising hostility to Simon in a series of reviews occupying the entire front page of the newspaper.[40] Simon's work, Broglie wrote, was appearing at a time when communication between philosophers and believers had broken down in an atmosphere of scorn and mistrust. "Some consider faith as a sign of limited intelligence, while others call doubt a vice of the heart." This "serious and conscientious book" offered an ideal opportunity to declare a truce. The work treated Christians not with derision but with respect, esteem, and even envy: "With such an adversary, we sincerely believe that it is useful and possible to carry on a discussion."[41]

Simon's work, Broglie wrote, raised the question whether "human reason, without revelation, left to its own discoveries, drawing only on itself . . . can give birth to a series of beliefs which fully deserve to be called a religion." Broglie began with Simon's definition of man's religious needs: "What man needs to know above all else . . . is whether God cares about him. We need God not only to give a foundation to metaphysics, but also to give hope and consolation to life."[42] His discussion would show, Broglie promised, that on examination, Simon's natural religion, in its conception of God, did not really respond to these needs. The God that Simon derived from an analysis of the idea of the absolute was "an abstract and insensitive God cloaked in ice."[43] The God that Simon detected through observation of the goodness and orderliness of nature was really an "irresistible machine," an "unshakeable will."[44] Simon did not have the right to identify such a *"nature divinisée"* with Providence.

In a second article, published in October 1856, Broglie continued this critique. He clearly registered his opposition to Simon's treatment of man's justification before God. Unaware of the place Simon reserved for divine grace in man's justification, and further prompted by his Christian sense of human

40. See Abbé P. Roux-Lavergne, "*La Religion naturelle* par Jules Simon," *L'Univers*, 28 July, 1, 10 August 1856.

41. Albert de Broglie, "*De La Religion naturelle* par Jules Simon," *Le Correspondant* 38, no. 5 (25 August 1856): 860–61.

42. Ibid., p. 864.   43. Ibid., p. 871.

44. Ibid., p. 882; Albert de Broglie, "*De La Religion naturelle* par Jules Simon (Deuxième Article)," *Le Correspondant* 39, no. 1 (1 October 1856): 7.

sinfulness, Broglie could not understand Simon's perorations about divine mercy, for how could "the God of reason . . . have the least pity for vice"?[45] Yet, Broglie's dominant concern, which must have pleased Simon, was to underscore all that the philosopher shared with Catholics. The irrationalism of the ultramontanes notwithstanding, "the great philosophical truths which M. Simon develops, and on which he mounts the whole edifice of natural religion. . . , these truths . . . we repeat, in agreement with all the doctors of the Church, are rational truths, truths of the reason, which reason alone, without any other aid can discover and demonstrate."[46] Catholics could hardly view with disfavor his attacks on materialism and on pantheism.[47] At the same time, Broglie tried to distinguish Simon from other deists. Despite his reservations about the philosopher's conception of God, he maintained that this being shared little in common with the "God of natural religion of novels and popular songs—a God who could hardly be charged with severity, whose principal character is compassion and even affability." Simon felt the "same indignation as the most severe Christian for such profanations of a God who is not merely good but Goodness."[48] Broglie even allowed himself a little liberty with the evidence to give *La Religion naturelle* a rather special interpretation. Many, he believed, would conclude from the book that Simon was proposing a new religion for the elite minds of the nineteenth century: "Nothing justifies our making this assumption about Simon's intentions, for his book exudes sincerity." He implied that Simon, like him, viewed natural religion as a temporary, personal position for a Catholic afflicted with grave uncertainties.[49]

Broglie's entire treatment of *La Religion naturelle* rested on an assumption, rooted in Catholic orthodoxy and reinforced by Simon's sentimental philosophic restraint, that natural religion was essentially a parasite of Christianity:

> It has never appeared except in union with a revealed religion: like those plants without substance or life, which can only grow attached to a sturdy trunk where they draw sugar. . . .

45. Broglie, "De *La Religion naturelle* par Jules Simon (Deuxième Article)," *Le Correspondant* 39, no. 1 (1 October 1856): 11–16, 35.
46. Ibid., p. 23.   47. Ibid., p. 8.
48. Ibid., pp. 17–18.   49. Ibid., p. 37.

This new purified form of natural religion has no more substance of its own than its predecessors.[50]

Although reason might verify the basic truths of Christianity,
it could not produce a stable faith, free from the anguish caused
by frequent sieges of confusion. Simon's admitted inadequacies
in formulating a suitable form of worship, even the discrepancy
between the claims he made for his God and his rational proofs,
suggested the degree to which his natural religion depended for
its vital forces on Christian culture. Since Simon admitted that
Christianity had previously served the development of the
intelligence, there was no reason to believe those services had
ceased. Indeed, the admiration that unbelievers might feel for
La Religion naturelle, while owing something to the force of
Simon's arguments, eloquently testified that "the reader is,
like the author, Christian without wanting to be, and without
realizing it."[51]

Catholics close to French university life also responded favorably to *La Religion naturelle*. Writing for the *Revue de
l'Instruction Publique*, Géruzez, the Catholic secretary of the
Faculty of Letters, lauded Simon as a welcome auxiliary in the
struggle against pantheism and materialism. "Much more
Christian than he thinks," Simon, like Rousseau, would initiate
a movement that would bring many unbelievers back to the
faith.[52] At the Faculty of Theology, Dean Henri Maret, formerly an editor of the Christian democratic *L'Ère nouvelle* (1848–
1850), treated *La Religion naturelle* in a lecture that inspired
an enthusiastic Morin to talk of an incipient "solution for our
religious debates." Although apprehensive about the strength
of the mocking ultramontane authoritarians, Morin encouraged
Catholics to look favorably upon Simon's efforts.[53] At the
Académie française, Montalembert joined Thiers, Rémusat,
and Guizot in an unavailing attempt to secure a prize for *La
Religion naturelle*. In this case, the Pope's reaction to the book

50. Ibid., p. 22.   51. Ibid., p. 35.
52. Eugène Géruzez, "La Religion naturelle par Jules Simon," *RIP*,
29 May 1856, pp. 114–17; Paul Gerbod, *La Condition universitaire*, p.
179.
53. Frédéric Morin, "Le Livre de *La Religion naturelle* et la faculté
de théologie," *RIP*, 19 February 1857, pp. 682–85; see also his "*Essai
critique sur 'La Religion naturelle'* par Michel de Castelnau," *RIP*, 4
November 1858, pp. 500–502.

is perhaps the best testimony to the attractiveness of this work to Catholics: On 9 May 1857, Pope Pius IX placed it on the *Index*.[54] Further public discussion between Catholic liberals and deists on this volume was now impossible.

III

In republican circles, Simon's plea for a spiritualistic republicanism oriented toward collaboration with modern Catholics elicited varied responses. His strongest support came from the *Revue de Paris*, where Simon was a member of the editorial board.[55] Indeed, after introducing *La Religion naturelle* to its readers in a prepublication review on 1 May the *Revue* became virtually the official patron of the book.[56] A month later, the "Bulletin bibliographique" called attention to Simon's book, which treated "one of the most pressing concerns of the present generation," and warned its readers against the "regrettably biased" review published by *La Presse*.[57] On 1 August the *Revue* published an appreciation of Simon's work by his friend the republican Jules Barni, a former *normalien* who had also been a member of Cousin's philosophic regiment.

Barni, unlike the Catholic critics, took the possibility of a self-sustaining natural religion for granted. He was in general agreement with Simon's major doctrines, although he felt the author's overly diffident treatment of reason invited misinterpretation.[58] Therefore, he sought to underscore the relevance of natural religion for contemporary religious difficulties. He identified natural religion with the true religious spirit—an attraction for the absolute that sprang from the "bottom of our hearts and . . . the depths of our reason," joining all men, re-

---

54. Roman Catholic Church, *Index librorum prohibitorum* (Vatican City: Typis polyglottis vaticanis, 1938), p. 442.

55. "*Revue de Paris*, Cinquième année," 1 April 1856, a brochure contained in *Revue de Paris*, April–May 1856 (Bibliothèque nationale, Z 21599). For Simon's relations with the *Revue de Paris*, see "Les Académiciens de mon temps," Maxime Du Camp Papers, 30, folio #388.

56. "*La Religion naturelle* par Jules Simon," *Revue de Paris*, 1 May 1856, pp. 350–62.

57. "Bulletin bibliographique," *Revue de Paris*, 1 June 1856, p. 147.

58. Jules Barni, "*La Religion naturelle* par Jules Simon," *Revue de Paris*, 1 August 1856, p. 37.

gardless of creed, under a universal moral law. The antithesis of this religious spirit was the theocratic spirit, which he associated with human superstitious propensites, dominating urges, and corporative instincts. Driven by this spirit, the Roman Catholic Church, although devoid of religious spirit, had attributed to itself exclusive rights to represent God on earth. This pretension justified its authoritarian intolerance in civil and ecclesiastical affairs and even a profound indifference to the dictates of the moral conscience.[59] Although sympathetic to the efforts of Voltaireans to rid humanity of this awful plague, Barni warned them not to confuse the religious spirit with the theocratic spirit. They should follow the lead of Rousseau and Voltaire, who understood that deism, not materialism or skepticism, provided the best foundation for human freedom and dignity.[60] In a second part, Barni supported Simon's critique of pantheism, especially from the moral point of view.[61] Thus, Barni strongly endorsed Simon's ideas but harnessed them to a restrained Voltairianism.

Despite Barni's qualifications, the *Revue de Paris* continued to show special solicitude for Simon. In October, Louis Ulbach, the director, prefaced a review of Charles Dollfus's *Essai sur la philosophie sociale* with a three-page apology for *La Religion naturelle*, a book he believed had suffered for its honesty and sincerity in a time of sharp polemics. Indeed, "freethinkers who have been only lukewarm toward *La Religion naturelle* will undoubtedly realize their mistake when they see how their reservations have encouraged the violence of our adversaries."[62]

For the *Revue de Paris*, the principal appeal of Simon's work lay in his eloquent formulation of a rational religious alternative to Catholicism, rather than in his deference to Catholic liberals. Yet, although the *Revue* was never anything but hostile to the ostensible liberalism of Montalembert, Broglie, and Falloux, it coupled its support for liberty of conscience

59. Ibid., pp. 27–33. 60. Ibid., pp. 35–36.
61. Ibid., pp. 38–44.
62. Louis Ulbach, "Chronique de la quinzaine," *Revue de Paris*, 1 October 1856, pp. 132–33. For further notices in the same vein, see Léon Laurent-Pichat, "Chronique de la quinzaine," *Revue de Paris*, 1 January 1857, pp. 479–80; "Chronique de la quinzaine: Bulletin bibliographique," *Revue de Paris*, 1 March 1857, p. 151; "Bulletin bibliographique," *Revue de Paris*, 1 October 1857, p. 501.

with the pledge to treat religious questions firmly but respect-fully.[63] At the same time, it welcomed Morin's tightly reasoned arguments in favor of Christian democracy.[64] The *Revue* did not, however, commit itself to Morin's position; it preferred to encourage debate on the relationship between Catholic and democratic principles. In general, with the exception of Barni's review of *La Religion naturelle*, the uncompromising Voltairean hostility toward the Church was conspicuously absent from the *Revue*.

Yet for Simon's purposes, the responses of *La Presse* and especially *Le Siècle* were much more important. For these newspapers could introduce his work to the people for whom it was primarily written. Peyrat's review in *La Presse* had been a disappointment; the response of *Le Siècle* would be decisive. Simon's apprehension mounted as time passed and the review did not appear. Although *Le Siècle* had praised *Le Devoir*, Simon had since been associated with the losing side in an internal struggle for power at the paper.[65] Then there was *Le Siècle*'s Voltairianism; would the newspaper extend its Voltairean suspicions of religious hypocrisy from Catholicism to natural religion? Yet there was also cause for optimism. Havin was the advocate of a "renovated Catholicism which would be very tolerant, very conciliatory, and regulated by the State."[66] The journalist who would write the article was Jourdan, a Saint-Simonian known for his religious feeling, an assiduous reader of the New Testament, especially the Gospel of John, the favorite of mystics.[67]

The review finally appeared on 6 July more than a month after Peyrat's disastrous critique. It was another disappoint-ment. *Le Siècle* was as respectful of Simon's personal integrity

63. "*Revue de Paris*. Cinquième année," p. 2. On Catholic liberals, see Louis Ulbach, "Le Parti Catholique, ses variations. —MM. de Mon-talembert, de Falloux et Veuillot," *Revue de Paris*, 15 August 1856; "Lettre de M. de Montalembert," *Revue de Paris*, 15 September 1856, pp. 605–9; Romain-Cornut, "Catholicisme et démocratie," *Revue de Paris*, 1 April 1857, pp. 426–30.

64. Frédéric Morin, "La Philosophie des sciences cherchée dans leur histoire," *Revue de Paris*, 1, 15 July 1856, pp. 351–79, 543–57.

65. Eugène Pelletan, "*Le Devoir* par Jules Simon," *Le Siècle*, 23 Janu-ary 1854; Léonor Havin, Paris, to JS, 5 July 1856, 87 AP 4.

66. Georges Weill, *Histoire de l'idée laïque au XIXe siècle*, p. 132.

67. Maxime Du Camp, *Souvenirs littéraires*, 2:144–45.

as it was hostile to his views. Jourdan defended the "firmness and loyalty of the celebrated philosopher's conviction" against *La Presse* and saluted Simon as a "deep thinker, a calm and firm writer, and an imperturbable logician." But, despite the philosopher's obvious commitment to a religion free from revelation and dogma, Jourdan balked at Simon's efforts to define and order the free religious spirit. Indeed, for Jourdan, natural religion was equated with the most radical religious individualism: "There are as many natural religions as there are believers, since there do not exist in the world two identical beings, two minds which see all things alike, two hearts which love and feel in the same way." Although man might agree on a universal morality, "religion as a form of worship, doctrines, conception of God, belief in a future life—that's another thing!" In such delicate matters of the conscience, "there is no middle ground possible between submission and absolute liberty, between a 'rule' and the absence of all 'rules.'"

With a Voltairean distrust of all priests and pastors, Jourdan insisted that natural religion is the "religion of those who . . . impatient with all yokes, wishing to submit to no director, follow no other rules of worship than those they impose on themselves." No sooner does Simon attempt to "regulate" the religious spirit than, as a "pontiff of natural religion," he is bitterly and tenaciously campaigning against pantheism. Moreover, Simon, with his unabashed admiration of Catholicism, and his doctrines, "borrowed with slight modifications from the Church," has provided, however involuntarily, a rationale for remaining Catholic. Although the Catholics of *L'Univers* will show their customary ingratitude, Jourdan concluded, Simon's book, "more Catholic than philosophical," was a "pure loss" for the cause of free thought.[68]

Jourdan's review underscored the profound differences between *Le Siècle*'s professed Christianity and orthodox Catholicism. The link that Simon established between ethics and deism was one of the bases of his efforts to reassure Catholic liberals of the depth of their common concerns. Since Catholics believed that ethics rested on a theological basis, Simon's firm deism was reassuring, if not totally satisfying. *Le Siècle*, on the other hand, was committed to a position that did not possess

68. Louis Jourdan, "*La Religion naturelle* par Jules Simon," *Le Siècle*, 6 July 1856.

the same credibility for Catholics. They could never accept Jourdan's belief that an ethical system could stand independently of any aspiration toward the divine.[69] Unsympathetic to *Le Siècle*'s deep-seated distrust of religious authority, they could not see the journal's ethically centered "Christianity" as anything more than a hypocritical technique of anti-Catholic polemic, a veil for a corrosive skepticism. And *Le Siècle*, which conceived of Christianity primarily as a doctrine of moral responsibility, could not accept Simon's advice and stop attacking the Church in the name of Jesus.[70]

*   *   *   *   *

In Parisian circles, Simon's efforts to stimulate a redefinition and consolidation of republican religious heterodoxy and to delineate a policy of conciliation directed at politically liberal and rationalistic Catholics met wth rather limited success. Although important elements among Catholic laymen were willing to open a dialogue, they found themselves extremely vulnerable to pressures from a more hostile hierarchy that, through the Pope, controlled the means of defining orthodoxy. Although the majority of republicans preferred some sort of theism to materialism or positivism and even hoped, for reasons both pragmatic and principled, to work out some form of modus vivendi with the Church, a Voltairean current ran deep in French republicanism. This current, the reflection of a profound distrust of the Church's political intentions, was difficult for Simon to combat, for even he considered an uncontrolled Church a clear and actual danger to the principles of modern liberalism. Republicans, living on the edge of the enormous shadow cast by the Church, understandably believed that the most significant cleavage in French intellectual life was between free thought and Catholicism. They could not accept Simon's view that the really crucial dividing line for republicans was between religious skepticism on the one hand, and the combined forces of religious and philosophic spiritualism on

69. Louis Jourdan, "La Loi morale," *Le Siècle*, 1 October 1856.

70. Louis Jourdan, "Christianisme et Catholicisme," *Le Siècle*, 9, 13 July 1856. See also *Le Siècle*'s response to the works of the Catholic democrats François Huet and J.-B. Bordas-Demoulin: Eugène Pelletan, "Variétés. Le Règne social du Christianisme," *Le Siècle*, 21 April 1854; Louis Jourdan, "Variétés. La Démocratie dans l'Église," *Le Siècle*, 9, 10 April 1855.

the other. The cause of reason, they believed, was too important
to confide to a spiritualistic philosophy closely associated with
university professors overcommitted to appearing irreproachable to Catholics.[71] Thus, they resisted an attitude that would
divide the philosophic camp. As Morin noted, Simon was more
applauded than followed by his republican associates.[72]

71. See the attitude of the *Revue de Paris* toward Victor Cousin:
Léon Laurent-Pichat, "Un Prix de 2,500 francs," *Revue de Paris*, 15
January 1855, pp. 161–79; Jean Wallon, "*Du Vrai, du Beau et du Bien,*
par M. Victor Cousin," *Revue de Paris*, 15 February 1854, pp. 497–526.

72. Morin, "Le Livre de *La Religion naturelle* et la faculté de théologie," *RIP*, 19 February 1857, p. 682.

CHAPTER VII

REPUBLICAN BUT RESPECTABLE
OPPOSITION, 1857–1870

Jules Simon's *La Politique radicale* (1868) and Gambetta's "Belleville Program" (1869) are often depicted as the two classical programmatic statements of the "Republic under the empire." On the surface, the two documents are markedly similar. Both demanded comprehensive powers for universal manhood suffrage, total liberty of thought and expression, freedom of assembly and association, the separation of Church and State, military reorganization, and the reform and expansion of public education—reforms that would have required nothing less than the dismantling of the whole authoritarian structure of the Second Empire. But for the purposes of this chapter, which attempts to define the distinctive character of Simon's republicanism in the years from 1857 to 1870, the differences in underlying intention are much more significant. Gambetta sought to rebuild the republican movement on the renewed forces of long repressed urban and southern radicalism. Simon, who sought to reassure Catholic notables, worked to shape another sort of republican movement. For him, republicans needed to achieve respectability, without losing broad popular support. The republican movement, he believed, should make a place in its front ranks for the old *classes dirigeantes* who had dominated French politics throughout the century. In their opposition to the empire, republicans needed to recruit that class of notables that, under the Second Republic, had all too often supported the Party of Order simply out of a deep-seated distrust of republican intentions.

In pursuit of this goal, Simon adopted a broad two-pronged strategy. First, he sought to reassure the notables directly by demonstrating that constitutional and civil liberty, not popular democracy, were the paramount republican values. As a straight-laced and sober *universitaire*, Simon might well make this appeal not only because of his past political connections in the Orleanist Left under the July Monarchy but also because he shared with the notables a pronounced social conservatism. The republican interest in popular education and the improvement of working-class conditions of life, he insisted, was essentially conservative; the object was to uplift an ignorant and volatile people, while counseling it against the illusory promises of atheistic socialism. This sort of republican policy, he believed, was the real key to the preservation of both liberty and a social order in which the social mobility of the talented few found its natural counterbalance in the immobility of the many. Second, Simon worked to moderate the republican movement, to prevent its identification with positivism, materialism, and atheism, and to temper its anticlericalism. To become attractive to the notables, republicans had to live down the classical stereotype that depicted democracy as the godless tyranny of numbers.

I

In *La Liberté de conscience* (1857) and *La Liberté* (1859), Simon set out, in a form intended to appeal especially to the notables, his fundamental political principles. Although *La Liberté* did contain a bland, classical defense of "natural rights," laissez-faire economics and representative government, the distinctive character of these works lay in their treatment of Catholicism, free thought, and tolerance. Amplifying ideas expressed in earlier writings, Simon sought to define a broad middle area, between the clerical *L'Univers* and the Voltairean *Le Siècle*, where Catholics and freethinkers, having renounced appeals to the secular arm as a means of propagating their particular views, might peaceably compete for the minds of nineteenth-century Frenchmen.

There was room for such an understanding between freethinkers and Catholics, he argued, because civil intolerance was not, as Veuillotists and Voltaireans believed, an integral or essential part of Catholicism. Indeed, civil intolerance in the Church ran against the grain of the true Catholic faith—it violated the Catholic principle of charity. Simon did not deny that the Church had a long historical record of such intolerance but maintained that this intolerance was the product not of the doctrine itself but rather of human weakness.[1] Like any deeply felt conviction about human destinies, the faith often inspired in its believers a "spirit of encroachment and propaganda"; this proselytizing spirit, embodied in a devoted, tightly organized clergy, had mistakenly turned, in its quest for converts, from persuasion and example to political coercion.[2] In modern times, however, according to Simon, most French Catholics had learned how to separate the essence of Catholicism from both the outmoded prejudices and worldly interests that clericalism represented. Thus, in reply to each fanatical outburst from L'Univers, "wise [Catholic] voices" preached "moderation, charity and the Gospel."[3]

Simon's advances to Catholic liberals were particularly cogent because he attacked not only Veuillot and his ultramontane followers but also the Voltaireans in republican ranks. The Voltairean view of Catholicism, he believed, was fundamentally false, for like the newspaper L'Univers, it grossly exaggerated the authoritarian elements in the faith.[4] Catholicism might represent the principle of revealed intellectual authority—to be a Catholic might mean to constrain, to stifle, and even to stupefy and to besot the reason. Monasticism and the Society of Jesus, in their almost military discipline, posed serious dangers for the human spirit. But, in the final analysis, he insisted, Catholicism was fundamentally a doctrine not of moral abdication and submission but of free will and personal responsibility. To underscore this conviction, he peppered his works with irreverences about Voltaire, his "prejudices," his "voluntary errors," his inability to grasp the "grandeur and ethical purity of Christianity," his taste in architecture, his "excessive" admiration for the philosopher Samuel Clarke, and his misunderstanding of Leibnitz's optimism.[5] And he called on the "Chris-

---

1. JS, La Liberté de conscience, pp. 85–86, 123; JS, Le Devoir, p. 375; JS, La Liberté, 2:290–94.

2. JS, Histoire de l'École d'Alexandrie, 2:303; JS, La Liberté de conscience, pp. 59–60; JS, Le Devoir, p. 395.

3. JS, La Liberté de conscience, pp. 228–29, 272–74; JS, La Liberté, 2:352.

4. JS, Le Devoir, pp. 394–95; JS, La Liberté de conscience, pp. 272–73.

5. JS, "La Tolérance," Revue nouvelle 1 (15 February 1864): 148–49; JS, L'École, p. 19; JS, La Liberté, 2:397; JS, Le Devoir, p. 132; JS, R.N., p. 24. For the fullest statements on Voltaire, see La Liberté, 2:125–27, 268–69.

tians" of *Le Siècle* to change their tone: "If you respect the Gospel as much as you say, respect the places where it is preached . . . churches filled with the name of the eternal and built for the glory of God and sanctification of men by a piety which, perhaps misguided in its expression, is nevertheless venerable in origin and aim."[6]

These semi-philosophic works constituted the backdrop for an intense and extensive effort to establish personal relations with Catholic Liberals and to convince them that there were elements in the republican party with whom they might work. While maintaining his republican contacts in the salons of Hippolyte Carnot, the Comtesse d'Agoult, and others, Simon began, after the elections of 1857, to hold his own "Thursdays," *habit noir, cravate blanche* affairs in his apartment on the Place de la Madeleine, where prominent men from the world of politics and letters gathered to talk and to sip tea, grogs, beer, or sugared water. In these salons, often preceded by a more intimate "dinner for twelve," the clever, witty, and entertaining host sought to create an environment in which republicans and Orleanists might become acquainted. In these years, Simon expanded his Orleanist connections beyond the sphere of such academicians and *universitaires* as Rémusat and the historian François Mignet to include the politically active Joseph d'Haussonville, and prominent liberal Catholics like Montalembert and Cochin.[7] When the Italo-Austrian War of 1859 raised the Roman Question once again, Simon, who was committed to the Italian national movement, let it be known that he was not opposed to the maintenance of the

6. JS, *Le Devoir*, pp. 394–95; JS, *La Liberté*, 2:406.

7. JS, "Mon Petit Journal," *Le Temps*, 9 January 1892; JS, *Le Soir de ma journée*, pp. 99–103; André Lavertujon, *Gambetta inconnu: cinq mois de la vie de Gambetta*, p. 120; Pierre Guiral, *Prévost-Paradol; pensée et action d'un libéral sous le Second Empire*, p. 316; Paul Gerbod, *La Condition universitaire*, p. 401; Louis Lafosse, "M. Jules Simon," *L'Illustration* 41 (4 April 1863): 217–18; J.-J. Clamageran, Paris, to Félix Pyat, 10 October 1859, J.-J. Clamageran, *Correspondance (1849–1902)*, p. 166.

On Simon's salon, see Jules Claretie, *La Vie à Paris, 1896*, pp. 177–81. On Simon's relations with liberal Catholics, see Charles de Montalembert, Paris, to JS, 19 September 1860, 87 AP 18; Nassau Senior, *Conversations with Distinguished Persons during the Second Empire from 1860 to 1863*, 2:119–27; Ernest Daudet, *Jules Simon*, p. 12; Augustin Cochin, Azy, to Alfred de Falloux, 23 September 1863, in Augustin Cochin, *Augustin Cochin, 1823–1872. Ses lettres et sa vie*, 1:350–51.

Pope's "modest kingdom."[8] By the early 1860s, two new news-papers, Auguste Nefftzer's liberal *Le Temps* and *Le Courrier du dimanche*, a weekly in which Haussonville was involved, had brought their support to such efforts to bring republicans and Orleanists together. In 1863, these newspapers would give journalistic backbone to republicans like Simon, who wished to challenge *Le Siècle*'s view of the electoral strategy best suited to the cause of liberal democracy.

Principles and personal interests were intertwined in the conflicts that divided the opposition in the spring of 1863 in a way so complex that they can hardly be unraveled. Yet as re-publicans competed in various ways for the few candidacies where they had some chance of success, one of the lines of cleavage concerned the attitude that republicans should adopt toward Catholicism. This question had important tactical im-plications, for Parisian republicans had to decide between a Liberal Union of republicans, Orleanists, and parliamentary Legitimists that would run one oppositional candidate in each district, and a single republican list negotiated among republi-cans. *Le Siècle* favored the second alternative, because it wished to make withdrawal of French troops from Rome the "link between . . . all groups."[9] Over the protests of the Voltairean Peyrat, *Le Temps* and *Le Courrier du dimanche* took the op-posing view. Noting that Havin's guidelines for democratic candidates included the evacuation of Rome and obligatory and free primary education, Nefftzer asked, "What would be, for example, *Le Siècle*'s attitude toward M. de Montalembert? Except for the evacuation of Rome and perhaps free and obli-gatory primary education, M. de Montalembert would prob-ably eagerly sign the full program."[10]

In this debate, Simon became one of the leading proponents of the Liberal Union. Although he had long worked to strength-en the ties between republicans and Orleanists, Simon had envisaged this rapprochement more as a force for molding pub-

8. JS, *La Liberté de conscience*, pp. 217–18; JS, *La Liberté*, 2:298; Alfred Darimon, *Histoire d'un parti. Les Cinq sous l'Empire (1857–1860)*, p. 276.

9. *Le Siècle*, 5 February 1863, quoted by Jean Maurain, *La Politique ecclésiastique du Second Empire de 1852 à 1869*, p. 636.

10. Alphonse Peyrat, "A. M. Nefftzer," *Le Temps*, 9 April 1863; Auguste Nefftzer, *Le Temps*, 18 March 1863. See also Taxile Delord, *Histoire illustrée du Second Empire*, 3:399–400.

lic opinion than as the basis of a concrete electoral agreement. For over a decade, Simon had argued that republicans, in protest against an illegitimate regime, should send no deputies at all to the *Corps législatif*. In 1857, he had run as an "abstentionist" and pledged, if elected, to refuse the required oath of allegiance to the empire and forfeit his seat in the *Corps législatif*.[11] By 1863, however, Simon's colleagues in the republican electoral or Carnot committee were, in the majority, ready to abandon abstentionism. Accepting this political reality, Simon turned his attention to persuading the committee to endorse some respected Orleanists as well as republicans.[12] A couple meetings in March 1863 between Simon and a few republican friends, and such Orleanist and Legitimist notables as Thiers, Montalembert, Changarnier, Daru, Berryer, Haussonville, Albert de Broglie, Victor de Broglie, Larcy, and Cochin produced no agreement. An accord was probably not possible, since Simon was not in the position to make any commitments that would draw united republican support, and the Orleanists and Legitimists believed that a Liberal Union would help the republicans in the countryside without aiding themselves commensurately in urban centers.[13]

In the end, *Le Siècle* rallied to a compromise solution suggested by *Le Temps*: on the second ballot, republicans should support that opponent of the empire who had received the most votes on the first ballot.[14] In early May, Simon swallowed his abstentionist scruples and accepted a candidacy in the eighth Parisian district. This change of position, made under pressure from Carnot, Havin, and other republicans, was never forgotten. The incident, blown out of all proportion over the years,

11. On Simon's unsuccessful candidacy of 1857 in the eighth district of Paris, see *Le Journal des débats*, 12, 13, 23 June 1857.

12. Georges Weill, *Histoire du parti républicain en France de 1814 à 1870*, pp. 366–67; Alfred Darimon, *Histoire d'un parti. Le Tiers parti sous l'Empire (1863–1866)*, p. 63.

13. The most important document on these maneuvers is Simon's famous "Charras letter" (JS to Col. Jean.-B. Charras, 8 April 1863, Darimon, *Le Tiers parti sous l'Empire*, p. 68). See also Delord, *Histoire illustrée du Second Empire*, 3:432; Albert de Broglie, *Mémoires du Duc de Broglie, 1821–1901*, 1:316–18; Cochin to Falloux, 22 March 1863, Cochin, *Augustin Cochin, 1823–1872*, 1:335; JS, "Mon Petit Journal," *Le Temps*, 5 February 1892.

14. Clément Duvernois, "Les Élections," *Le Temps*, 20 March 1863; Auguste Nefftzer, *Le Temps*, 26 March 1863.

always suggested to suspicious French politicians that Simon's moderation was more a matter of personal ambition than of principle. In the subsequent campaign, the candidate reiterated many of the themes of *La Liberté*, and unlike Havin, remained silent on the Roman Question.[15] Supported by *Le Siècle* and *Le Temps*, Simon saturated his district with photographs of himself and marched to a landslide victory over the official candidate Koenigswarter.[16]

Simon was willing to court the notables so readily because despite his republicanism, this middle-class *universitaire* shared many of their anti-democratic inclinations. A respectable Republic, Simon believed, would assemble a progressive "aristocracy of intelligence and probity," which a courageous and suffering people would recognize not as a servant but as a physician. With the assurance of a bourgeois used to counseling his own domestics, and accustomed to thinking in terms of social rank and even "caste," Simon viewed himself as one of the natural leaders of a democracy that required even more guidance than respect.[17] The people, he believed, would turn for leadership to those who understood the popular thirst for education and would accept the harsh teachings of classical economic science from men who had demonstrated a real concern with the improvement of working-class conditions.

Like his political colleagues, Simon did not know much about the people, especially about the problems of the rural population. But he was relatively knowledgeable about urban industrial workers, for in the late 1850s, he had studied at first-hand the factories and working-class quarters of such industrial centers as Lyons, Mulhouse, Reims, Lille, and Rouen, as part of the preparation for the writing of *L'Ouvrière* (1861), a study of female workers and, more broadly, of the living conditions of workingmen. Appalled by what he saw, he wrote

15. Léon Séché, *Jules Simon; sa vie et son oeuvre*, pp. 82–83; JS, "Aux électeurs de la 8ᵉ circonscription. Candidature de Jules Simon." See *Le Temps*, 19 May 1863 for Léonor Havin's electoral circular.

16. Louis Jourdan, "L'Oeuvre de M. Jules Simon," *Le Siècle*, 20 May 1863; *Le Temps*, 3 June 1863.

17. Simon first used the phrase "aristocracy of intelligence and probity" in his study of Plato's *Republic*: JS, *Études sur le théodicée de Platon et d'Aristote*, p. 217; JS, "Aux électeurs des Côtes-du-Nord" (1848). [JS], "L'Assemblée nationale," *LP* 3 (15 April 1849): 413; JS, *Le Devoir*, pp. 74–75, 130, 167–68.

that his "worst fears had everywhere been surpassed . . . ,"
and that he would carry for the rest of his life the mark of the
suffering he had witnessed. In fact, however, his inquiry did
not shake in the least his conviction that the requirements of
classical economic theory should set the parameters for all attempts to improve working-class conditions. Insulated by his
own intellectual rigidity, the occupational hazard of the professional philosopher, and more generally by the prejudices of
his class, Simon melancholically viewed this sort of social in-
justice, not as cause for scandal, but as part of a larger pattern
of life's injustices. Heaven, he consoled himself, would set
things right. Although Simon knew that material poverty was
an irreducible obstacle to human self-improvement, he never
showed the imaginative sympathy of his liberal English counterpart John Stuart Mill, who was once moved to write, "the
restraints of Communism would be freedom in comparison
with the present condition of the majority of the human race."[18]

Despite this firsthand view of working-class misery, Simon
considered the enormous inequalities between rich and poor,
between bourgeois elite and the common people as natural—
the God-given lot of man. Classical economics appealed to him
as a science of productivity but especially as a doctrine of liberty. Based on the "sacred right of private property," which
Simon viewed as the material buttress of the personal independence of a man and his family, this doctrine was the key to
a socioeconomic system in which, on the whole, all elements
found their proper place. In this system, the interests of the
capitalist and worker were not opposed but complementary,
even when, as Simon admitted, a factory worker could hope,
at the very best, to earn little more than the absolute minimum
required to sustain himself and his family.[19] In this view, the
proper role of public authority was limited to helping men
prepare themselves for their economic struggle, especially
through education and vocational training, and to regulating

18. JS, L'Ouvrière, pp. i–ii; John Stuart Mill, *Principles of Political
Economy*, in *Collected Works of John Stuart Mill*, ed. J.M. Robson (Toronto: University of Toronto Press, 1965), 2:209.

19. JS, *Le Travail*, pp. 53–54; JS, "Cités ouvrières," *Dictionnaire
général de la politique*, ed. Maurice Block, 1:347; JS, L'Ouvrière, pp. 23,
308. For a later, equally grim view, see JS, Paris, to Domenico Galati, 6
September 1882, *Le Temps* (20 September 1882).

child labor and hygienic conditions in factories. Simon opposed on principle most forms of direct public and private assistance because he believed that they removed incentive, the "spur to work," and interfered with the smooth functioning of the economic system. Thus, as a member of the Labor Committee of the Constituent Assembly in 1848, Simon opposed the National Workshops from principle and policy, voted against inserting the principle of *Droit au travail*, a state guarantee of remunerative work, into the Constitution of the Second Republic and opposed, as a violation of the "right to work," such measures as a Ten Hours Bill.[20] The alternative to the existing social hierarchy was a tyrannical socialism, the annihilation of society, "property destroyed, the family . . . weakened, nature mutilated, eternal justice violated."[21]

This natural inequality of condition, reflected in general, although by no means in every particular case, the differences in both talent and moral fiber that distinguished men from one another. Without talent or character, a family could not forever retain a place of social prominence nor could a man advance from the lower ranks in the open society created by the French Revolution. So strong is Simon's sense of the "undeniable" moral inequality of men, an inequality that education could counteract but not abolish, that he maintains this view even at the risk of weakening the case for his stern insistence on man's moral responsibility. Man must blame himself for much of his suffering, for one half, at least, derives from his own faults and moral failings.[22] Yet Simon sees that such moral inequalities have been amplified by the terrible pressures of modern industrial life. Under conditions where both men and women have been obliged to work in factories, he argues in *L'Ouvrière*, large numbers of urban workers have been unable to maintain their family lives and have sought refuge in stupefying drunkenness and debauchery.[23] Indeed, accepting a management viewpoint, he reports that in certain

20. JS, *La Liberté*, 1:384; *Procès-verbaux du Comité du travail à l'assemblée constituante de 1848*, p. 55; [JS], "Publications relatives à l'organisation du travail," *LP* 1 (15 May 1848): 588–89; JS, *L'Ouvrière*, p. 23; JS, *La Liberté*, 2:77–79.
    21. JS, "Aux électeurs des Côtes-du-Nord" (1848).
    22. JS, *R.N.*, pp. 208, 221; JS, *Le Devoir*. p. 201.
    23. JS, *L'Ouvrière*, p. 170; [JS], "L'Assemblée nationale," *LP* 2 (15 September 1848): 300.

industrial centers, the corruption of the working class has reached the point where an increase in wages would provoke not a general moral improvement, but still new prodigies of depravity.[24]

For Simon, the visits to the working quarters of France's great industrial centers were like visits to an uncivilized country—to a world of ignorance, rudeness, and appetite, where man was cut off from all "that has ever been thought, felt and discovered: everything is missing here to make one's way in the world and to endure the world."[25] The worker appeared to the professional moralist as a kind of moral child, a creature with a dormant reason, at the mercy of the "blind," "violent" demands of passion.[26] Without the restraining discipline of reason, the worker was always vulnerable to the rages of the passions, whose insatiable thirst for power, glory, and pleasure threatened to level the whole social order. This "instinct for equality," which Tocqueville identified with an emerging democratic spirit, was for Simon, to a large degree, a product of ignorance.[27] The people, he believed,

> are generous, proud; they have noble aspirations; but their ideas, like their sentiments, are not yet perfectly clear. . . . More accustomed to feel than to think reflectively, they are more like children than men, so that, despite their generous and heroic nature, it is rather easy to precipitate them into certain vices.[28]

In his understanding of popular violence, Simon insisted on the distinction between leaders and followers, between *meneurs* or ringleaders and ignorant victims. In June 1848, he had taken up arms, as a member of the National Guard, to defend the Cavaignac government. On the basis of conversations with insurgents, as the fighting was ending, he believed that the June days were the work of a revolutionary nucleus, a revo-

24. JS, *L'Ouvrière*, pp. 125–26.
25. JS, "L'Instruction et les bibliothèques populaires," *RDM*, 2d series, 47 (15 September 1863): 351. See also JS, *L'École*, pp. 224–25; JS, *Le Devoir*, p. 207; JS, *L'Ouvrière*, p. 353.
26. JS, *L'Ouvrière*, pp. 277–78, 360; JS, *La Liberté*, 1:221; 2:232.
27. JS, *La Liberté*, 1:317–20; JS, "La Révolution de 1848," *Dictionnaire général de la politique*, ed. Maurice Block, 2:866–71.
28. *Annales de l'association pour le progrès des sciences sociales. Congrès de Gand, 1863*, pp. 575–78.

lutionary party, a "dedicated battalion of hardened conspirators" that had called the people of Paris to the barricades in 1834, 1839, and in February 1848. This party, the party of Auguste Blanqui and Étienne Cabet, did not represent a doctrine, but only a set of instincts, a "religion of self-interest" parading behind an incoherent collection of socialist hallucinations about "work in common, life in common, with the State as the only entrepreneur." Inspired by the irresponsible rhetoric of socialist theoreticians, the people, "enlightened enough to see that something is wrong but not to discuss a remedy, both presumptuous and incompetent," delirious with hunger, animated by a love of danger and an instinct for opposition, chose the path of blood and ruins. To repel the assault of what the National Assembly termed these "new barbarians," Simon was prepared to support the full demands of the Cavaignac government, including the Transportation Decree, which provided that all prisoners, except the leaders of the insurrection, would be transported without trial. Later, there would be a time for pardons.[29]

The future of liberty, Simon believed, hinged on the response of the French Liberal and republican elite to the challenge posed by the threatening conditions of the emerging urban and industrial age. The working classes were not mentally or morally prepared to deal with the new industrial conditions, he warned in July 1848; cannon, while repressing the symptoms of this modern disorder, was not a permanent cure. Under the conditions of modern economic competition, republicans needed to support a legislation that would develop the spirit of self-help by enlightening minds and fortifying characters. The time for middle-class moralizing was over, for under present conditions, hardly any worker was disposed to listen: "speeches, a thousand times more powerful in the service of evil than good, only exalt their passions, and never repress them."[30] Since most common people, Simon believed, "lack moderation and learning," the task of the republican lawmaker was to assemble in a manner compatible with respect for individual liberty, a network of legal and cultural forces that would but-

29. [JS], "L'Assemblée nationale," *LP* 2 (15 July 1848): 97–117; JS, "La Révolution de 1848," *LP* 1 (15 March 1848): 319.

30. [JS], "L'Assemblée nationale," *LP* 2 (15 July 1848): 97; JS, *L'Ouvrière*, p. 363.

tress the embattled reason in its struggle against the "violence of passions."[31]

With Jean Macé, the founder of the *Ligue de l'enseignement*, Simon was the leading republican champion of popular instruction under the Second Empire and in the early years of the Third Republic. In his advocacy of free and obligatory primary education, Simon acted on the belief that reading, writing, and arithmetic were forms of power that would aid the lower classes to combat, although not entirely to escape, the cruel necessities of their lot. In the 1860s and 1870s, he worked indefatigably for the *Société pour l'instruction élémentaire*, which founded lay private primary schools, for the *Association philotechnique*, which sponsored adult courses, and, with the publisher Hachette, for the *Société Franklin*, which established popular libraries. In articles, speeches, and books like *L'École* (1865), he repeatedly affirmed his belief that all popular suffering was far from irremediable, and his commitment to the conscientious improvement of all that might be ameliorated in human affairs. Yet especially in the realm of *éducation*, of moral as opposed to intellectual development, Simon's sense of the enormous natural differences among men in intelligence, virtue, and social condition all but overshadowed his republican faith in their natural civil and political equality. Popular education, he believed, in its efforts to moralize the demoralized should not disturb the moral convictions, embedded in Catholic tradition, of the great mass of the French population.

Simon's sense of the intellectual and moral gulf between the *bourgeoisie classique* and the people was so acute that he came dangerously close to adopting a religious double standard. For the public record, Simon denounced the religious hypocrisy of social conservatives who cynically attempted to use Catholicism as a means of police.[32] Nothing could justify the efforts of "old Voltaireans" to encourage the propagation of a religion that they considered false.[33] For Simon, however, the

31. JS, *La Liberté*, 1:221.
32. JS, *Le Devoir*, pp. 398–99; [JS], "L'Assemblée nationale," *LP* 3 (15 November 1849): 453; JS, "La Tolérance," *Revue nouvelle* 1 (15 February 1864): 148; JS, "Préface," *La Politique radicale*, p. 29.
33. "Old Voltaireans" and "Voltaireans" are not to be confused. Old Voltaireans was a nineteenth-century expression that denoted men like Thiers, who rejected Catholicism as false, but utilized it as a means of social control over the lower classes.

Catholic religion, although false in form, was true in its essential moral and metaphysical content. Catholic dogma, which contained the essential spiritualist verities in the form of revelation, was majestically simple, sublime, and profound.[34] And Catholic moral doctrines, which Simon, unlike Voltaireans, identified with the ethics of the New Testament, constituted a system of values that was "pure and really humane." Jesus, he insisted, preached a truly liberal and democratic doctrine, an ethics of universal fraternity summed up in St. John's "These things I command you, that ye love one another." This doctrine of charity, respectful of the opinions and property of others and committed to the equality of all before God, contrasted sharply with the authoritarian politics and religious fanaticism of the Clerical party.[35] In fact, Simon so admired the New Testament that he regarded it as a book of moral teachings sacred not only for Catholics but "for almost all men . . . for all those who appreciate the grandeur and *douceur* of this kind of teaching."[36]

Simon thus viewed the New Testament as a popularized version of his purely philosophic Le Devoir. The people, or at least the working class and the peasantry, were incapable of grasping a purely philosophic moral teaching. In religious and philosophic matters, they proceeded not by rational thought and discussion but rather by feeling and imagination. Befuddled by the slightest philosophic abstraction, the people "are not intellectually mature; they do not have the time to gain full control of their ideas." Thus, they "need others to think for them; they need casuistry, whether it comes from established customs, or laws, or a positive religion."[37] The early Christians, in their battle with classical philosophy, understood this fact and did not leave their doctrine "at the mercy of a [philosophic] demonstration." "They preach their Gospel in God's name. . . . A God become man, witnesses of his life

34. JS, *l'École d'Alexandrie*, 1:156; JS, *La Liberté*, 2:294, 298; JS, *La Liberté de conscience*, p. 10.

35. JS, *La Liberté*, 2:343–44; JS, *La Liberté de conscience*, pp. 274–79; JS, *La Liberté*, 1:290–91; JS, *Le Devoir*, p. 320.

36. JS, *Corps législatif*, 19 May 1864, *Le Journal des débats*, 20 May 1864; see also JS, *L'École*, p. 410.

37. JS, *l'École d'Alexandrie*, 1:169–70, 2:185. See also JS, "Liberté," *Dictionnaire général de la politique*, ed. Maurice Block, 2:198–99.

and death . . . the promise of heaven, the fear of hell, that is a pillow on which the people can rest their heads."[38]

This complex attitude toward the Catholicism of the people found its most dramatic expression in 1862 and 1863, when Simon, as the secret director of a widely read popular illustrated magazine, *Le Journal pour tous,* surreptitiously attempted to counterbalance Renan's attacks on the traditional Catholic portrait of Jesus.[39]

In his famous lecture of 21 February 1862, and in his *Vie de Jésus* (1863), Renan argued that Jesus was an "incomparable man" who taught a doctrine of unparalleled moral purity, an absolute and even "interplanetary" religion of the spirit; but like all mortal men, the Galilean reformer was obliged to confront the moral dilemmas of practical politics. To further his work of moral regeneration, he had, under pressure from his followers, permitted himself to condone a number of false miracles or "pious frauds," particularly the resuscitation of Lazarus. To counter this portrait of Jesus, which Catholics found scandalous, Simon published an article entitled "The Death of Jesus Christ." Here Simon presented as historical truth an account of the crucifixion, based primarily on St. Matthew's especially miraculous version, and concluded with an assertion of Jesus' divinity. And in April 1863, on the eve of the publication of the *Vie de Jésus,* Simon published Chateaubriand's portrait of Jesus—not an incomparable mortal but a human God whose douceur, charity, tolerance, and love, expressed even in his miracles, were an inspiration to man's moral imagination.[40] Such behavior, overly clever at best, and duplicitous at worst, reflected the moralist's highly undemo-

38. JS, *l'École d'Alexandrie,* 1:168–69.

39. Simon was the director of the *Journal pour tous* from its inception in 1855 until 1865. André Oheix, "Un Coin de bibliographie simonienne, Jules Simon au *Journal pour tous,*" *Revue historique de l'Ouest,* pp. 139–45; Dossier Jules Simon, Hachette Archives; Gustave Vapereau, "Lahure (Auguste-Charles)," *Dictionnaire universel des contemporains* (Paris: Hachette, 1878), p. 1013.

40. Vincente [JS], "Variétés. La Mort de Jésus–Christ," *Journal pour tous,* 19 April 1862, pp. 95–96; "Jésus–Christ. Par Chateaubriand," *Journal pour tous,* 4 April 1863, pp. 23–26. The passage comes from François Auguste René Chateaubriand, *Génie du christianisme. Oeuvres complètes* (Paris: Pourrat, 1836), 3:113–20.

cratic sense of the vast social distance separating a civilized bourgeoisie from a barbarous people.

Moralisation and progress for the workingman, Simon expected, would flow naturally from an intensified public commitment to education, especially at the primary level. But schooling alone was not enough. Like other middle-class moralists, Simon attached great importance to the maintenance of the conjugal family among the lower classes. The emotional rewards of a solid family life, he believed, would give male and female workers the incentive to endure the hardships of their condition. Although Simon was too attached to the dogmas of classical economics to advocate the outlawing of female labor in factories, he hoped to strengthen domestic bonds by facilitating the workers' acquisition of property. If factory workers were given the opportunity of owning their lodgings, the center of domestic life, they would develop the virtues of self-discipline, thrift, foresight, and sobriety.

This objective could and should be obtained without substantially altering the relations between labor and capital. Although Simon favored the abrogation of the Le Chapelier Law, which forbade workers to associate in order to negotiate salaries, he hoped that the right of combination would be used with restraint. He insisted that workers respect the right to work of others and opposed strikes as counterproductive.[41] Rather than attempt to gain a larger share of the profits of production, Simon urged workers to associate in various forms of producers' and consumers' cooperatives. Thus, in 1864, he joined with Orleanists to publish a manual on cooperatives, *Des sociétés de coopération et leur constitution légale*, and with Léon Walras, he founded the *Caisse d'escompte des associations populaires, de crédit, de consommation, de production*. Simon was president of the *Société coopérative des habitations à bon marché*, founded in Paris in 1867, and also created with Walras the *Société coopérative immobilière*, the first cooperative of its kind in France. In 1865, he journeyed to England to gather material for *Le Travail*, a book on the cooperative movement.[42] In the same year, Simon, who belonged to

41. JS, "Ouvrier, ouvrière," *Dictionnaire général de la politique*, ed. Maurice Block, 2:455; JS, *La Liberté*, 2:50–53; Theodore Zeldin, *Emile Ollivier and the Liberal Empire of Napoleon III*, pp. 79–85.
42. Jean-Baptiste Duroselle, *Les Débuts du catholicisme social en*

many workers' mutual aid societies, gave the working-class militant Ernest Fribourg a subscription to support the foundation of an international social-science association for the furtherance of the rights of labor, and a year later, opened his purse again to help send a French delegation to the first international congress of this association. By this subscription, he became a member (number 606) of the First International, a society that, the embarrassed politician was later obliged to admit, was to become a "universal strike agency."[43] For Simon, cooperative efforts should produce quite different results. Through association, sturdy laborers would gain the habits and incentives to cope with the hardships of their lot. They would give up the drunken carousings of the local cabaret for the chaste pleasures of the family garden.[44]

France, 1822–1870, p. 639; Jean Gaumont, *Histoire générale de la coopération en France*, 1:470, 539, 554; 2:198; Jean Maîtron, ed., *Dictionnaire biographique du mouvement ouvrier français*, 9:135.

43. Maîtron, ed., *Dictionnaire biographique*, 9:135; "Déposition de M. Jules Simon" (31 August 1871), Commission d'enquête sur les actes du Gouvernement de la défense nationale. *Annales de l'Assemblée nationale*, 23:435–36.

44. Simon's concern with the conjugal family as a crucial "school of duty" caused him to devote considerable attention to the woman question. Women, he believed, were destined by nature to set the moral standards of society as devoted mothers, obedient wives, and industrious homemakers. Industrialization, which drew women out of the home into the factory, threatened to undermine their ability to perform this fundamental social role. To offset such pressures, Simon looked to formal education to provide women with the skills and knowledge that would enable them to continue, in adverse modern conditions, to perform their traditional social function. With these social, as opposed to professional, goals in mind, Simon was an early advocate of public primary and secondary education for girls. As one might expect of a *universitaire*, he insisted that the State, not the Church, should take a leading role in this enterprise. Although these activities won him the sympathy of some elements in the nascent woman's movement, Simon did not support most of the goals of nineteenth-century feminists. Unlike the middle-class feminist Ernest Legouvé, he defended with hardly a criticism those parts of the Civil Code that gave married women an extremely subordinate position in French law. While favoring the principle of equal pay for equal work, he nevertheless accepted as a natural consequence of laissez-faire economics the general French practice of paying women less than their male counterparts for the same work. Needless to say, he was irrevocably opposed to the few feminists who advocated the woman suffrage. In his attitude toward the condition of

II

After the elections of 1863, Simon encountered increasing difficulties in his efforts to maintain close ties with Orleanist notables. At first, he and other republican deputies meeting regularly at the home of their colleague Alexandre Marie collaborated with Thiers in efforts to obtain a minimum program of "necessary liberties."[45] But the Convention of 15 September 1864, which revived the Roman Question, and the publication of the Papal *Syllabus of Errors* (1864), which proscribed liberalism and modern civilization, increased religious tensions and made collaboration between Catholics and freethinkers more difficult than ever. At the same time, Simon found that his efforts to champion the cause of public primary education underscored the lines separating proponents of a liberal but Catholic France from men like himself, advocates of a lay France, tolerant and respectful of all positive religions.[46] Finally, the development of a dynastic opposition, a Third party between the republicans and the governmental majority, clearly showed that the Liberal Union, while serving marked propagandistic purposes, combined too many conflicting elements

women, as in his view of the condition of the working classes, Simon's reformism operated totally within the confines of a seemingly uncritical acceptance of the existing social hierarchy.

For Simon's writings on women and the family, see *La Liberté*, 1:211–83; *L'Ouvrière*; "De la famille," *Revue des cours littéraires*, 6, no. 19 (10 April 1869): 295–96; *La Femme du vingtième siècle*. For Simon's advocacy of girls' education, see especially *L'École*, pp. 115–206; "L'Organisation de l'enseignement secondaire pour les jeunes filles, par M. Camille Sée," *Séances et travaux de l'Académie des sciences morales et politiques*, 110, no. 12 (December 1878): 927–30; "De l'éducation des filles. Rapport de M. C. Sée sur le projet de loi presenté à la Chambre des Députes," *Séances et travaux de l'Académie des sciences morales et politiques*, 112, no. 10 (October 1879): 557–60.

For two informative and thought-provoking discussions of nineteenth-century French feminism, see Karen Offen, "The Male Feminist Phenomenon in Mid-Nineteenth Century France. The Case of Ernest Legouvé (1807–1903)" (Third Berkshire Conference, June 1976); Claire G. Moses, "Feminism as a Phenomenon of Time and Place" (Second Berkshire Conference, October 1974). These papers may be consulted in the Schlesinger Library, Cambridge, Mass.

45. Darimon, *Les Cinq sous l'Empire*, p. 201.

46. Félix Hémon, *Bersot et ses amis*, p. 201; Darimon, *Le Tiers parti sous l'Empire*, pp. 274–75.

to serve as a tool of republican political action in the *Corps législatif*. The Third party was hostile to Napoleon III's personal power, but, like Thiers and many of his followers, identified republicanism with socialism and viewed a liberal empire as a bulwark of social conservatism. For Simon, the idea of a liberal empire was a contradiction in terms. An edifice based on the destruction of freedom could not take liberty as a crown. As liberal notables moved toward the Third party, Simon turned to fashioning the moderate republicanism that was to prove more attractive to some of them in the 1870s.

One aspect of this effort to moderate the republican movement was, of course, Simon's continued effort to maintain the deistic current in French republicanism. His task was difficult, for in the 1860s, philosophic spiritualism began to appear both intellectually dated and politically irrelevant to an element in the republican movement that, with the support of the younger generation, was rapidly gaining strength. These men, taking for their intellectual heroes the chemist Marcellin Berthelot, the anatomist Charles-Phillippe Robin, Comte, Renan, and Littré, adopted materialistic and scientistic theses. In such republican journals as *La Pensée nouvelle*, *La Libre pensée*, *La Rive gauche*, *Le Travail*, *Les Écoles de France*, and *Le Candide*, they uncompromisingly defended the methods and findings of positive science. But unlike Littré, who founded his *La Philosophie positive* in 1867 to popularize his own particular blend of Comtism and liberalism, they usually underscored their anti-spiritualistic animus by linking the defense of the positive method with an aggressive materialism and Voltairianism. In opposition to this current, Simon published three new editions of *La Religion naturelle* and supported other republican deists like Henri Carle, editor of the weekly *La Libre conscience* (1866–1870), and Jules Favre, his colleague in the *Corps législatif*. Atheists and communists, he wrote Hugo in 1868, were scaring the bourgeoisie and reinforcing the empire.[47]

By opposing materialism and positivism as the "fanaticism of negation," Simon reminded conservative notables that not

47. Sauva, "Nota," *La Libre conscience*, 23 May 1868; Sauva, "Chronique. Anniversaire de la fondation du journal," *La Libre conscience*, 30 May 1868; JS, Paris, to Victor Hugo, 7 October 1868, Victor Hugo Papers, #3255, Musée Victor Hugo.

all republicans were atheists. He was not able, however, to dissociate republicanism so easily from the views expressed in an important republican journal *La Morale indépendante* (1865–1870). Founded by a prominent republican Freemason and former collaborator of Proudhon, Marie Alexandre Massol, the journal advocated the separation of God, ethics, grace, and justice. The moral law, Massol explained in the first issue, is an imperative "consistent with reason, inscribed in our hearts, and its voice dictates our rights and our duties, turns us away from evil." The moral action is an expression of a man's sense of himself as free and responsible before his fellow men. In the past, Massol argued, the moral energy of man suffered the enervating effects of the theistic metaphysical and religious "hypotheses" to which ethics had been linked.[48] From this point of view, Massol was sympathetic to positivism, which also sought to free ethics from such hypotheses. But he believed that "social feeling" or "altruism," the basis of positivist ethics, did not provide an adequate basis for the defense of man's natural rights. "Independent morality" was not to be associated with the broader range of doctrines connected with either materialism or positivism.[49]

Massol was eager to secure Simon's approval for his enterprise. In a review of the sixth edition of *La Religion naturelle*, Massol inquired whether Simon really understood ethics as a derivative or consequence of certain notions of ontology and theodicy? Ostensibly, Massol believed, Simon was one of those University philosophers who tended "to judge a man's morals by his metaphysical and religious position." For them, materialists who professed an ethics of duty were either confused or secretly hedonistic. In the affairs of day-to-day life, consequently, such official philosophers believed that one could not trust a materialist, a positivist, or a pantheist, even if he professed pure ethical views, for these notions rested on a foundation that would not stand up under stress.[50]

This challenge embarrassed Simon on a number of levels.

48. Alexandre Massol, "La Morale indépendante," *La Morale indépendante*, 6 August 1865.
49. Alexandre Massol, "Bulletin," *La Morale indépendante*, 23 May 1869.
50. Alexandre Massol, "La Religion naturelle par Jules Simon (Nouvelle édition)," *La Morale indépendante*, 11 February 1866.

On the philosophic level, his own natural religion and natural ethics were inextricably intertwined; man's deepest ethical impulses, he believed, originated not in the voice of conscience but in the loving desire to do God's will. Although deists like Jourdan at *Le Siècle* and Pelletan at *Le Tribune* applauded *La Morale indépendante* in the belief that the ethical imperative existed independently of other metaphysical considerations, Simon must have thought that, in general, such a view diminished man's sense of God's role in ethical life. On the political level, this challenge obliged Simon to comment on the integrity of his agnostic and atheistic political allies. Reluctant to give any encouragement to materialism and atheism, Simon ignored Massol's call for explanations. Finally, in the preface to *La Politique radicale*, published in May 1868, he conceded that the Stoics had been at once materialists and men of high moral standards.[51]

It was not until the election year of 1869 that, under pressure from the Left, Simon attempted a fuller response. At a public Sunday lecture, sponsored by the *Association philotechnique*, Simon announced his intention to speak on duty, but not in a metaphysical manner: he would limit himself to one element of common experience, man's innate idea of justice. Throughout history, Simon asserted, the greatest obstacle to ethical behavior was not a lack of understanding of the principle of justice but rather a failure to understand fully the circumstances in which the principle was to be applied. And in a great show of contrition, he admitted having argued that men who professed his ethics of duty without accepting a corresponding metaphysics were either unthinking or insincere. Such an argument, he acknowledged, was worthless, unintelligent, and detestable, refuted by the existence of the materialistic Stoics.[52]

This speech satisfied Massol, who declared Simon's endorsement complete and published a long excerpt from the lecture.[53] In fact, however, Simon's speech was little more than a con-

51. JS, "Préface," *La Politique radicale*, pp. 31–32.

52. JS, "Le Devoir," *Revue des cours littéraires de la France et de l'étranger*, 6, no. 12 (20 February 1869): 179–81. This speech also appeared as a pamphlet, "Le Devoir" (Paris, 1869).

53. Alexandre Massol, "Bulletin," *La Morale indépendante*, 21 February 1869; Alexandre Massol, "Bulletin," *La Morale indépendante*, 28 February 1869.

ciliatory equivocation, an embarrassed obfuscation that served
his political need to maintain contact with the younger elements
in the republican movement. Simon had accepted Massol's
view of ethics only with a vague but all-important qualification. While granting Massol that there was much in the So-
cratic identification of virtue and knowledge, Simon insinuated
that virtue was not simply a matter of knowledge. A man of
limited intellectual ability who sought to act justly with an
upright heart would generally reach a higher level of ethical
achievement than a man of mere knowledge.[54] Although Simon
did not say so, *heart* was, in his work, a code word for two
related and mutually supportive loves, the love of God and the
love of justice. Independent morality, Simon knew, might suf-
fice for Cato, and even for a Littré, or a Jules Ferry, but how
many men were made to this measure? As he said to another
popular Parisian audience a few months later, metaphysics,
out of favor at the moment, was nevertheless the "basis" of all
truth.[55]

In the realm of practical politics, as opposed to theoretical
discussion, Simon was more effective in his efforts to contain
the influence of the kinds of attitudes underlying the program
of *La Morale indépendante*. The key to Simon's moderate political strategy, in the 1860s and in succeeding decades, was his
constant defense of the primacy of the principle of liberty of
conscience against the competing claims of the laic principle.
"Total liberty," even "radical liberty," were, from his perspective, much more suitable republican rallying cries than independent morality. For in politics, the tenets of independent
morality logically implied "laicity," the systematic dissociation
of public patronage from all religious doctrines, including those
of natural religion. For if men's moral lives were really autono-
mous, metaphysical or theological "hypotheses" were of no
interest to the legislator concerned only with the rights and duties of citizens. Most republican leaders believed that no real
liberty of conscience could ever be definitively achieved without the rigorous application of the laic principle. Simon, on the
other hand, sensitive to Catholic apprehensions and eager to
defend the idea of God, sought to strengthen the republican

54. JS, "Le Devoir," *Revue des cours littéraires*, p. 179.
55. JS, "De la famille," *Revue des cours littéraires de la France et de
l'étranger*, 6, no. 19 (10 April 1869): 295–96.

commitment to liberty of conscience against threats inherent in laicity. In his opposition to independent morality, as in the efforts that led ultimately to his opposition to the Ferry Laws in the 1880s, Simon worked to ensure that laicity did not become a *machine de guerre* against religious and philosophic theism.

Simon's political reservations about the doctrines of independent morality and laicity rested on two considerations. On the one hand, he believed that republicans were overextending the laic principle. While they used the term *laïque* to denote the dissociation of public power from all theological or philosophic conceptions of the divine, Simon preferred to use the term in a more limited sense. He agreed that the State should not sponsor an official religion or an official metaphysics, but he denied that the State should be atheistic or neutral. Although created for and by the people, the modern State formulated and enforced the law in the name of justice. And justice, Simon insisted, was linked in the moral universe and in the common sense of most men to natural religion, to "doctrines shared by all religions, the existence of God, Providence, and the immortality of the soul."[56] For the most part, Simon believed, French society was already "essentially and irrevocably *laïque*." The notion of a State religion had disappeared with the Restoration; the lay University had taken root in French society; and in general, the government left the citizenry to "seek their salvation as they choose."[57] On the other hand, even measures that Simon favored, like the secularization of the curriculum of primary schools and the elimination of the special status that the concordatory Church occupied in French legislation, were bound to strike the Church as persecutory and to jeopardize his efforts to construct a republicanism attractive to modern Catholics. The time was not right to provoke extensive debate about such issues.

This manner of envisaging the relationship between liberty of conscience and laicity, which was absolutely central to Simon's cultural vision, was the hallmark of Simon's republican liberalism. To refuse priority to liberty of conscience, even for Catholics, and to turn to laicity as the fundamental principle

56. JS, *La Liberté de conscience*, p. 175; *L'École*, p. 233; JS *La Liberté*, 2:272; JS, *R.N.*, pp. 455–57.
57. JS, *La Liberté*, 2:352.

regulating the relations of Church and State was, in Simon's view, a retreat from liberalism.

In the 1860s, Simon was still able to exercise a significant influence in support of his conception of liberalism. The publication of his *La Politique radicale*, with its program for "total" or "radical" liberty, crowned his continuing efforts to assert his leadership over the younger generation of republicans. Particularly after 1865, he had made a concerted effort to consolidate his relations not only with Ferry but also with Gambetta and his close associates Henri Allain-Targé, Clément Laurier, Eugène Spuller, and Henri Brisson. Despite his wide range of acquaintances in Orleanist circles, Simon was able, according to Allain-Targé, to induce these younger men "hopefully . . . to put . . . [him] in a separate category, to follow his lead, and to contrast him with his colleagues, M. Jules Favre and M. Ernest Picard."[58] Simon's particular approach to politics helps explain his success. In contrast with Émile Ollivier, who associated liberty primarily with a series of institutional arrangements that he felt could be grafted onto the institutions of the Second Empire, the philosopher and the former abstentionist in Simon identified liberty with a quality of civic awareness shared by a whole people. No people could be really free, he believed, if it received its liberties piecemeal from an arbitrary regime; he insisted that a liberal political regime had to pay homage to the principle of self-government, even if it felt obliged to regulate and restrict this principle in practice. From this viewpoint, Louis Napoleon's letter of 19 January 1867, which announced the regime's intention to embark on a new program of liberal reforms, was totally insufficient. France needed republicans who could use the new reforms to destroy the liberal mirage created by Ollivier and the Third party.

The Roman Question provided Simon with the opportunity to formalize his rapprochement with the younger group. In accordance with the Convention of 15 September 1864 between the imperial government and Italy, the French had agreed to withdraw their troops from Italy within two years in return for an Italian promise to respect the territorial integrity of the Papal States. By the fall of 1867, however, the accord had broken down, and the French government was obliged

58. Henri Allain-Targé, "Souvenirs d'avant 1870," *Revue de Paris*, p. 14.

to dispatch an expeditionary force to protect the Pope against Garibaldi and his volunteer army. After the French victory at Mentana, the Italian government, although sympathetic to Garibaldi, was willing to participate in a congress of Catholic powers to find a settlement for the Roman Question. The French government, with the support of the Senate, sought to find a solution that would both respect the rights of Italy and preserve the Pope's independence.

In preparation for the debate on the matter in the *Corps législatif*, Simon consulted with his younger republican associates. Allain-Targé wanted Simon to demonstrate "that the intervention is illegal and contrary to the principles of 1789, because it is religious and not political, and because the government does not have the right to use the public force, which our *laic* society has given it, to further any religious opinions or interests whatsoever." In addition, the situation offered, he believed, a fine chance to "preach separation of Church and State and liberty of conscience."[59] On 3 December in the *Corps législatif*, Simon demanded, for the first time, the separation of Church and State.[60] For both Simon and the younger men, the Roman imbroglio showed what problems would attend any effort to treat France's religious problems on any basis but liberty of conscience and laicity. Simon's emphases, however, were his own. He treated the question of separation primarily in terms of liberty of conscience, while his young supporters leaned more heavily on the principle of laicity.

Simon prefaced his remarks with an expression of his respect for Christianity and for "all beliefs which are equally sincere." But, he argued, Catholic arguments that the principle of liberty of conscience justified the defense of the Pope's temporal power rested on a false premise. To protect the Catholic faith, it was necessary that the Pope not be a subject, but there was no need for him to be a king. The very existence of a unified Italy implied, however, that so long as the Pope retained his temporal power in the Papal States, he would be dependent on France or some other power. Since the present French policy could not possibly guarantee the Pope's spiritual independence,

59. Henri Allain-Targé, Paris, to his father, 3 December 1867, Henri Allain-Targé, *La République sous l'Empire; lettres, 1864–1870*, p. 142.

60. For Simon's earlier, negative treatments of the question of separation, see JS, *La Liberté de conscience*, pp. 42–45; JS, *La Liberté*, 2:366.

Simon urged defenders of the Pope to choose between two alternatives: the destruction of Italy or the search for another means of defending the principle of religious liberty.[61] Taking the second alternative as the sole viable one, Simon put practical considerations aside and raised the discussion to a more theoretical level. He insisted that the solution did not lie in a concordat between the Italian State and the Roman Catholic Church. Indeed, the futility of the empire's Roman policy served to dramatize the inadequacy of concordats as instruments of public policy. For "the principle of our Roman intervention, of our protection which the Pope has requested and accepted, is identical with the principle of concordats." In both cases, the State offered the Church part of its temporal force in return for a part of the Church's spiritual force. The results were also the same. Even when liberty of conscience was not violated, the Church lost the possibility of complete autonomy in the management of its own affairs and was compromised by its close association with less principled political regimes. The only remaining solution was separation of Church and State.[62]

Simon ended with a call to Catholics to accept the fundamental principles of modern civilization, the separation of the spiritual and the temporal, and liberty of conscience. Without using the term *laicity*, he insisted that the true liberal program was "free churches in a free State." Frenchmen, he declared, could not respect a religion that, in alliance with the State, often seemed little more than a means of police. "The spiritual power can live from now on by appealing to the principle of liberty. . . . If it does not appeal to it, this power becomes the enemy of the principles upon which modern civilization rests, and we will be obliged to become its enemy." Freed from the Concordat, the Church would become "the greatest power of the nineteenth century."[63] Confronted with the dynamism of an emancipated Church, Frenchmen would be obliged to eliminate all restraints on liberty of speech and press. As a gauge of his commitment to liberty of conscience, he was demanding liberty for the Church as a first step toward total liberty.[64]

In subsequent months, Simon repeatedly rose in the *Corps*

61. JS, "La Séparation de l'Église et de l'État" (3 December 1867), *La Politique radicale*, pp. 47–54.

62. Ibid., p. 58.   63. Ibid., p. 65.

64. Ibid., p. 73.

législatif to defend the theses of "total liberty" in debates concerning freedom of assembly and of the press. Although Simon had himself always opposed the Voltairean manner in discussions of religious and philosophic issues, he sponsored and spoke in support of an amendment abrogating Article 8 of the Law of 17 May 1819, and by implication, Article 1 of the Law of 25 March 1822. These press laws, which punished "outrage to public and religious morality" and "outrage or ridicule" of an officially recognized religion, were the bêtes noires of Voltaireans, for they provided the juridical basis for the prosecution of writers who openly and explicitly identified Catholicism with fraud and hypocrisy. As Simon himself observed, in another context, under these laws, Voltaire, if he had lived in the nineteenth century, would have spent his life in prison.[65] In Simon's view, the "right to insult" a religion or a philosophy, to subject it to ironic and sarcastic mockery, was implicit in the right of free thought. To limit free discussion of religious and philosophic questions was to sterilize inquiry and to hinder the progress of knowledge.[66]

In May 1868, Simon published *La Politique radicale*, a collection of speeches preceded by an important programmatic "Préface." In his choice of a title, Simon made a concession to the resolutely republican rhetoric of his friends.[67] But in both tone and substance, the book reflected Simon's preoccupation with restraining the republican movement. For Simon, the term *radical* meant first and foremost "liberal," even "ultraliberal," not democratic. In his "Belleville Program," Gambetta would salute the sovereign people as the source of all political authority; Simon, in contrast, insisted that the ultimate authority in politics, even in a regime based on universal suffrage, was the rational judgment of the people and their representatives. In politics as in philosophy, the only true authority was not the deafening roar of a numerical majority, nor the blinding command of a divine right ruler, but the quiet voice of the trained

---

65. JS, "Liberté," *Dictionnaire général*, ed. Block, 2:197; see also JS, *La Liberté*, 2:326.
66. JS, "Suppression du délit d'outrage à la morale publique et religieuse" (20 February 1868), "Droit de réunion" (13 March 1868), *La Politique radicale*, pp. 141–58, 357–94.
67. Allain-Targé, "Souvenirs d'avant 1870," *Revue de Paris*, p. 15; Allain-Targé to JS, 16 February 1868, 87 AP 17.

reason. Rejecting the "Jacobin" identification of liberty with the decrees of a single, popularly elected Convention, Simon called on republicans to work to foster the broadest possible use of man's "right to think and to speak freely to bring about the peaceful formulation and revision of the laws governing a society."[68] While Gambetta would look forward to a republican era of social equality and laicity, Simon discussed social and religious questions in a way intended to allay the fears of conservatives who identified radicalism with an atheistic socialism. On the tactical level, also, Simon's program was reformist rather than revolutionary. Although radicals should underscore their fundamental hostility to the regime by avoiding any formal alliance with the Third party, and although they should be wary of half measures and compromises, Simon called on republicans to support those partial reforms that seemed to "make the achievement of total liberty more imminent and inevitable."[69]

In his advocacy of "total liberty," Simon succeeded, for a while, in maintaining his influence over the younger republicans.[70] In June 1868, Allain-Targé founded the *Revue politique* and enlisted Challemel-Lacour as editor, with Gambetta, Brisson, Spuller, Ferry, Vacherot, Despois, Barni, Seinguerlet, and Simon as collaborators. The *Revue*, Allain-Targé anticipated, would defend in the press the ideas and the policies that Simon would defend in the *Corps législatif*. The young lawyer and his friends hoped to push Simon toward a more militant opposition to the regime.[71] Events, however, soon freed these younger republicans from their dependence on the cautious Simon; indeed, when the republican subscription to honor the martyred republican, Dr. Baudin, catapulted the *Revue politique* and Gambetta into the national limelight in the last months of the year, Simon lost his ascendancy over this group. Increasingly distrusted by an exigent Parisian working-class republicanism Simon would from now on find himself obliged to deal on a

68. JS, "Préface," *La Politique radicale*, pp. 1–3.
69. Ibid., pp. 6, 8, 11, 33–34.
70. Jules Ferry, "Bibliographie. *La Politique radicale*, par M. Jules Simon (Librairie internationale)," *Le Temps*, 17 June 1868.
71. Allain-Targé, Paris, to his father, 20 May 1868, Allain-Targé, *La République sous l'Empire*, pp. 172–73; Weill, *Histoire du parti républicain*, p. 385.

more equal basis with Gambetta and his friends. Challenged in the Parisian electoral campaign of 1869 by the candidacy of the revolutionary socialist, Jules Vallès, a protégé of Delescluze's *Le Réveil*, Simon struggled to maintain his ascendancy over his constituency. Using tactics of verbal obfuscation that almost suggest panic, he attempted to convince the working classes of his concern for their problems by characterizing his liberal humanitarian sympathies as "socialist."[72] It was at this time, as we have seen, that he sought to draw closer to younger republicans by a deceptive overture to Massol and *La Morale indépendante*.

III

Under the empire, Simon's religious sensibilities, political liberalism, and social vision coalesced in a sincere, coherent, and highly personal republicanism. As a moderate, he sought to bring together enlightened conservatives and liberal republicans in the hope that a common commitment to civil and political liberty would overshadow and ultimately soften other conflicts. This task, which aimed at reconciling groups often considered irreconcilable, required, under the best of conditions, consummate political skills. In the service of such complex and relatively unconventional views, even Simon's strengths, like his oratorical prowess, tended to inspire as much distrust as admiration. After listening to one of his speeches, with its ingratiating gestures to almost all parts of the chamber, many republicans drew the conclusions of Anatole France:

His art is flawless. When the Greeks spoke to the people, they apparently were accompanied by a flutist. When M. Jules Simon speaks, a delicious flute accompanies him, but it is invisible, and sings on his lips. M. Jules Simon is a philosopher. . . . He knows when to forget it. He knows everything. Insinuating, ironical, tender, vehement in turn, he has all the devices of an orator. When he comes up to the speaker's

72. J. Mahias, "Le Mouvement électoral à Paris et dans la Seine," *L'Avenir national*, 14 May 1869; Maurice Reclus, *Jules Favre, 1809–1880*, p. 233; Charles Du Bouzet, "Chronique," *Le Temps*, 12 March 1869; letter of P. Barthélemy, Paris, to *Le Siècle*, 22 March 1869 (published in *Le Temps*, 26 March 1869).

platform, he seems overwhelmed. Leaning over the podium, he looks over the audience with expressionless eyes which will soon be charged with flashes of lightening; he draws out the sounds of a stifled voice which little by little revives, swells up, then becomes damp with tears, or roars like melodious thunder. He is master both of himself and of his audience. Emotional but vigilant, he seizes on interruptions and carries them along in the movement of his thought, like a river sweeping off branches thrown to it. He uses everything. He is the great artist whose subtle genius transforms everything which he touches, and has only to fear his very perfection.[73]

His professorial proclivity for the stern language of conscience, duty, and principle, moreover, magnified the significance of those real or apparent shifts in position (like his abandonment of abstentionism) that are part of any moderate politics, however principled, which seeks to remain in contact with the possible. Finally, Simon was given to a kind of unction, and a sentimentality that often verged on the maudlin; a journalist summed up a view of Simon that was widespread in the political class when he noted his "talent at concealing his thoughts while opening his heart."[74]

Despite this image, due as much to his centrist positions as to his personality, Simon's political speeches and extensive travels and public lectures won him a widespread popularity. In the elections of 1869, he was generally regarded as one of the leaders of the republican opposition and was easily elected in Paris and Bordeaux.[75] Yet there was no simple correlation between his personal popularity and support for his vision in its totality.

Among Catholics, Simon appealed to republicans who, like the family of Waldeck-Rousseau, viewed the faith as a question of conscience but not of politics. These universal suffrage Catholics, to use Littré's phrase, were religious and laic, as attached

73. Anatole France, "Hommage à Jules Simon," *Revue encyclopédique* 6 (1896): 433.

74. Fulbert Dumonteil, "Jules Simon," *La Presse*, 25 August 1871.

75. Simon chose to represent the second district of Bordeaux. For electoral statistics, see "Simon (François-Simon-Jules Suisse)," *Dictionnaire des parlementaires français*, ed. Adolphe Robert et al., 5 (Paris: Bourloton, 1891): 323.

to Catholic practice as they were opposed to "government of priests." Simon's relations with Catholic liberals of Orleanist background, however, were much more ambiguous. As an opponent of the empire, a defender of the principle of liberty of conscience, and an opponent of atheism, Simon was a useful auxiliary. But for men like Albert de Broglie and Montalembert, hemmed in by the *Syllabus of Errors* and the necessity of defending the Pope's temporal power, there was not sufficient ground for a lasting alliance. Finally, despite Simon's social conservatism, the "burgraves" associated him with a republicanism that they considered by far too democratic. In general, Simon believed, the Roman Question imposed severe limits on his ability to attract Catholic liberals. As he wrote his wife from Montpellier, where he was a candidate in the 1869 elections, "success would be assured, if I would promise not to attack the Pope's temporal power, but that is quite out of the question."[76]

Among republicans, Simon's services to the democratic opposition won him an extensive following that included even the Voltairean readers of *Le Siècle* and *L'Avenir national*. In his efforts to moderate republican anticlericalism, however, Simon appealed particularly to liberal middle-class elements that, without necessarily sharing his philosophic views, appreciated his progressive and conciliatory approach to cultural politics. In this respect, Simon not only found support at Nefftzer's *Le Temps* but also was able to work easily with positivist republicans like Lavertujon, the editor of *La Gironde*, and Ferry, from 1865 to 1869, a prominent journalist at *Le Temps*.

Simon met the capable Lavertujon in 1859, at a time when *La Gironde* was beginning to attract attention as a leading liberal provincial newspaper. Lavertujon, who resided in Paris and commuted frequently to Bordeaux by rail, soon became a regular at Simon's Thursday "dinners for twelve" and a close political adviser. United by a common hostility to the regime, and by a moderate and practical liberalism, the two men put aside their philosophic differences. In 1863, Simon, Carnot, Ferry, and other members of the *Comité général démocratique de Paris* vigorously supported Lavertujon's unsuccessful lib-

76. Pierre Sorlin, *Waldeck-Rousseau*, pp. 113–16; JS, Montpellier, to Mme. Jules Simon, October 1868, 87 AP 8.

eral candidacy at Bordeaux.[77] In subsequent years, Simon occupied a privileged position in *La Gironde*'s "Correspondance de Paris" and, in 1868, Lavertujon, his father-in-law, Gustave Gounouilhou, the owner of *La Gironde*, and others convinced Simon to accept a candidacy in one of the Bordeaux electoral districts. During the campaign of 1869 against the official candidate Blanchy, a prominent Bordeaux *négociant*, *La Gironde* not only gave Simon full coverage but also published, in serialized form, his *La Peine de mort*.[78] His campaign was marked by a "moderation" and a "relative reserve" that in the eyes of the embarrassed attorney general had effectively rallied support even from the business community and from large landowners.[79]

Simon's relations with Ferry were also especially cordial. In the 1860s, even before he ran for public office, the talented Ferry played an important role in the republican movement as a journalist and legal expert on electoral laws and practices, and he quickly established close relations with Simon and with a wide range of both older and younger republicans. From the frequent collaboration between Simon and Ferry grew a long-lived association, based on mutual admiration, similar political styles, and even affection, in which the younger Ferry always retained a certain "nuance of deference" toward his older patron. Indeed, when Ferry delivered his celebrated speech at the Salle Molière (10 April 1870) for the *Société pour l'instruction élémentaire* in which he pledged to devote his career to the cause of popular education, he began with a salute to Simon, with whom he shared the platform, as a past master of the popular lecture.[80]

Despite his personal successes, Simon sensed in 1869 that republicanism had reached a critical stage. In their eagerness to broaden their electoral appeal, republicans might, he feared,

77. Lavertujon, *Gambetta inconnu*, pp. 119–20; *La Gironde*, 24 May 1863; J. Massicault, "Élections," *La Gironde*, 19 May 1863; JS, *Corps législatif*, 19 November 1863, *Le Journal des débats*, 20 November 1863.

78. Gustave Gounouilhou, "Correspondance de Paris, 2 février, 1864 (résumé)," *La Gironde*, 4 February 1864; JS, "Mon Petit Journal," *Le Temps*, 18 August 1892; "*La Peine de mort*, par Jules Simon," *La Gironde*, 5–12 May 1869.

79. Reports of 15, 18, 31 May 1869, A.N. BB[18] 1786.

80. Maurice Reclus, *Jules Ferry, 1832–1893*, p. 159; Jules Ferry, *Discours et opinions de Jules Ferry*, 1:284.

give in to the urgings of Gambetta and his followers, who wished to accentuate republican anticlericalism. As Simon explained to Juliette Adam in mid-1869, this "fanatic atheist" thought nothing of pitting a "Voltairean country" against the clergy. "Gambetta," he added, "is inventing religious hatred, as if there were not enough political hatred. The two together are too much." For the bourgeois *universitaire*, the loud, gregarious, and socially ill-mannered Gambetta, with only a smattering of general culture to cover his "fathomless ignorance," posed an authoritarian threat to the "aristocracy of talent and probity" that might rightfully claim the leadership of the republican movement. And he interpreted Gambetta's decision to challenge the tested republican veteran Carnot in the elections of 1869 as proof that the ambitious young politician placed personal political advantage above republican principle. Most important, Gambetta, both in personal style and democratic rhetoric, represented precisely that image of a demagogic republicanism that so frightened the established notables whom Simon had been courting for over a decade. Such a judgment was not entirely disinterested, since Gambetta posed a threat to Simon's popularity in the country, and to his influence over men like Lavertujon and Ferry, who had close ties with both political leaders.[81]

In the period between the elections of 1869 and the fall of the empire, Simon continued his attempts to restrain Gambetta and his followers by enrolling them under the banner of "total liberty."[82] But his efforts to build a republicanism attractive to both the notables and the people hindered his ability to maintain his influence over the younger republican politicians who felt that the movement should court the forces of urban

81. Juliette Adam, *Mes sentiments et nos idées avant 1870*, p. 376; Maxime Du Camp, "Les Académiciens de mon temps," Maxime Du Camp Papers, 30, fol. #388; JS, "*Les Petits papiers* de M. Hector Pessard," *Le Journal des débats*, 21 June 1887. Other writings by Simon on Gambetta repeat the same themes: JS, "Gambetta," *Figures et croquis*, pp. 26–55; JS, "Page d'histoire," *Le Passant*, 3 January 1883, 87 AP 14.

82. Simon sought to involve Gambetta in a projected republican monthly, *La Liberté totale*, but the journal was never published. JS, Ostende, to Gambetta, 12 August 1869, Gambetta, Villeneuve, to Lavertujon, 30 August 1869, Lavertujon, *Gambetta inconnu*, pp. 9–14; Jules Ferry, Ems, to JS, 12 August 1869, Jules Ferry, *Lettres de Jules Ferry, 1846–1893*, pp. 73–74.

and rural radicalism. The fall of the empire in September 1870 would give Simon access to power under new political conditions, and another chance to win French opinion to a Republic more socially conservative and liberal than radical and democratic.

CHAPTER VIII

THE MINISTRY OF PUBLIC INSTRUCTION, WORSHIP, AND FINE ARTS, 1871–1873

On 16 February 1871, Adolphe Thiers, head of the executive power, requested Simon to accept the portfolio of the minister of public instruction, worship, and fine arts in his new cabinet. Thiers wanted to establish a broadly based government capable of inducing the republican urban population as well as the more conservative countryside to accept an inevitably cruel treaty of peace. He hoped to persuade republicans that their best strategy was to capitalize on the division between Legitimists and Orleanists in the monarchist majority to show the country that a popularly elected assembly could conclude a peace and could tranquilize the nation. "If the Republic loses this opportunity," he told his weary, discouraged, and hesitating colleague, "it will be the republicans' fault, and not mine."[1]

Thiers, with his customary shrewdness, knew his man. Unlike many in Orleanist circles, he understood that Simon was more a liberal parliamentarian than a radical democrat. *La Politique radicale*, he knew, was best read not as a revolutionary program but as a declaration of general principle designed to aid the republican party maintain its identity in the face of the progressive liberalization of the Second Empire. The moderate character of Simon's republicanism was also apparent in his activities as minister of public instruction in the Government of National Defense. Uncomfortable with popular democracy and too attached to legal forms to initiate revolutionary activity, Simon was obliged to assume a secondary, although not insignificant, role in the inner councils of the government. In both his own administration and in the more general discussions of

1. Gustave Simon, "Jules Simon: notes et souvenirs (Documents inédits), Partie III," *La Revue mondiale*, 160, no. 6 (15 March 1926): 115; JS, to Adolphe Thiers, 20 October 1875, Adolphe Thiers, *Le Courrier de M. Thiers*, p. 423.

policy, Simon used his influence to oppose Gambetta's efforts to give the "revolution of 1870" a marked republican character. Resisting these pressures to identify the defense of France with an explicit republicanism in administration and legislation, he insisted that the government should appeal to Frenchmen of all political persuasions. Privately convinced that *guerre à outrance* would succeed not in expelling the Prussians but only in bringing France to social revolution, he looked beyond the inevitable negotiated settlement to the election of a representative assembly that might appropriately decide the momentous questions raised by the republican program. Such different attitudes had led to a dramatic confrontation between the two men in Bordeaux in early February, when Gambetta attempted to use his powers as minister of the interior to deny the suffrage in the impending elections to all those who had served the Second Empire. Supported by the government in Paris and aided by Lavertujon, who was one of its under secretaries, Simon had secured Gambetta's resignation; only his tact and Gambetta's self-restraint had averted a disastrous civil war.[2]

2. The Government of National Defense, a provisional government caught between the Prussians on the one hand, and pressures from both Parisian popular democracy and Léon Gambetta on the other, faced political problems of extreme complexity. In these circumstances, existing sources often do not shed much light on the policies of a figure like Simon, who played a much less prominent role in the government than either Gen. Louis-Jules Trochu or Jules Favre. The most comprehensive discussion of the internal politics of the Government of National Defense in Paris is Henri Guillemin's three-volume *Les Origines de la Commune*. Guillemin correctly associates Simon with the more moderate elements in the government: Trochu, Favre, Picard, and Ferry. But, convinced that the French could have won the war, he depicts these men as traitors who were more willing to come to terms with Bismarck than to risk jeopardizing bourgeois class interests in the extended mobilization that a true *guerre à outrance* would require. I accept neither Guillemin's high estimate of French military potential in 1870 and 1871, nor his portrayal of the psychology of these republican politicians.

For sources that suggest Simon's rather narrow interpretation of the government's mandate, see: JS, Paris, to Léon Gambetta, 9 January 1871, Joseph Reinach Papers, #197–200, n.a.fr. 24910; JS to [?], [October–November] 1870, 87 AP 9 II (9); Amaury Dréo, *Gouvernement de la Défense nationale, 4 septembre 1870–16 février 1871. Procès-verbaux des séances du conseil. Publiés d'après les manuscrits originaux de M. A. Dréo*, p. 573.

On Simon's confrontation with Gambetta, see: Léon Séché, *Jules*

The elections of 8 February 1871 at last gave France an elected assembly, but, overwhelmingly monarchical in composition, the National Assembly hardly augured well for republican prospects. In fact, republicans associated with the Government of National Defense had done badly at the polls, and Simon himself, defeated in Paris and in the Gironde, just managed to gain election in the Marne. Still, Thiers's offer gave Simon the opportunity to resume his efforts—this time as a minister in a regime that was republican in all but name—to rally republican deists, academic spiritualists, and Catholic liberals under the banner of liberal republicanism. Now that the Third party had disappeared, Simon was eager to strengthen the ties between republicans and Thiers and his followers. He might also perform real services for public education; the disorganization of the educational system, caused by the war and related events, he feared, might offer a pretext for a minister belonging to the Right to reorganize in a manner favorable to clerical influences.[3] The strength of the Catholic monarchist element in Thiers's majority would minimize the possibilities of far-reaching educational reform, but a man dedicated to the principle of liberty of conscience might ward off mischievous proposals emanating from the Right. At the same time, Thiers's proposal appealed to his strong sense of patriotism; could he refuse to aid in the work of national reconstruction?

After securing assurances that he would be master in his own administration, and that other republicans would belong to the cabinet, Simon accepted Thiers's offer.[4] At that time, no one could have predicted that Thiers's ministry would last until May 1873. In the cabinet, Simon's intellectual agility and appreciation of subtleties enabled him to become the most influential of Thiers's advisers. But Thiers, enjoying a tremen-

Simon; sa vie et son oeuvre, pp. 129–80; for other extended accounts, see Frank Brabant, *The Beginnings of the Third Republic in France*, pp. 39–60; J. P. T. Bury, *Gambetta and the National Defence*, pp. 245–64; Guillemin, *Les Origines de la Commune*, 3:382–410.

3. JS, *The Government of M. Thiers, from 8 February, 1871 to 24 May, 1873*, 2:262. Jacques Gouault, *Comment la France est devenue républicaine; les élections générales et partielles à l'Assemblée nationale, 1870–1875*, pp. 71, 80, 217.

4. Gustave Simon, "Jules Simon: notes et souvenirs (Documents inédits), Partie III," *Revue mondiale*, p. 115; JS, *Le Soir de ma journée*, pp. 160, 218; JS, *Thiers, Guizot, Rémusat*, p. 74.

dous ascendancy over the French nation and its Assembly, dominated French political life, and set the parameters of most public policy. As minister of public instruction, worship, and fine arts, Simon worked in bureaucratic shadow, relatively shielded from the public view.[5] In the course of the next two and one-half years, the republican cause made great progress, but Simon was less successful in his efforts to use his particular office to rally freethinkers and Catholics around his vision of a liberal and spiritualistic republic. Such disappointing results were a measure of the magnitude of the obstacles against which he struggled.

As minister of worship, Simon worked to lay the foundations for a reconciliation between the French Church and the Republic. Despite the protests of the Right, he had refused to yield the jurisdiction over the Ministry of Worship that he had exercised during the Government of National Defense.[6] Just as the Republic and the Church could coexist in an atmosphere of mutual respect, so a spiritualistic philosopher could direct the Ministry of Worship in a manner acceptable to believers and unbelievers alike. Simon himself was aware that the Concordat of 1801, and the Organic Articles of 8 April 1802, the fundamental laws regulating the relations between the French State and the Church, would severely limit the effectiveness of such an effort. For Simon's task could not be reduced simply to an impartial enforcement of a law accepted by all. The Concordat was the product of prolonged and difficult negotiations between Napoleon I and Pope Pius VII and, like most treaties, had been understood somewhat differently by each party. The Papacy had never formally recognized the Organic Articles, a supplementary body of regulations on Church affairs, which Napoleon I had imposed on the Church after the Concordat had been drawn up. In subsequent years, the Church had, with the tacit approval of the State, succeeded in circumventing or ignoring many of these articles.[7] In this situ-

5. JS, "Mon Petit Journal," Le Temps, 17 December 1892.
6. Camille de Meaux, Souvenirs politiques, 1871–1877, p. 37.
7. For an interesting discussion of the state of nonobservance of the Organic Articles during the Second Empire, see the memorandum of M. de Rayneval, an ambassador to Rome during the Second Empire: "Mémoire sur la législation ecclésiastique française et la situation de l'Église de France. . . ," A.E., Mémoires et documents: Rome, vol. 117 (see Abbreviations, p. viii).

ation, any effort to enforce certain Organic Articles, like the article that required the Church to seek official authorization prior to the publication of some kinds of Papal bulls in France, struck Catholics as vindictive rancor, while failure to enforce such articles provoked the wrath of many anticlerical republicans. Caught between these forces, Simon grudgingly yielded to Catholic pressures more often than not.[8]

Although Simon inclined toward a strict interpretation of formal matters relating to the essence of the Concordat, both Catholic opinion and his own respect for religious liberty narrowly circumscribed his range of options in actual practice. The Concordat gave the French government the power to nominate bishops and archbishops. Since the nominee could not take his seat until he had received canonical institution from the Pope, it had become customary for French officials to consult with representatives of the Pope before formally naming a candidate. Failure to employ this device of *entente préalable* had led to a series of deadlocks in the 1860s. During his ministry, Simon maintained close relations with Flavio Chigi, the Papal nuncio, and even exchanged lists of candidates. Simon reached some form of *entente préalable* for eight of the eleven bishops and all of the five archbishops whom he named to seats in metropolitan France during his ministry. As for the three bishops who do not seem to have received this preliminary approval, one, Théodore Legain, bishop of Montauban, was known for his sympathy for *L'Univers* and Papal infallibility and was appointed before Simon and the nuncio had entered into relations with one another. In the case of another, Denis Nouvel, bishop of Quimper, Simon exceeded the Pope's fondest wish by the precedent-breaking nomination of a Benedictine monk.[9] As for the third, Alexandre Sébaux, bishop of Angoulême, Simon acted on the warm recommendation of Joseph Guibert, archbishop of Paris, and the Pope, in this case as in the others, did not protest. Such a display of solicitude disappointed many republicans who repeated stories of how their minister had taken to kissing the hands of prelates. Others repeated a remark attributed to Bishop Félix Dupanloup: "Jules Simon will become a cardinal before I do."[10]

8. JS, *The Government of M. Thiers*, 2:476–79.
9. Jules-Alexis Des Michels, *Souvenirs de carrière (1855–1886)*, p. 85.
10. Adrien Dansette, *Histoire religieuse de la France contemporaine*,

Republicans were not well situated to judge Simon's actions properly. In fact, particularly in his appointment of bishops and archbishops, he sought to limit the power of the most authoritarian elements in the Church. At a minimum, he tried to imitate the policies of his recent predecessors and sought to fill episcopal vacancies with men who, whatever their theological nuance, were moderate and conciliatory in temperament. Although Simon's sympathies lay with that element in the French episcopacy that had fought at the recent Vatican Council for the rights of bishops and churches and against the claims of Papal supremacy, he proved willing to accept ultramontanes who were likely to refrain from converting their offices into centers of Legitimist or Bonapartist agitation. Thus, on the nuncio's recommendation, he named Félix Fruchard, bishop of Limoges, a man who had voted for Papal infallibility at the Council, to the archbishopric of Tours; "a distinguished prelate, a good administrator, who," he wrote Thiers, "has never caused trouble for the government."[11] He resisted pressure from the nuncio to name well-known Legitimist ultramontanes like Jean-Baptiste Caussette, vicar general of Toulouse, and François de Cabrières, vicar general of Nîmes, to the bishoprics of Bellay and Mende, respectively.[12] And he yielded to Thiers and the nuncio on the appointments of such zealous ultramontane Legitimists as Léopold Léséleuc de Kérouara, the titular chanoine of Quimper, to Autun, and François de la Bouillerie, the bishop of Carcassonne to Bordeaux, only after an effort to assure certain limitations on their political activities.[13] Although Adolphe Tardif, Simon's director of worship,

---

p. 358. The principal sources for Simon's relations with the Papal nuncio came from 87 AP 10 I (1), especially Mgr. Flavio Chigi, Versailles, to JS, 8 May 1871, JS, Versailles, to Mgr. Chigi, 9 May 1871, Mgr. Chigi, Paris, to JS, 11 August 1871, Mgr. Chigi, Versailles, to JS, 1 September 1871. See also A.N. F19 2459 and F19 2609; Jacques Gadille, *La Pensée et l'action des évêques français au début de la IIIe République, 1870–1883*, 1:285–88.

11. JS, Paris, to Adolphe Thiers, 5 September 1871, Adolphe Thiers Papers, #233, n.a.fr. 20623; see also Dossier Fruchard, A.N. F19 2588.

12. Dossier Caussette, A.N. F19 2618; Mgr. Chigi, Versailles, to JS, 1 September 1871, 87 AP 10 I (1); JS, Versailles, to Thiers, 1872, #171, n.a.fr. 20625.

13. Mgr. Chigi, Versailles, to JS, 1 September 1871, 87 AP 10 I (1); JS, Versailles, to Thiers, 5 September 1871, Thiers Papers, #233, n.a.fr.

might admit that "a particularly emphatic *gallican* has caused and will cause more trouble for the government than a moderate ultramontane," their recommendations suggest that both found "immoderation" a vice particularly widespread among churchmen of ultramontane persuasion.[14]

While blocking the appointment of men too closely identified in his mind with the shrill authoritarianism of *L'Univers*, Simon also hoped to push some of the more liberal churchmen, usually opponents of Papal infallibility, into positions of leadership in the episcopacy. In principle, Simon denied the right of the government to appoint bishops on the basis of their doctrines, but he also defended the right of the State to pressure the Pope to accept, at least in a few cases, nominees of unquestioned fidelity to the Church, who might greatly contribute to national reconciliation. In his most notable effort in this direction, Simon sought to fill the seat of archbishop of Paris with Dupanloup, bishop of Orleans, the leader of the European opposition to Papal infallibility at the Vatican Council of 1870. More recently, *L'Univers* had openly accused Dupanloup and his friends at *Le Correspondant* of advocating "a free Church in a free State."[15]

The news of the death of Georges Darboy, archbishop of Paris, at the hands of the Communards had hardly become public when the Pope and his emissaries began to signal their opposition to Dupanloup's promotion.[16] Simon and Thiers discussed the matter in early June, and Simon wrote a letter formally reiterating his belief that an ultramontane appointment would "deeply sadden all the members of the upper clergy who still are resisting ultramontane doctrines," and might do great damage to the French Church. Of Dupanloup, he wrote:

20623; JS, Paris, to Thiers, 15 October 1872, Thiers Papers, #167, n.a.fr. 20625.

14. Simon's private papers contain a memorandum, dated 18 July 1870, drawn up by Tardif, which registers the votes of the members of the French episcopacy at the Vatican Council and discusses the current meaning of the distinctions between ultramontane and Gallican, 87 AP 10 I (5).

15. *L'Univers*, 8 March 1871, quoted in Alfred de Falloux, *Augustin Cochin*, p. 358.

16. JS, Versailles, to Thiers, [early June] 1871, A.N.F¹⁹ 2459; Bernard d'Harcourt, Rome, to Jules Favre, 4, 5 June 1871, A.E., *Correspondance politique: Rome*, vol. 1051.

The bishop of Orleans is clearly the most important member of the French clergy. His turn of mind is more decisive than conciliatory; but he understands all questions (even non-religious ones), he values liberty, he can stand up against the excesses of certain Catholics when other less eminent bishops dare not, and he has a deserved reputation for courage and ability which, especially at Paris, would facilitate his administration.

The government should name Dupanloup immediately, before the nuncio could build up other candidacies, and the Pope would be obliged, albeit grudgingly, to give him canonical institution. As a gesture of conciliation, the government might then appoint several notorious ultramontanes to other (and lesser) posts.[17] Thiers continued to hesitate, however, and the Papal pressure against Dupanloup mounted. In the third week in June, Théodore Forcade, bishop of Nevers, wrote Simon from Rome that the Pope would refuse to institute any bishop who had said "*non placet,* or . . . who had abstained at the last session of the Council."[18] Exasperated by this opposition, Simon wrote Thiers another letter, probably never sent, reporting that the nuncio had informed him that the Pope would not institute such men for any seat in France whatsoever. Reminding Thiers of the government's responsibilities toward "enlightened Catholics" and their representatives in the episcopacy, he called on Thiers to deal firmly with the ultramontanes, "this party, which yields to firmness, but which becomes imperious and threatening when one obeys it . . . [and] will create every day greater and greater difficulties." He concluded by reminding Thiers that a "great bishop at Paris is almost a transformation of the French Church."[19]

About that time, Dupanloup, unwilling to lend himself to a maneuver that might cause the Pope such displeasure, wrote Thiers to announce that he would not accept the seat at Paris even if it were offered him.[20] Thiers, for his part, while sharing

17. JS, Versailles, to Thiers, [early June] 1871, A.N. F.[19] 2459.

18. Théodore Forcade, bishop of Nevers, Rome, to JS, 21 June 1871, 87 AP 10 I (1).

19. JS, Paris, to Thiers, [late June] 1871, 87 AP 10 I (1).

20. François Lagrange, *Vie de Mgr. Dupanloup, évêque d'Orléans,* 3:233; for Thiers's reply, see Thiers, Versailles, to Félix Dupanloup, 11 July 1871, Adolphe Thiers, *Thiers au pouvoir (1871–1873),* p. 83.

Simon's sympathy for Dupanloup, was unwilling to provoke a confrontation with the Pope that might jeopardize his efforts to induce the Pontiff to accept gracefully his decision to regularize diplomatic relations with the Italian government and to reassure the Catholic elements of his majority.[21] In a cabinet meeting on 14 July, Simon made one more effort to convince Thiers and his ministers to name Dupanloup but was voted down.[22] Instead, the government named Joseph Guibert, the archbishop of Tours, Simon's alternative candidate who, absent from Rome at the time of the vote on Papal infallibility, would not seem too disfavorable either to Gallicans or the Pope.[23] Thus, Thiers was able to sweeten his message informing Pope Pius IX of his intention to name Guibert by reminding the Pope that he had not obeyed "preferences which would have led to other choices."[24] The Pope agreed to give his formal approval to Guibert who had refused to accept the government's nomination without first consulting the Pope's emissaries.[25]

Despite this setback, however, Simon continued to seek advancement for members of the French clergy sympathetic to the twenty-five French churchmen who had refused the *placet* at Rome. In September, when the appointment of a new archbishop of Auch was under consideration, Simon set aside the nuncio's recommendation of an ultramontane candidate and proposed Bishop Colet of Luçon, a man who had abstained in the vote on Papal infallibility. Like Dupanloup, however, Colet notified the government that he would not accept the appointment.[26] Later in the month, Simon sought to correct the impression created by the promotion of two ultramontane bishops to Auch and Tours, by naming to the bishoprics of Bellay and Limoges protégés of Darboy, the former archbishop of Paris,

---

21. For indications of Thiers's concerns, see Bernard d'Harcourt, Rome, to Thiers, 29 July 1871, Thiers Papers, #120, n.a.fr. 20622.

22. JS, "Mon Petit Journal," *Le Temps*, 28 January 1891.

23. JS, Paris, to Thiers, [late June] 1871, 87 AP 10 I (1); the register of candidates in the ministry describes him as "neutral—not at Rome at the moment of the vote. The first bishop to condemn *L'Univers*," A.N. F[19] 1330*.

24. Jules Favre, minister of foreign affairs, Versailles, to Bernard d'Harcourt, 14 July 1871, A.E., *Correspondance politique: Rome*, vol. 1052.

25. Joseph Paguelle de Follenay, *Vie du Cardinal Guibert*, 2:516–17.

26. JS, Paris, to Thiers, 5 September 1871, #233, JS, Paris, to Thiers, 21 September 1871, #234, Thiers Papers, n.a.fr. 20623.

and of Cardinal Mathieu, the archbishop of Besançon, both prominent opponents of the *placet*. Darboy's friend, Alfred Duquesnay, was so discreet that he was acceptable even to the nuncio, but Mathieu's friend Louis Besson, the superior of Saint François-Xavier College at Besançon, was a notorious Gallican. When the cabinet accepted Simon's choices in late September, it appeared that the minister had finally succeeded in giving "Gallicans a sign of . . . [the government's] sincere desire not to exclude them from the episcopacy." However, before the nomination became official, Besson wrote Simon to denounce as calumny rumors that associated him with Gallicans and declared himself more ultramontane than ever. When it became clear that the nuncio would oppose this nomination, Simon suggested that the government look elsewhere rather than engage in a struggle for "a candidate who so unexpectedly declares himself ultramontane."[27] Thus, Simon's efforts to utilize the powers given him by the Concordat to shape a more liberal French episcopacy foundered on the demands of domestic and foreign politics, the resistance of the Pope, and the scruples of the more liberal elements in the French Church.

In early 1873, Simon set in motion a plan calculated to show the Republic's favor for the lower clergy by giving tenure to *desservants* over fifty years of age who had served the same parish for ten years. This plan, aimed at the lowest and most numerous segment of the French clergy, was of old republican vintage. Edgar Quinet, Pascal Duprat, and Jules Favre had been its advocates during the Second Republic; now, in a "Circular of 7 January 1873," Simon asked the French episcopate what they thought of the plan.[28] The response of the episcopate, as Simon must have foreseen, was cautious, for the question affected the authority of bishops and raised questions of legal jurisdiction between the government and the Papacy. If Simon really expected to bring about a quiet reform, as he subsequently declared, his hopes were dashed when the circular appeared in *Le Français* with an attack by the archbishop of Rennes.[29] Still, as Tardif had anticipated, publicity of this initiative could

27. JS, Paris, to Thiers, 21 September 1871, #234, JS, Paris, to Thiers, 6 October 1871, #235, Thiers Papers, n.a.fr. 20623; Dossier Besson, A.N. F19 2550.

28. "Circulaire du 6 janvier, 1873," 87 AP 10 I (4).

29. "Circulaire du 7 février, 1873," 87 AP 10 I (4); A.N. F19 2655.

not fail to give Simon's friends on the Left an opportunity to heap their sarcasms on the archbishop: "To give new dignity to the lower clergy, through tenure," wrote *Le Siècle*, "to break ...the humiliating yoke imposed by ultramontane policies, and which reduces the lower clergy to little more than an instrument in the hands of the episcopacy: How audacious! How improper! How sacrilegious!"[30]

For republicans, however, reform of the educational system, especially at the primary level, was the surest means to the related goals of Republic and French regeneration. In the fall of 1871, at Saint-Quentin, Gambetta demanded for the people "a good amount of education, of well-taught, obligatory, free and ... absolutely lay instruction."[31] Such demands met strong conservative opposition, for many on the Right were convinced that French misfortunes were the product of a moral degeneration that they associated with rationalism, republicanism, and with the weakening of the French Church. Questions related to the reform and administration of France's system of primary education were Simon's principal preoccupation during his first eighteen months as Thiers's minister of public instruction. Following in the steps of his friend, Carnot, minister of public instruction in 1848, he sought to strengthen public education by making primary instruction obligatory for all children between the ages of seven and thirteen and by taking steps to free the primary schoolteacher from political pressures. Eager to support French republicans who favored lay instruction, without however discriminating against Catholics, Simon sought to guarantee freedom of conscience for Catholics and freethinkers alike in educational matters. Thus he developed an elaborate procedure for the exercise of local options between lay and religious public teaching personnel. Such a policy, he hoped, would make the Republic attractive to Catholic liberals.

This question of local option between schoolteachers drawn from the ranks of laymen and from Catholic religious teaching orders, was, Simon later admitted, the most thorny problem that his administration faced in 1871.[32] The collapse

---

30. "Paris, 3 mars," *Le Siècle*, 4 March 1873; a note for JS from Adolphe Tardif, headed "Systèmes divers," 87 AP 10 I (4).

31. Maurice Gontard, *Les Écoles primaires de la France bourgeoise (1833–1875)*, p. 215.

32. "Déposition de M. Jules Simon" (31 August 1871), Commission

of the empire on 4 September had provoked the formation of revolutionary municipal councils in several French cities. On 14 September the Committee of Public Safety of Lyons voted to replace all members of Catholic teaching orders serving in its public schools with laymen; only laymen, it believed, could teach in a manner fully in accordance with the republican spirit. In the following months, cities like Toulouse, Saint-Étienne, and Chambéry followed the Lyons example. Sometimes, as at Lyons and Saint-Étienne, local authorities also decided to change the program of instruction, which, in accordance with the Falloux Law of 15 March 1850, included a prescribed amount of religious instruction.[33] In the spring and summer of 1871, other municipal councils in Vichy, Toulon, Besançon, Valence, Narbonne, and elsewhere also declared their intention to change the character of the personnel in their communal schools.

Such procedures were in violation of the existing legislation on the substitution of one category of primary schoolteacher for another. According to this legislation, the prefects decided upon the category of schoolteacher after consulting the municipal councils. In the earlier years of the empire, the municipal councils had the right to express their wishes only when a place became open through death, dismissal, resignation, or the creation of a new school. Since the prefect could often make replacements of one teacher by another of the same category before any of these conditions occurred, the municipal councils had little power to change the status quo. As the empire became more liberal, Duruy reinterpreted the existing body of law in a sense that allowed the municipal council to express its desires whenever it chose. The prefect was then obliged to investigate whether the opinion of the municipal council really reflected the desires of the population, and final decision in this case reverted to the minister of public instruction. After 4 September the Government of National Defense theoretically

---

d'enquête sur les actes du Gouvernement de la défense nationale, *Annales de l'Assemblée nationale*, 23:442.

33. Maurice Gontard, "Une Bataille scolaire au XIXᵉ siècle; l'affaire des écoles primaires laïques de Lyon (1869–1873)," *Cahiers d'histoire*; "Les Subventions scolaires," *Le Français*, 19 October 1871; Charles Zévort, "Note sur la substitution d'une catégorie d'instituteurs à une autre," A.N. F¹⁷ 9196.

maintained the new jurisprudence but left the final decision in the hands of the prefect. Although this jurisprudence was more responsive to the desires of local communities, it had serious educational and political drawbacks. On the pedagogical level, it posed a threat to administrative continuity in primary schools; in times of political uncertainty, oscillations in political opinion would provoke constant changes in the category of personnel teaching in public schools. On the political level, it heightened tensions between municipal councils and prefectoral authority. For as Simon's associate Charles Zévort pointed out, how could a prefect of a government that purported to draw its legitimacy from universal suffrage declare the will of a popularly elected municipal council unrepresentative?[34]

The Government of National Defense, itself born at the *Hôtel de ville* in Paris, could hardly maintain this jurisprudence against a determined municipal council, let alone a revolutionary commune like Lyons. Preoccupied with matters of defense, reluctant to raise divisive political questions and without the kind of authority a popular election might supply, the government resignedly let local circumstances largely determine the official response to the pretensions of municipal councils. Some prefects, like Armand Duportal at Toulouse and Paul Challemel-Lacour at Lyons, formally recognized and approved the actions of the municipal councils.[35] Others, like the prefect of Loire at Saint-Étienne, withheld approval of similar actions. But they did not interfere with the execution of these questionable decisions.[36] In Paris, Simon himself clashed with the mayor of the eleventh arrondissement, Jules Mottu, who had proclaimed "purely lay teaching" and excluded the congregationists from their nine communal schools. Unwilling to challenge

34. The best discussions of this legislation and jurisprudence are Auguste Silvy, *La Délégation du Ministère de l'Instruction publique à Tours et à Bordeaux. Compte rendu présenté à M. le Ministre de l'Instruction publique, des Cultes et des Beaux-Arts*, pp. 90–93, and Charles Zévort, "Note sur la substitution d'une catégorie d'instituteurs à une autre," A.N. F[17] 9196.

This jurisprudence was based on Article 31 of the Law of 15 March 1850, Article 5 of the Decree-law of 9 March 1852, the ministerial circulars of 9 April 1852 and 2 March 1853, Article 8 of the Law of 14 June 1854, and the ministerial circular of 12 July 1862.

35. Auguste Silvy, *La Délégation du Ministère de l'Instruction publique à Tours et à Bordeaux*, pp. 93–94.

36. Ibid., Appendix, no. 10.

directly the militants of the faubourg Saint-Antoine, Simon first sought to conciliate Mottu by promising funds to support new lay schools in the district and by appointing him to a commission to formulate a legislative package dealing with all aspects of primary education. When these inducements proved ineffectual, Simon demanded that Gambetta revoke him and backed his request with a threat to resign if he did not receive satisfaction.[37] Subsequent conflicts of a similar nature in the third and fourteenth arrondissements, as well as the reelection of the martyred Mottu in early November, were harbingers of the difficulties Simon would face as a member of Thiers's cabinet.

This new government could hardly afford to do anything that might exacerbate tensions between the republican municipalities of southern France and the conservative Assembly. Especially after the Commune, Thiers was eager to reassure moderate republicans that he was not conspiring against the Republic.[38] In cities like Lyons and Toulouse, prefects, rectors, and deputies warned that political tempers were at the flash point and urged prudence and temporization.[39] The vigor of

37. The Mottu controversy was an important political episode in the history of the Government of National Defense and it fell directly under Simon's jurisdiction.

For an excellent account of Simon's policies with regard to Mottu and to broader educational questions, see Gontard, *Les Écoles primaires*, pp. 208–11. For source material on Simon's confrontation with Mottu, see especially: JS, *Souvenirs du quatre septembre. Le Gouvernement de la défense nationale*, 2:122–23; draft of a letter from JS to Favre in late October 1870, 87 AP 9 X; JS, Paris, to Favre, 1 December 1870, A.N. F[19] 2005.

For the fullest contemporary discussions, see: Mgr. Maurice d'Hulst, *Les Maires et les écoles pendant le siège*; Clarisse Coignet, *Rapport présenté au nom de la Commission des dames chargée d'examiner les questions relatives à la réforme de l'instruction primaire*; Abbé Louis-Antoine Lesmayoux, "L'Enseignement primaire," *Le Correspondant*, 86, no. 1 (10 January 1872): 104–48.

38. Thiers, Versailles, to Jacques Hénon, mayor of Lyons, 1 September 1871, Thiers, *Thiers au pouvoir*, pp. 107–9.

39. Philippe Le Royer, Versailles, to JS, 16 April 1871, Edmond Valentin, prefect of Rhône, Lyons, to JS, 21 August 1871, A.N. F[17] 9173; Charles de Kératry, prefect of Haute-Garonne, Toulouse, to JS, 3 June 1871, Adolphe Gatien-Arnoult, rector of the Academy of Toulouse, Toulouse, to JS, 6 June 1871, A.N. F[17] 9174.

the resistance raised by the *Frères de la Doctrine Chrétienne* also gave the government room to maneuver. In Lyons, the *Frères* established private schools that were attracting a clear majority of the city's school population.[40] In Toulouse, they obtained a court order permitting them to remain at least temporarily in the public buildings; deprived of municipal funds, they were nevertheless attracting more pupils than the public lay schools.[41] At the same time, they had appealed to the provisional Council of State against the alleged illegality of the actions of the municipal councils.[42]

The minister of public instruction was vested by law with the power to annul the actions of the municipal councils. To adopt this path of action, however, would have provoked serious confrontations with numerous municipal councils; these councils, although oblivious to certain legal niceties, did articulate the long-thwarted desires of urban populations for change in public education. Simon therefore hoped to reach negotiated settlements with the municipalities.[43] His objective was not the status quo ante for all municipalities that had overstepped their powers; instead, he hoped that he might induce municipal councils to reintegrate a number of congregationist schools into their public-school system without necessarily eliminating the new lay schools that they had just created.[44] At the same time, he hoped that the promise of a new law reforming the procedures for the appointment of schoolteachers would induce the offending municipal councils to accept such a compromise. Using the jurisprudence of the late empire as a guide, he instructed prefects faced with disputed municipal decisions to try to determine "whether the decisions of the municipal as-

40. L. Aubin, inspector of the Academy of Lyons, Lyons, to La Saussaye, rector of the Academy of Lyons, 9 March 1871, A.N. F[17] 9173.

41. Vidal-LaBlache, inspector of the Academy of Toulouse, Toulouse, to JS, 4 March 1871, Auguste Silvy, director of primary instruction, "Note pour M. le Ministre," [December 1871], A.N. F[17] 9174.

42. Silvy, "Note pour M. le Ministre," [December 1871], A.N. F[17] 9174; Gontard, "Une Bataille scolaire au XIXe siècle," p. 281.

43. JS, Paris, to Kératry, prefect of Haute-Garonne, 13 June 1871, A.N. F[17] 9174.

44. Aubin, inspector of the Academy of Lyons, Lyons, to JS, 14 October 1871, A.N. F[17] 9173; JS, Paris, to Laporterie, prefect of Var, 26 August 1871, A.N. F[17] 9175; Auguste Silvy, "Note pour M. le Ministre, Paris, 4 mars, 1872," A.N. F[17] 9175.

semblies came from a surprise vote and whether they accurately reflected the opinion of the majority of the population."[45] As the summer wore on, the minister slightly refined these instructions. In his letters outlining certain tests that prefects might use to determine the opinion of the majority of the population, Simon gave great weight to those that indicated the attitudes of fathers of families. He urged prefects to note particularly the current distribution of children in public and private schools run by different categories of teachers. He also urged prefects to consult their Departmental Council of Public Instruction; created by the Falloux Law to survey public instruction at the departmental level, this body was composed of relatively conservative notables, including several churchmen.[46] Ideally, the ratio of public schools with lay personnel to public schools with religious personnel would correspond to the preferences of fathers of families in the community. In questions of local option, Simon's concern with national reconciliation and liberty of conscience came into conflict with the respect for universal suffrage that was another of the bases of his republican convictions.

This approach involved the prefects in long and difficult negotiations. In the meanwhile, more sources of conflict arose over municipal option in such cities as Toulon, Besançon, and Valence. By August, Catholics at both the authoritarian *L'Univers* and the liberal *Le Français* were growing impatient and were beginning to pressure Simon, the sole remaining republican in the cabinet, to take a firmer line against the municipalities.[47] On 21 August, two monarchist deputies, Alfred Monnet and Baron Chaurand, raised a related question in the National Assembly, and Simon narrowly averted an unfavor-

45. JS, Paris, to Valentin, prefect of Rhône, July 1871, (copy), A.N. F[17] 9173; see also a reference to instructions of 18 July 1871 in a letter from Laporterie, prefect of Var, Draguignan, to JS, 23 August 1871, A.N. F[17] 9175.

46. JS, Paris, to Valentin, prefect of Rhône, July 1871; JS, Paris, to Valentin, prefect of Rhône, 17 August 1871, A.N. F[17] 9173. For a thoughtful analysis by a prefect of the problem posed by the jurisprudence of the empire, see Laporterie, prefect of Var, Draguignan, to JS, 23 August 1871, A.N. F[17] 9175.

47. *L'Univers*, 4 August 1871; "Les Écoles de Lyon," *Le Français*, 4 August 1871.

able vote by giving assurances that the law would be applied.[48] By this time, it was becoming apparent that the National Assembly would revise legislation in this area only after a long and difficult debate. Therefore, on 28 October, Simon issued an administrative circular that spelled out "a liberal, but exact, interpretation of the law as it still exists." This circular, resting on the jurisprudence of the late empire, sought to give "municipal councils full opportunity to give their opinion, while confiding to the departmental councils the task of protecting those educational interests which are at stake." Stressing the need for prefects to act in accordance with the "wish of the population," which was virtually equated with the wish of the fathers of families, the new jurisprudence took advantage of an article in the Falloux Law to give the departmental councils the task of ascertaining this desire.[49]

Simon presented this jurisprudence as a measure of decentralization (for it reinforced the role of local authorities in the prefect's decisionmaking process) that provided maximum safeguards for liberty of conscience. Ignoring many real issues involved in the conflicts at Lyons and Toulouse, he suggested that these conflicts stemmed from the confusion of powers that the centralizing policies of the empire had created.[50] Yet most contemporaries viewed this circular in terms of concrete political conflicts paramount in everyone's mind: How would this circular affect laic and Catholic interests? For Gambetta and all republicans sympathetic to the demands of popularly elected municipal councils, the circular was suspect. It gave too much weight to a departmental council dominated by religious interests and a conservative magistracy. Such councils were bound to be hostile to the laic mood of the French populace. Indeed, in subsequent months these departmental councils played an important role in imposing compromises on municipal councils who were determined to subsidize no congregationist primary school.[51] For the Thierist newspaper Le National, the initiative

48. Gontard, "Une Bataille scolaire au XIXe siècle," p. 280.
49. "Circulaire aux préfets sur la nomination des instituteurs," Bulletin administratif de l'Instruction Publique, 4 November 1871, pp. 298–302.
50. Ibid., p. 300.
51. "Questions d'instruction primaire," La République française, 19 March 1872; "Paris. 8 novembre," La République française, 8 November

granted to municipal councils, against the jurisprudence of the early empire, suggested to the contrary, that the aim of Simon's administration was to substitute lay teachers for congregationists.[52]

For Simon, the politics of the question were considerably more complex. France was living under a regime that was republican in all but name, and a loyal body of lay schoolteachers, protected from the pressures of monarchist municipal councils, could become an important source of support. On 27 May, Martial Delpit, Dupanloup, and others on the Right had revived the stipulations of the original Falloux Law in a legislative proposal that guaranteed the municipality's right to select both the category and the personnel of their teaching staffs.[53] Such a strategy was based on Catholic confidence in the Church's ability to influence municipal councils in the vast majority of French communes, whatever might happen in the large urban areas. To the excited inspector of the Academy of Bordeaux, Delpit's proposal aimed at "ruining the University. For [the Catholics] prefer to the University, anarchy, the unknown, communistic tendencies even, because they hope eventually to extend their control over all village and city councils."[54] Delpit's proposition terrified many lay schoolteachers, who heartily seconded Simon's efforts to raise them above partisan politics.[55] Speaking before the National Assembly in July, Simon had declared his opposition to the current legislation and the Delpit proposal that both delegated the appointment and advancement of schoolteachers to authorities outside the domain of the Ministry of Public Instruction.[56] Now, in

---

1871; Adolphe Michel, "Paris, 27 novembre," *Le Siècle*, 28 November 1871.

52. Eugène de Germiny, "De la nomination des instituteurs communaux," *Le Français*, 9 November 1871.

53. "Proposition de loi relative à la nomination des instituteurs communaux et à la surveillance des écoles primaires, présentée par MM. Delpit, l'Évêque d'Orléans, et plusieurs de leurs collègues," A.N. C 3129 #1199.

54. Belin de Launay, inspector of the Academy of Bordeaux, Périgueux, to JS, 13 June 1871, A.N. F[17] 10900.

55. "Note sur le Projet de loi de M. Delpit, 1871," F[17] 10900.

56. JS, National Assembly, 17 July 1871, *Annales de l'Assemblée nationale*, 4:118–20.

his circular, he gave the departmental council, where the University was well represented, a primary role in the resolution of questions of municipal option. At the same time, he resisted Catholic demands for a simple return to the status quo ante and pressed for inclusion of both kinds of schools within large public school systems. He evidently hoped that the supervision of a liberal government would help avert local conflicts that might arise if one category was public and the other private.[57] In public elementary education, laymen and members of religious orders might labor side by side under the tricolor of the liberal Republic.

From the point of view of Gambetta and of the republicans of both *La République française* and the more moderate *Le Siècle*, such collaboration was suspect; convinced that the Republic and the Church represented opposing principles and interests, they felt such compromises only played into the hands of the Right. This view was shared by the municipal councils of the cities of Lyons and Toulouse. Both refused to accept their departmental councils' compromise proposals; these proposals insisted on the incorporation of both lay and congregationist schools within the public system but gave lay education a much stronger position than it had occupied before 4 September 1870.[58] Municipalities found it difficult to accept such compromises, because of the principles involved and the added expense that they incurred. By refusing these compromises, they left themselves open for more reactionary forces to impose a return to the status quo ante at a later date.[59] In the short run, at least, it was not the departmental councils but rather the municipal councils in Lyons and Toulouse that were serving the cause of reaction. Moreover, evidence gathered from the most contentious cases handled by the departmental councils

57. This seemed to be a common opinion in University circles. See Vidal-LaBlache, "Délibérations du Conseil Départemental de l'Académie de Toulouse," 4 November 1871, A.N. F[17] 9174; Aubin, inspector of the Academy of Lyons, Lyons, to La Saussaye, rector of the Academy of Lyons, 9 March 1871, A.N. F[17] 9173.

58. On Toulouse, see Vidal-LaBlache, "Délibérations du Conseil Départemental de l'Académie de Toulouse," A.N. F[17] 9174; on Lyons, see Gontard, "Une Bataille scolaire au XIXe siècle," pp. 270, 284.

59. "Décision du Conseil d'État du 7 février, 1873," A.N. F[17] 9174; Gontard, "Une Bataille scolaire au XIXe siècle," pp. 284–89.

in a dozen departments suggests that Simon's policies responded to ambiguous and inchoate emotions widespread in liberal and republican circles. Many Frenchmen feared clerical domination without denying to the Church an influential place in their private and public lives.

The most impressive example of this ambivalence in popular psychology was the general acceptance of Article 23 of the Falloux Law, which required the inclusion of religious teaching in the curriculum of the primary schools. As interpreted by the regulations of 17 August 1851, this article ensured that in most public primary schools, education would be profoundly Catholic. Numerous provisions had a religious content, but three were particularly important: (1) the law required students to recite prayers drawn from the diocesan catechism at the beginning and end of both the morning and afternoon school sessions; (2) the curriculum necessarily included instruction in religious history, based on books approved by ecclesiastical authorities, and the recitation of the catechism; (3) the schoolteacher was obligated to take his students to the local Church on Sundays and religious holidays and to supervise their conduct while they were there.[60] Only the municipal councils of Paris (during the Commune), Lyons and Nantes actually voted to introduce a totally laic curriculum in their public schools. In Lyons, moreover, the Municipal Council, led by republicans like Hénon and Désiré Barodet, was unyielding on the question of lay personnel but was in agreement with the government's demands for obedience to the law in the realm of curriculum.[61] Undoubtedly, both guile and the fear of setting a precedent in local determination of curricula, which would redound to the benefit of Catholics, underlay the moderation of some; yet it seems probable that popular pressure was simply stronger for lay personnel than for laic programs.

At the same time, there were other indicators of a similar state of mind. Between 1871 and 1872, Jean Macé's *Ligue de l'enseignement* sponsored a series of petitions eventually signed by millions of French citizens, in favor of the reform of primary education. These petitions indicated that many more Frenchmen were willing to support the principles of obligation

60. Édouard Lecanuet, *Les Dernières années du Pontificat de Pie IX, 1870–1878*, pp. 345–46.
61. Gontard, "Une Bataille scolaire au XIXᵉ siècle," pp. 280–81.

and gratuity than the principle of a broadly defined laicity.[62] In Lyons, the efforts of the Municipal Council to introduce a laic curriculum in the public schools met the opposition of the famous *Société d'instruction primaire de Lyon* that, prior to 4 September, had directed most of Lyons' lay public schools. In the face of this resistance, the Municipal Council withdrew its financial support from the *Société*'s schools. According to University sources, important segments of the populace of Lyons, recognizing the quality of education given by the *Société*, were willing to pay to continue to send their children to the *Société*'s schools that had become private, rather than to send them to the public lay schools of the municipality.[63] In the same way, in Roanne (Loire), where the Municipal Council had founded a number of new lay schools and dismissed the congregationists, Eugène Rendu, the Catholic inspector general found only words of praise for the care with which the new teachers observed the religious requirements of the program.[64]

The case of Besançon, where a republican municipal council sought to strengthen lay education in its primary schools, is indicative of the kind of support that Simon found for his ideas in the French provinces.[65] Spread out over a hillside extending down to the Doubs River, the city of Besançon maintained three congregationist schools and two lay schools serving 951 and 384 boys respectively during the 1870 to 1871 academic year. In August 1871, however, the Municipal Council voted to convert the city's largest congregationist school, the Arsenal, located in the upper city, into a lay school and to abolish a small lay school located nearby. The response of the Catholic personnel to this action was a petition, containing three thousand signatures, demanding the Municipal Council to revoke its decision. The prefect, after a trip to Paris to consult with Simon, sought to persuade Louis Fernier, the sympathetic republican deputy mayor, to induce the council to reconsider. But the mayor replied that the council could not and

62. Louis Capéran, *Histoire contemporaine de la laïcité française*, 1:26.

63. JS, Paris, to Valentin, prefect of Rhône, July 1871; L. Aubin, "Notes sur les écoles de Lyon," A.N. F[17] 9173.

64. Eugène Rendu, Roanne, to JS, 14 July 1871, A.N. F[17] 9175.

65. The material for the following account is drawn from a dossier of letters and documents contained in A.N. F[17] 9197.

would not, and if the deliberation was annulled, it would resign en masse. When the council refused to change its deliberation from a decision—clearly illegal—to an opinion, the prefect
issued a decree dated 19 October 1871 annulling the initial
decision of the Municipal Council.

The affair did not end here. Although the Municipal Council
did not resign, it began to harass the congregationist schools
on a number of minor matters. It appealed the prefectural
decree of 19 October to the Council of State. And, taking advantage of a vacancy due to the death of the principal of a
congregationist school in the Battant district of the lower
city, it formally notified the prefect of its opinion that the
school should come under lay supervision. Following the direc-
tions in Simon's circular of 28 October, the prefect conferred
with the Departmental Council, which advised rejection of the
Municipal Council's request. The Battant school, it declared,
was popular in the city, and its proximity to the lay public
school, the Grenier, guaranteed the rights of fathers of families. The Departmental Council also, however, reopened the
Arsenal issue; it formally noted that although an equitable balance existed in the lower city, in the upper city there were two
congregationist schools of considerable size and a small lay
school. Creation of a new lay school or the redistribution of
facilities in the upper city would create a better balance. The
prefect, however, followed only that part of the deliberation
that enabled him to name a congregationist teacher to the vacancy at the Battant school.

In January 1872, the affair again came to the attention of Simon and his aides. Influenced by a letter from the rector of the
Academy of Besançon and by a conversation with the republican representative from Doubs, Albert Grévy, they decided
to try to work out a compromise along the lines suggested by
the Departmental Council. Grévy and other deputies had convinced them that equity in the number of public schools in each
category was the real desire of public opinion:

> If [the administration] rejects the demand of the Municipal
> Council, it will make it seem as if the alleged illegality of the
> first deliberation was only a pretext, and that it really wants
> to assure the absolute and permanent predominance of
> congregationist teaching in Besançon. That would lead to

conflict between central and local powers and to trouble in the city.[66]

Simon wrote the prefect and asked him to work out an agreement with the Municipal Council that would establish an equilibrium between the different categories of public school in Besançon. Efforts at a settlement broke down, however, in face of the prefect's inflexibility and the Municipal Council's determination to transform the Arsenal into an enormous model school. In late April, Simon sent Inspectors General Faye and Jacquinet to Besançon to assist in reaching an agreement. After paying their respects to Cardinal Mathieu, archbishop of Besançon, the two emissaries were able to reconcile the desires of the conflicting parties: the Municipal Council would have its school in the upper city at the Arsenal and would finance an addition to the nearby congregationist school, St. Jean. The Municipal Council also formally committed itself to an evenhanded policy toward the two kinds of public school. The moderation of both parties made the settlement possible. The Municipal Council wanted to ensure the availability of lay education to the city's citizens without imposing it upon all; Cardinal Mathieu, eager not to jeopardize his chances of obtaining funds to enlarge the local seminary, used his influence to win Catholic acceptance of the settlement. It was with republicans like those of the Municipal Council and with Catholics like the moderate Cardinal Mathieu that Simon hoped to build a Republic.[67]

Although Catholic liberals were often hard pressed to find fault with Simon's policies as minister of worship or with his treatment of the delicate question of municipal option, they rejected Simon's efforts to forge a new Liberal Union. After the war, Catholic liberals had regrouped around Albert de Broglie and the newspaper *Le Français*.[68] The Government of National Defense and the Commune had only confirmed their distrust of the masses. They called on all truly liberal forces to rally to the defense of "moral order." Conservative and moderate republicans, they believed, should accept their leadership in the

66. Albert Grévy, "Note de M. Grévy sur l'affaire de Besançon," A.N. F[17] 9197.
67. Césaire Mathieu, archbishop of Besançon, Besançon, to JS, 11 July 1872, 28 October 1872, 87 AP 10 I (1).
68. "Les Subventions scolaires," *Le Français*, 19 October 1871; Eugène de Germiny, *Le Français*, 9 November 1871.

struggle to maintain such social bulwarks as the Church against the attacks of Gambetta and the Radicals. Attached to an image of a society that was Catholic in culture but was tolerant of freethinkers, *Le Français* was eager to rally philosophic spiritualists to its cause.[69] Simon might have been an ideal ally on many issues of mutual concern, but his activities in the last years of the empire and in the Government of National Defense had identified him in their minds with the threatening new wave of popular democracy. Even his confrontation with Gambetta in early February 1871 could not induce them to revise their opinion.[70] Convinced of his reprehensible complacency toward the most antisocial forces, they took advantage of news revealing Simon's fortuitous link with the International Workingmen's Association to label him the "very pope of socialism."[71] Frustrated by Simon's opposition to the efforts of the Right to confide control over primary education to local notables, these social conservatives convinced themselves that Mottu had been right when he said that "basically, Jules Simon is with us."[72]

In the Right Center, this distrust of Simon's intentions heightened anxiety about the possible ramifications of Simon's impending law on primary education. At the time of the formation of Thiers's cabinet, Catholics had fearfully questioned the wisdom of giving power to a man closely identified with the cause of obligatory and free primary education for boys and girls between the ages of seven and thirteen.[73] Even the Pope had called the matter to Thiers's attention.[74] Many Catholics saw such a law as an opening wedge, which would result in the banishment of the Church from public education and the laicization of the curriculum. The actions of the *Ligue de l'en-*

69. See its favorable treatment of Henri Martin in "Les Prières publiques et le parti républicain," *Le Français*, 28 May 1871.

70. *Le Français*, 11 February 1871.

71. *Le Français*, 31 October 1871; Abbé Louise-Antoine Lesmayoux, "L'Enseignement primaire," *Le Correspondant*, 86, no. 1 (10 January 1872): 104.

72. *Le Français*, 11 August 1871; Abbé Lesmayoux, "L'Enseignement primaire," *Le Correspondant*, 86, no. 1 (10 January 1872): 115; "Jules Simon," *Le Correspondant*, 86, no. 3 (10 February 1872): 393–412, *passim*.

73. Meaux, *Souvenirs politiques*, p. 79, note 1.

74. Pius IX, Rome, to Thiers, 2 July 1871, Thiers, *Le Courrier de Monsieur Thiers*, p. 460.

seignement, which, impatient with Simon, had inaugurated a campaign of petitions favoring obligatory, free, and lay education during the fall of 1871, could only awaken further apprehensions in such Catholics. While some newspapers like *Le Temps* petitioned for obligation, others like *Le Siècle* and *La République française* were demanding obligation, gratuity, and laicity.[75] Eager to allay Catholic fears, Thiers assured Dupanloup in November that all the ideas that the law contained were approved by the Catholic liberal, Augustin Cochin.[76]

In the formulation of his new law on primary instruction, finally presented to the National Assembly on 15 December 1871, political and financial circumstances forced Simon to give up his hope of providing for gratuity as well as obligation. Yet in his mind, the law was eminently republican; as early as 1847, he had written that "the real way to emancipate men is to enlighten them. A new school does more for liberty than a new law."[77] Although Gambetta's *La République française* found the law totally inadequate, the moderate republican newspaper *Le Siècle* applauded: "This is the only important law which the present government has proposed so far."[78] The bill was fashioned, however, to soothe Catholic apprehensions.

In addition to the absence of gratuity, deemed threatening to Catholic private schools, the bill did not require obligatory attendance in a school but only obligatory instruction. It defined a procedure by which parents might teach their own children; at the age of thirteen, the child would demonstrate before State officials that he had acquired a rudimentary knowledge. In the matter of penalties for fathers who failed to comply, the new proposal, still judged too severe by a man like Guizot, was nonetheless more lenient than the law Simon had proposed in 1870.[79] In his introductory remarks before the Assembly,

75. Gontard, *Les Écoles primaires,* p. 216.
76. Thiers, Versailles, to Dupanloup, bishop of Orleans, 9 November 1871, Thiers, *Le Courrier de Monsieur Thiers,* pp. 460–61; in a letter of 30 October to the *Impartial du Loiret,* Dupanloup attacked the principles of gratuity and obligation in primary education (*Le Français,* 2–3 November 1871).
77. JS, "La Réforme électorale," *LP* 1 (15 December 1847): 104.
78. *Le Siècle,* 18 December 1871; *La République française,* 27 December 1871.
79. "Projet de loi sur l'instruction gratuite et obligatoire, et sur l'enseignement technique" (24 February 1870), #232 A.N. C 1144.

Simon presented the bill as a measure of national regeneration. According to the statistics of 1866, one-eighth of French children were illiterate; more widespread instruction would protect France against aggression without and subversion within. Resisting republican demands that the program include classes in ethics, Simon reminded the Right that the present program, including the religious instruction, reflected his belief that "moral training is more important than instruction, and France needs good citizens as much and more than scholarly ones." Education of girls would strengthen the family. Frenchmen would learn a "wise liberty."[80]

Simon's proposal served the needs of republican propaganda, but it had little chance of success before the conservative Assembly.[81] Even before its presentation, *Le Français* called for Simon's resignation and suggested that almost any sanction in support of obligation violated the sacred rights of fathers of families.[82] In early January, the Assembly formed a commission dominated by the opponents of obligation to consider all aspects of Simon's law, including articles that gave a firmer legislative base to Simon's jurisprudence on municipal options, required the *brevet de capacité* for all public schoolteachers within a certain fixed time, and confided the nomination of primary schoolteachers to agents of the Ministry of Public Instruction. In the following months, the commission, chaired by Dupanloup, developed counterproposals strengthening local authorities' power over the choice of schoolteachers and omitting obligation. But the government was reluctant to take up a question that would mean a defeat for Simon, and it fell before the matter ever came up for debate.[83] In this case, as in so many others, fear of the intentions of the Left imposed severe limitations on Catholic liberalism. As Simon later observed,

> Catholics, even when they are liberal, cannot abandon the habit of considering their clergy in the light of a public authority intended to maintain a good understanding with the

80. "Projet de loi sur l'instruction primaire," *Annales de l'Assemblée nationale (Annexes)* 6 (1872): 186–94.

81. JS, *The Government of M. Thiers*, 2:100.

82. "Les Conseils généraux et l'enseignement primaire," *Le Français*, 1 December 1871; *Le Français*, 6 December 1871.

83. Gontard, *Les Écoles primaires*, pp. 217–25.

secular power, as its ally and its neighbor, but in no sense to be under its control. Their liberalism consists in not demanding the subordination of the State. The bill gave great prominence to State influence in primary schools, and that was quite sufficient to render it suspect.[84]

By the beginning of 1872, Simon's failure to win the confidence of Catholic liberals was readily apparent. In February, Le Correspondant published an unsigned and intemperate article attacking the minister for his democratic and anti-Catholic sympathies.[85] The events of the following months led Thiers to conclude that fusion of monarchist parties would not take place. When he began to urge the Assembly to build a conservative Republic, the distance between the Right and Thiers's more liberal ministers widened some more. Simon's subsequent reforming efforts would necessarily be restricted to the limited administrative channels that were available to him. From the days of the early empire, Simon had shown an interest in curriculum reform at the secondary level. In Le Devoir, he criticized the French habit of envisaging the University more as a manufacturer of doctors, lawyers, and engineers than as an educator of men of virtue and probity. The University itself reflected this attitude, for French youth received there "a very mechanical education, which at the most, develops the memory. . . . Children so trained repeat or copy, but do not think."[86] In the early 1850s, the regime's proscription of philosophy gave a partisan flavor to Simon's charges that the University did little to develop the powers of will and of critical thought in its students. When Simon came to power, however, he proved his sincerity on this point; even though philosophy had long since been restored to the curriculum, he assembled a group of scholars well versed in pedagogy to aid him in his efforts to reorient teaching in the University. Although he was powerless to change educational requirements without the approval of a High Council of Public Instruction that existed only in pending legislation, he did have considerable latitude in the realm of methods.

84. JS, The Government of M. Thiers, 2:105.
85. "Jules Simon," Le Correspondant, 86, no. 3 (10 February 1872): 393–412.
86. JS, Le Devoir, pp. 410–11.

On 27 September 1872, after consultation with Thiers, Simon issued a "Circulaire aux MM. les proviseurs sur l'enseignement secondaire" that called for greater emphasis on history, geography, and on modern languages, both French and foreign.[87] In the teaching of modern languages, pedagogical emphasis would shift from rote learning of grammatical rules to an understanding of their underlying principles. In addition, he gave a more general directive urging teachers to de-emphasize written exercises, which often became mechanical, in favor of more vigorous dialectic with their students. To help make room for his additions to a crowded school day, Simon proposed the abolition of the famous Latin verses, which absorbed two hundred hours a year, and a reduction of the time spent on translation from French to Latin: students should learn to read Latin, but they did not need to know how to write Latin verse or prose.[88]

The circular received widespread applause in most republican circles. If La République française suggested that structural changes in the University should have first priority, Le Siècle heralded measures that would extricate the University from the "rut of jesuitical routine."[89] Carnot sent his congratulations.[90] On the Right, however, Dupanloup, traditionally a vigorous defender of classical studies within the Church, denounced the circular as "the definitive overthrow of French education." Ignoring Simon's declaration that classical studies were "the basis of all liberal instruction," the impulsive Dupanloup insisted that the circular was illegal, for such wide-ranging reforms required the approval of the High Council of Public Instruction.[91] Dupanloup found support for his opposition not only at Le Français but also in academic circles. In L'Instruction Publique, the successor to the Revue de l'Instruction Publique, the Catholic liberal Alfred Blot expressed a distrust that

87. Étienne Vacherot, Paris, to JS, 13 September 1872, 87 AP 7.
88. "Circulaire aux MM. les proviseurs sur l'enseignement secondaire," reprinted in JS, La Réforme de l'enseignement secondaire, pp. 399–430.
89. La République française, 27 October 1872; Charles Bigot, Le Siècle, 3 October 1872.
90. Hippolyte Carnot to JS, 8 October 1872, 87 AP 2.
91. "Lettre de Mgr. l'Évêque d'Orléans" (6 October 1872), Le Français, 9 October 1872; JS, "Circulaire aux MM. les proviseurs," La Réforme de l'enseignement secondaire, p. 412.

appealed both to the more conservative academic rank and file committed to age-old patterns of classical education and hostile to ministerial interference in their proper domain, and to those who found Simon too sensitive to democratic influences. At *Le Journal des débats*, where Paul Leroy-Beaulieu applauded Simon's measures, the academician Alfred Cuvillier-Fleury prophesied "the ruin of the humanities . . . the victory of a political sect which seeks to bring society down to the level of those inferior groups who did not care to raise themselves."[92] After a second attack by Dupanloup in late December, Nathaniel Johnston, a member of the Right Center, interpellated Simon in the Assembly and secured Simon's promise to refer his circular to the High Council of Public Instruction as soon as possible. Cast into the realm of the provisional, the reforms fell victim to the overwhelming inertia of the academic system.

Both Simon and Thiers fell from power in late May as pressure from the Right mounted. Although Simon was able to adjust to Thiers's political virtuosity, the philosopher in him always yearned for a different style of government.[93] He had hoped that large segments of the majority that Thiers held together by his personal power might soon coalesce in a coherent centrist majority committed to the twin ideals of political and intellectual freedom. He appealed to those who rejected the authoritarianism of both the extreme Right and Left, to Catholics who only asked that modern liberties offer equal protection to believers and unbelievers, to republicans whose liberalism often rested on both sympathy for sincere religious belief and distaste for clerical encroachment in the secular realm. He appealed to the many for whom all issues had not yet been joined —to those who were republicans but not uncompromising laics, to those who were Catholics but not doctrinaire monarchists. Since the terrain of reconciliation was to be the Republic, his primary problem was to win the confidence of Catholics. For Catholic leaders, however, the Government of National Defense was to blame for unleashing the irreligious and antibourgeois forces that eventually made the Commune. They believed that a constitutional monarchy would temper popular passions more effectively than the Republic. In an atmosphere dominated by such misgivings, it was difficult for such Catho-

92. Paul Gerbod, *La Condition universitaire*, pp. 528–32.
93. JS, *Thiers, Guizot, Rémusat*, p. 158.

lics to take Simon at face value. Just as his natural religion appeared more as a weapon against the Church than as an expression of genuine religious sentiment, so his efforts in educational and religious reform struck many as dangerous threats to a crucial social barrier. Simon's relation with Thiers, who dominated the cabinet, further hindered his efforts to establish a clear image; for it was easy to credit Simon's moderation to Thiers while viewing his more republican actions as pale shadows of his real intentions.

In this difficult situation, Simon worked with a skill that prompted the admiring Thiers to salute him as "the capable man, par excellence."[94] Although he achieved some success in his effort to resist clerical pressures, his more long-range goals required time and tranquility—rare elements in nineteenth-century French political life.

94. Thiers, Paris, to JS, 18 May 1873, Séché, *Jules Simon*, pp. 198–99.

CHAPTER IX

The Campaign for the Conservative Republic, 1873–1886

Thiers's dictum that "*La République sera conservatrice ou elle ne sera pas*" perfectly suited Simon's political tastes. After the fall of the "Government of Monsieur Thiers," he turned immediately to the task of developing the kind of "just, conciliatory, and *aimable*" republicanism that, he hoped, would reassure the old *classes dirigeantes*, the notables who had dominated French politics throughout the century.[1] Recent history, he argued in his *Souvenirs du quatre septembre* (1874), an anti-Bonapartist apology for the Government of National Defense, had demonstrated both the patriotism and scrupulous liberalism of most republicans; this government had, under difficult conditions, struggled mightily against the same revolutionary and socialist forces that were later to make the Commune.[2] The key element in Simon's appeal to hesitating notables was, as always, the promise that republicans would know how to adopt, even against Radical pressures, a tolerant and respectful attitude toward the Church. With these aims in mind, Simon favored the creation of a "second chamber," in which the notables would gain a special voice for their interests; and after the adoption of the Constitution of 1875, he took the lead in defending the prerogatives of the Senate against possible encroachment by the Chamber of Deputies.

This Conservative Republican or moderate strategy did not of course preclude collaboration with Gambetta in defense of the republican cause against the various forms of clerical mon-

1. JS, speech delivered at Cette (Hérault), 6 October 1875, *Le Temps*, 10 October 1875.
2. JS, *Souvenirs du quatre septembre. Le Gouvernement de la défense nationale.* This work appeared in serial form between 1 April 1874 and 13 July 1874 in the new Conservative Republican newspaper, *Le Dix-neuvième siècle.*

archism. But on a day-to-day level, Simon and other moderates worked to contain Gambetta's influence over the republican movement. The aim was to maneuver this tribune into a position where he would be obliged to jettison his more Radical followers. This anti-Gambettist animus rested not merely on personal rivalry, as has often been supposed, but on differing conceptions of the men and measures most appropriate for the emerging French Republic. Simon's efforts to build up the appeal of the Republic for men who had exercised political authority under previous regimes was diametrically opposed to the rhetoric and much of the practice of Gambetta and his political associates at *La République française*. In his famous Grenoble speech of 26 September 1872, Gambetta had announced that the coming of the Republic meant the accession to power of men drawn from new, previously passive social strata, the *nouvelles couches sociales* and, with several references to the sad experiences of 1848, advised republicans to elect only proven republicans to represent them. Republicans should not be taken in by newly republicanized members of the old *classes dirigeantes*, men who were most likely "pseudo-republicans, men with the word Republic on their lips, but the monarchy in the bottom of their hearts." They should vote not for the "conservative Republic" or the "constitutional Republic," but for the "democratic Republic."[3] The Church and the Senate were, in Gambettist eyes, essentially monarchist institutions, to be combated rather than courted by all republicans worthy of the name.

Simon's politics were thus highly suspect to Gambetta and *La République française*, even though they were often obliged to work closely with him. And they made no secret of this distrust. "Those who have known him for a long time," one of their most vehement attacks began,

> know that for this philosopher, this professor of ethics, this republican, this democrat, everything has been an instrument to help him seek his fortune, a mask put on or taken off according to the need, a theatrical disguise to don or put aside according to his interest. His philosophy, which no professional philosopher can mention with a straight face, was both a front and a merchandise. His ethics, a sentimentalized

3. Léon Gambetta, *Discours et plaidoyers politiques*, 3:100–119.

Stoicism, were a vehicle for his ambitious vanity. . . . Free thought and pious effusiveness, socialism and classical economics, the International and the Institute, politics and literature, have all served as stepping-stones for his march to fortune.[4]

In the years between the fall of Thiers's cabinet in 1873, and the crisis of 16 May 1877, Simon and his moderate allies were able to muster the political strength to oblige Gambetta to impose one compromise after another on his more militant followers. Sheer parliamentary arithmetic, not Thiers's paternalistic advice, required Gambetta to take moderate demands seriously. Both in the National Assembly and in the chamber of 1876, the moderates of the Left Center and Republican Left greatly outnumbered Gambetta's followers in the Republican Union and the Extreme Left.[5] In the press, moderate republicanism was well represented by *Le Temps, Le Dix-neuvième siècle,* and by a transformed *Le Siècle,* now under Simon's political direction.[6] Throughout these years, Gambetta cleverly managed to restrain his followers without sacrificing his general popularity. But his hold on the chamber became virtually uncontestable only after the upsurge of clerical activity in 1877 and the ensuing crisis of *Seize Mai.*

The elections of October 1877 strengthened Gambetta's Republican Union at the expense of the moderates and ended the close collaboration of Simon and Ferry. In 1879, with the Senate in republican hands at last, Ferry would inaugurate a program of broad educational reform that, contrary to Simon's more centrist preferences, rested squarely on an alliance of the Republican Left and the Republican Union. Despite Ferry's insistence, rooted in his own Comtian outlook, on the distinction between clericalism and Catholicism, Simon bitterly fought this educational legislation. Unable to appreciate the

4. "Paris, 8 novembre," *La République française,* 8 November 1871; see also "Paris, 27 décembre," *La République française,* 27 December 1871; *La République française,* 21 May 1873.

5. Alain Bomier-Landowski, "Les Groupes parlementaires de l'Assemblée nationale et de la Chambre des Députés de 1871 à 1940," *Sociologie électorale,* ed. François Goguel, Georges Dupeux, p. 76; André Daniel, *L'Année politique, 1876,* pp. 46–51.

6. Simon was political director of *Le Siècle* from 1 August 1874 until early January 1877, Jules Simon Dossier, A.P.P. B A/1270.

moderate spirit that informed this program, he viewed Ferry as a dupe who, in his efforts both to temper and to utilize Voltairean anticlericalism, had actually become the tool of Gambetta and his followers. This opposition to the laic laws effectively precluded any possibility of Simon's inclusion in any future republican cabinet. This chapter attempts to view republican politics in the period between 1873 and 1886 through Simon's eyes, and to describe the obstacles he faced in his unsuccessful efforts to assemble a Conservative Republican majority.

I

Simon's task would have been greatly facilitated if Catholics had not seemed so deeply involved in the monarchist cause. The Government of 25 May 1873, under the direction of Albert de Broglie, intensified republican anxieties, for it linked Catholic "moral order," social defense, and monarchism. Especially after the threatening pronouncements of Broglie's extreme allies, some republicans were ready to believe that a Catholic restoration was imminent. At *La République française*, Challemel-Lacour and other Gambettists prepared to repell what appeared to be a mounting clerical onslaught. Even though *La République française* was not a Voltairean newspaper, Gambettists generally believed that the necessities of republican defense more than abstract questions of liberal principle, should govern their policy toward the Church. Thus, when Comte Jaubert's proposed law on the liberty of higher education came up for debate in late 1874, Gambetta and his followers, unlike Simon, Ferry, and the Republican Left, opposed the consideration of a law based on the principle that any Frenchman might establish an institution of higher learning.

Challemel-Lacour expressed the thinking of some Gambettists when he denied that liberty of education was a bona fide right and added that only Catholics were in a position to profit from a law that would enable them to propagate, to the detriment of the republican cause, a Catholic spirit that was none other than the spirit of the *Syllabus*. Other Gambettists, like Paul Bert, recognized liberty of education as a natural right but, apprehensive of the political use to which the Church would turn such a liberty, announced their intention to oppose any such measure unless it was accompanied by a full-scale program to reorganize and develop the State system of higher education.[7] Even the formal establishment of the Republic in January 1875 was scant reassurance for Gambetta and his followers. As the law on liberty of higher education, specially tailored to favor Catholic initiatives at the expense of those of freethinking laymen, moved toward passage, Gambettists prepared to launch a campaign "against the clericals, to unmask their doctrines, and to show the country, using Belgium as an example, the decadence toward which liberty of education is leading France." When the bill passed on 12 July, *La République française* consoled its readers by reminding them that the future belonged to the "sons of Voltaire and of the French Revolution" and by calling for the dissolution of the Assembly.[8]

The first great manifestation in this effort to alert the public consciousness to the threat of clericalism was the induction, on 8 July 1875, of Littré and Ferry into the Masonic Lodge, Clémente-Amitié of the Grand Orient of France. In the eyes of the presiding officer, Charles Cousin, the admission of Littré, whom Dupanloup had made the symbol of free thought, was reminiscent of the entrance of Voltaire into the Freemasonry on the eve of the French Revolution. Gambetta, who gave the major address before two thousand attendants, called on freethinkers everywhere to imitate Littré and to join "the great fight of science against obscurantism, of liberty against fanaticism." Littré for his part, adroitly sidestepped the comparisons drawn between himself and Voltaire, and delivered a scholarly lecture on the positivist conception of agnosticism.[9] Overshadowed by these republican luminaries, Ferry never got the chance to deliver his carefully prepared profes-

---

7. Paul Challemel-Lacour, Paul Bert, National Assembly, 3, 4, 5 December 1874, *Annales de l'Assemblée nationale* 35 (1874): 16–26, 43–49, 67–68.

8. Léon Gambetta, Paris, to Arthur Ranc, 20 August 1875, Léon Gambetta, *Lettres de Gambetta, 1868–1882*, no. 248; J. P. T. Bury, *Gambetta and the Making of the Third Republic*, pp. 249–50.

9. Bury, *Gambetta and the Making of the Third Republic*, p. 249; A. Caubet, "Réception d'Émile Littré dans la Franc-Maçonnerie," *La Phillosophie positive* 15 (September–October 1875): 161–69; see also Émile Littré, "Variétés. Loge la Clémente-Amitié," *La Philosophie positive* 23 (September–October 1879): 310.

sion of faith, "Des devoirs de l'homme envers ses semblables." In this short address, Ferry outlined his positivist conception of a new ethics that substituted altruism or love of humanity for that love of God on which religious and philosophic spiritualists constructed their "servile and inadequate" ethics. Alluding to the controversy over the reference to the Grand Architect of the Universe in the Constitution of the Grand Orient, Ferry insisted that Masonry, with its emphasis on tolerance and charity, was unconsciously positivist, a carrier of the new ethical spirit summed up in the phrase "independent morality." At the same time, Ferry sought to reassure his friend and ally Simon, who, perhaps for political reasons, had chosen not to attend such a militantly anticlerical ceremony. Citing Comte, who had insisted that man's only right is to do his duty, Ferry suggested that such was also the thought of "one of the great ethics professors of our time, who is not a positivist, but who has arrived at identical conclusions by other means." And without citing Simon by name, he quoted from *Le Devoir*, "the task of our forefathers was to establish our rights; our task must be to teach and spread the idea of duty." [10]

This accentuated anticlericalism troubled Simon and other republicans like Juliette Adam, who feared that the republican policy toward the Church would become "anti-liberal, untowardly . . . and concocted in such a way as to make the Republic detested." [11] Placed on the defensive in the councils of

10. Jules Ferry, "Des devoirs de l'homme envers ses semblables," published in Louis Legrand, *L'Influence du positivisme dans l'oeuvre scolaire de Jules Ferry; les origines de la laïcité,* pp. 238–43; Louis Capéran, *Histoire contemporaine de la laïcité française,* 1:8; JS, *Le Devoir,* p. 384.

Simon belonged to the Lodge *Réveil maçonnique* (Boulogne-sur-Seine) of the Scottish Rite, which he joined on 3 July 1870. From 20 March 1874 until his resignation from the Masonry in early 1881, Simon served on the Supreme Council of the Scottish Rite. The Scottish Rite, the conservative wing of French Masonry, did not imitate the Grand Orient of France which, in 1877, removed the references to the Grand Architect of the Universe and to the immortality of the soul from its statutes. See Édouard Lecanuet, *Les Dernières années du Pontificat de Pie IX, 1870–1878,* p. 270, note 2; Jules Simon Dossier, A.P.P., B A/1270; Mildred J. Headings, *French Freemasonry under the Third Republic,* pp. 44–45.

11. Juliette Adam, *Nos amitiés politiques avant l'abandon de la revanche,* p. 262; *Le Temps,* 9 September 1874.

the Left, Simon took a tenured position in the newly constituted Senate on 16 December 1875. For the wily parliamentarian, just past sixty and eager to escape the burdens of electoral
politics, the Senate promised to be a most fitting base for his
future efforts to exert a moderating influence on the anticlerical
exuberances of universal suffrage. On the same day, he entered
the *Académie française*, where, appropriately, he succeeded the
distinguished Liberal Charles de Rémusat. Indeed, in the
Paris elections of April 1873, Rémusat had championed the
cause of the Conservative Republic against Désiré Barodet,
the petit bourgeois "priest eater," who, as mayor of Lyons, had
become the hero of Radical republicans.

In the elections of 1876, a republican electorate implicitly
ratified the narrowly passed constitutional laws of 1875.
Alarmed by the republican victory in the chamber but confident of the support of the president of the Republic, Maréchal
MacMahon, and of the anti-republican Senate, the Right, led
by Broglie, adopted a strategy calculated to provoke the republicans into discrediting themselves in the eyes of the country. After the short-lived cabinet of the veteran, Catholic, Left
Center politician Jules Dufaure, Broglie, intent on exposing
the "latent radicalism" of republicans, persuaded the impatient
Maréchal to call Simon to power.[12]

This is not the place to present a full political history of
Simon's cabinet of 13 December which ended in the constitutional crisis of the "16th of May." In otherwise detailed accounts, most historians have, however, neglected to explore
Simon's political calculations and expectations both at the
time he took power and during the course of his ministry. Taking the cabinet's tragic climax as their point of focus, most
have accepted the clichéd view of Simon as an overly clever and
ambitious republican moderate who, partly because of a personal dislike for Gambetta, had accepted the premiership
under obviously impossible conditions.[13] Simon himself, how-

12. Charles Alan Grubb, "The Politics of Pessimism: A Political
Biography of Duc Albert de Broglie during the Early Third Republic,
1871–1885," (Ph.D. diss.), pp. 555–57, 565–67.
13. Gabriel Hanotaux, *Histoire de la France contemporaine (1871–
1900)*, 3:633–724; Fresnette Pisani-Ferry, *Le Coup d'état manqué du
16 mai 1877*, pp. 136–67; Daniel Halévy, *La République des ducs*, pp.
195–329. See also Louis Capéran, *Histoire contemporaine de la laïcité*

ever, saw things differently; for him, the oscillations of centrist politics were not improvised expedients designed merely to save the cabinet, but rather measures consistent with a broader Conservative Republican strategy.

Although the political situation in early December 1876 was hardly ideal, Simon thought that it offered real possibilities for a man of his temperament and opinions. Like other republican moderates, he envisaged the next two years as a period during which republicans might demonstrate their ability to handle day-to-day problems of government and administration. In any case, republicans would not be able to launch their program of legislative reform until 1879, when, after the senatorial elections, they would presumably control the Senate. The new government would also have to prove, once and for all, to men who thought like Broglie, that it was capable of containing radicalism, and Simon felt himself to be particularly well suited to hold republican anticlericalism under tight rein. He anticipated that his indisputable republican credentials and his widespread reputation would give him more leverage than Dufaure over the republican majority. He would base his government on Marcère's Left Center and Ferry's Republican Left, which after the elections of 1876 almost constituted a majority in the chamber.[14] In close contact with Ferry, Simon hoped, through the exercise of power, to demonstrate the political viability of his sort of liberalism and to convince those who might be attracted to Gambetta that the future lay with a more moderate policy. For the practical Ferry, such hopes were not unfounded in December 1876. By judicious use of his patronage powers as minister of the interior, especially in the realm of prefectures and sous-prefectures, Simon could, he confidently predicted, reduce Gambetta's following from about one hundred to fifty.[15] As a final consideration, Simon knew that

française, 1:48–79; Maurice Reclus, Le Seize mai, pp. 18–46; Alexandre Zévaès, Au temps du seize mai, pp. 102–15.

For Léon Séché's accounts, which focus, for the most part, on the crisis itself, see Jules Simon; sa vie et son oeuvre, pp. 203–29, and Jules Simon. Souvenirs personnels, pp. 87–106.

Simon's fullest account is in Le Soir de ma journée, pp. 227–49.

14. Guy Chapman, The Third Republic of France. The First Phase, 1871–1894, pp. 162–63.

15. Jules Ferry, Versailles, to JS, 30 December 1876, Paul Raphaël, "Trois lettres inédites de Jules Ferry," Revue historique.

should he fail in his efforts, he would, as premier, be well situated to ensure that the onus for the fall of his government fell on the Right.

To succeed in this situation, Simon would have had to acquire the kind of personal ascendancy, both in the chambers and in the country, which Thiers had turned to such advantage between 1871 and 1873. Such was not to be the case. Gambetta and his followers viewed the aged Thiers as a necessary and temporary evil but not as a rival. By taking power under present conditions, the Gambettists believed, Simon expressed his willingness to allow Broglie and the Maréchal to use him as a republican weapon against Gambetta and the real republican movement. Indeed, Simon's ministry began with a dramatic victory over Gambetta and the Republican Union on the issue of the fiscal rights of the Senate. And in January 1877, when Simon supported the efforts of the moderate groups to remove Gambetta from his powerful position as president of the budget commission of the chamber, the Gambettists did not hesitate to ally with Bonapartists in order to save Gambetta and to give the Republican Union a position in the commission that greatly exceeded the group's power in the chamber.[16] Although Simon received solid support from Ferry, who published a remarkable series of "Lettres parlementaires" in *La Gironde,* his cautious and conscientious liberalism, which struck many as no more than a parliamentary balancing act, never generated the kind of republican enthusiasm that might have permitted the formation of a strong ministerial party. Caught between the conservative Senate and the republican chamber, Simon exhausted himself in efforts to convince his republican colleagues that he was doing all in his power to further their cause.[17] Indeed, as time passed, pressure mounted on the leadership of the Republican Left to join with Gambetta in a forceful manifestation of republican principle.

The heightening of religious tensions, provoked by events beyond Simon's control, brought the cabinet to crisis. The origin of this controversy was not in France, but in Italy, where, on 12 March, Pope Pius IX called on the faithful to pressure their governments to support him against the anticlerical Italian

16. Hanotaux, *France contemporaine (1871–1900),* 3:659–61, 668–69.
17. Ibid., p. 684; Paul Cambon, Besançon, to Jules Cambon, 22 April 1877, Paul Cambon, *Correspondance, 1870–1924,* 1:80.

government. In France a portion of the clergy, led by the intemperate bishop of Nevers, inaugurated a petition campaign in support of the Pope. The government, while making no effort to exploit the petitions for anticlerical purposes, quietly but firmly insisted that the campaign stay within the strict bounds of legality. Gambetta, who sensed that republicans shared his desire for a sharper, more dramatic rebuff to "clerical intrigues," induced the three groups of the Left to interpellate Simon on the issue. On 3 May, in the chamber, Simon defended his policy as both firm and liberal, but he could not satisfy even his moderate allies. On the following day, Gambetta, in one of the most important speeches of his career, described the dangers that the Church presented for the Republic and concluded with the battle cry "Le cléricalisme, voilà l'ennemi!" In the course of subsequent debate, Simon vehemently declared both his own determination to combat the clerical threat and his faith in the Maréchal's loyalty to the constitution by dramatically tearing up a copy of Bishop Dupanloup's La Défense sociale et religieuse that had impertinently reminded Simon that he exercised power only as the servant of the Maréchal. After a futile attempt to induce the triumphant Gambetta to include the word confidence in the ordre du jour, a humiliated Simon was obliged to swallow a motion that summoned the government to "repress" all "clerical manifestations." Simon's government, now doomed to appear as a front for Gambetta to the Right, and as a front for MacMahon to the Left, was henceforth living on borrowed time.[18] On 16 May 1877, the Maréchal found a pretext to dismiss him and initiated a crisis for which the Right never succeeded in disavowing responsibility.

In the electoral campaign that succeeded the "16th of May," a united Left fought the Right in the name of parliamentary principle; despite its legality, MacMahon's dismissal of a premier supported by the majority of the chamber seemed to expand the role of presidential prerogatives in the Constitution of 1875. Most republicans viewed the Maréchal's coup de tête as part of a plot engineered by Legitimist, Orleanist, and Bonapartist forces who were linked only by a common clericalism. Since he was not a member of the Chamber of Deputies, Simon

18. Hanotaux, France contemporaine (1871–1900), 3:697–709.

was not well situated to play a major role in the bitter electoral battle against the administrative pressures of the Broglie-Fourtou "ministry of combat." While Simon occupied himself with an ultimately unsuccessful effort to establish *L'Écho universel*, his former ministerial newspaper, as a major Conservative Republican force, Gambetta directed the republican electoral campaign.[19]

Although republicans were victorious in the elections of October 1877, the *Seize mai* crisis dealt a serious blow to Simon's political fortunes. While he would have conceded that the Maréchal's coup did not create republican anticlericalism, Simon believed that the events of 1877 induced republican elites to adopt a particularly harsh attitude toward the Church. "The 16th of May," he later wrote, "caused Article 7."[20] This view, which contrasts with that of modern historians who have placed the turning point in 1875, 1851, and even 1789, expresses Simon's reflections on his own experience. For the veterans of the brutal electoral battle of 1877, the Conservative Republic, with its conciliatory attitudes toward the old *classes dirigeantes*, was bound to appear out of touch with the realities of French political life. Indeed, Simon had encountered many ready to believe, as *La République française* insinuated, that he, "former minister of Maréchal MacMahon," was almost an accomplice in the coup![21] Simon's publication of *Le Gouvernement de M. Thiers* in 1878, which reminded readers of Thiers's (and Simon's) services to the republican cause, was unlikely to change many minds. For the Gambettists, Thiers, with his long history of compromise with Catholic and clerical forces, was not the appropriate model. Denouncing "the growth of a spirit which is not only clerical but *vaticanesque*, monastic, congregationist, and *syllabiste*," these men eagerly awaited the moment in 1879 when republicans would gain control of the Senate and the laic campaign could begin at last.[22]

19. A.N. F[18] 341.
20. JS, "Public Education in France," *Contemporary Review* 42 (November 1882): 665; JS, "Mon Petit Journal," *Le Temps*, 16 September 1891.
21. "Paris, 17 mai," *La République française*, 18 May 1877; "Paris, 23 mai," *La République française*, 24 May 1877; *La République française*, 27 May 1877, 4 June 1879, 17 February 1880, 4 February, 5 July 1881.
22. Capéran, *Histoire contemporaine*, 1:112.

II

As minister of public instruction in the moderate republican cabinet of Charles Waddington, Jules Ferry turned in early 1879 to the task of shaping a wide variety of republican proposals for educational reform into a series of coherent pieces of legislation. On 15 March 1879, the twenty-ninth anniversary of the hated Falloux Law, he presented his first legislative measures, including a proposed reform of the Law of 12 July 1875 on Liberty of Higher Education. Its main provisions were reasonable enough to most republicans: the proposal deprived the newly founded Catholic universities of the title "university" and placed the granting of degrees prerequisite for entry into the professions under the exclusive control of the University. Article 7, which concerned secondary and primary education, was another matter and, in the eyes of Simon and other republican moderates, gave the whole piece of legislation an inordinately anticlerical and even irreligious cast. According to this article, members of unauthorized religious congregations were forbidden to participate in public or private education and to direct any educational establishment. This provision rested on a legal distinction between authorized and unauthorized congregations. The Concordat and Organic Articles had provided for the regulation of religious orders "authorized" by the government, but the Church, refusing to recognize the legitimacy of the Organic Articles, had subsequently established in France numerous religious orders without requesting a formal authorization from the government. These orders existed under the general legislation governing the formation of associations in France. Legal, but "unauthorized," such orders as the Society of Jesus had assumed a substantial role in French secondary and primary education. In secondary education, where the University and the private Catholic colleges attracted an equal number of students, the Jesuits directed 42 percent of the Catholic colleges.[23] In primary education, the most important Catholic teaching order, the *Frères des écoles chrétiennes*, was authorized, but other important teaching orders, like the Marists, were not. The probable consequences of Article 7 were difficult to foresee clearly, for the government might have de-

23. André Latreille and René Rémond, *Histoire du Catholicisme en France*, 3:435.

cided to authorize certain orders. But it was clear to all that the measure would seal the fate of the Jesuits and raise serious questions of principle.

As in the case of the French State's earlier campaigns against the Jesuits, Article 7 provoked bitter controversy. According to many members of the episcopacy, the congregations were integral parts of the Church and indispensable auxiliaries of the clergy. To attack them was to violate the Concordat, liberty of education, and liberty of conscience. Some like Théodore Forcade, archbishop of Aix, accused the government of seeking to "dechristianize the world."[24] Catholic laymen in the department of Nord, the first to create a Catholic university, initiated a petition directed especially against Article 7 and rapidly gathered almost two million signatures. The majority of General Councils, taking up the issue in the spring pronounced against the measure.[25] For Ferry, however, Article 7 was not an attack on the Catholic religion but rather a relatively mild measure of republican defense against the regular clergy in general and the Jesuits in particular.

With a conviction that rested firmly on the findings of positivist historical science, Ferry argued that the Society of Jesus constituted not a religious but a political threat to the Third Republic. Citing the attacks on the principles of political liberty and laicity to be found in Jesuit historical textbooks, he argued that the followers of Loyola were the shock troops of the theocratic spirit, the soul of political Catholicism, the organizing force behind the Clerical party. Buttressed by the theory of "indirect power," they sought to make the Church the ultimate arbiter of political life. Article 7, he believed, satisfied the secret desires of most French Catholics and a large portion of the secular clergy who, in their heart of hearts, accepted universal suffrage and the principle of laicity and regarded the *Syllabus of Errors*, that "jesuitical work of the Jesuits," as a misfortune for the Church.[26] He sought to neutralize the influence of an element in the Church that insisted on teaching doctrines permanently threatening republican in-

24. Ibid., p. 458.
25. Capéran, *Histoire contemporaine*, 1:171.
26. Jules Ferry, Chamber of Deputies, 26, 27 June 1879, *Annales* 7 (1879): 170, 190–99; Ferry, Senate, 5, 6, March 1880, *Annales* 3 (1880): 204, 243–46.

stitutions. But, he protested, the government meant no harm to the Catholic faith, the religion of a great number of French citizens. His arguments easily convinced a majority in the chamber, and the bill moved on to the Senate in mid-July. The Senate selected a commission composed of four supporters of the bill, four opponents, and Simon, who supported the parts of the bill dealing strictly with higher education, but opposed Article 7. Simon, as the mediator between the two groups, was elected president of the commission.

Unable to finish its work before 3 August when the parliamentary vacation began, the commission was obliged to await the fall before submitting its report. Meanwhile the heated campaign ran its course in the country. In addition to Catholic interests, moderate republican opinion, represented by newspapers like *Le Temps*, *Le Constitutionnel*, and *Le Moniteur*, and by such prominent republican legislators as Littré, Étienne Lamy, Léon Renault, Agénor Bardoux, and Alexandre Ribot, was highly critical of Article 7. To combat such opposition, Ferry and other republican orators undertook extensive speaking engagements throughout the country. While the ardent Bert predicted that Article 7 and the Ferry Laws would do for clericalism what carbonic sulphur had done for phylloxera, Ferry toured the Midi to the cry of *"Vive Article 7."*[27]

On 8 December 1879, Simon finally submitted the commission's report. The three members of the Right and two republicans, Simon and Voisins-Lavernière, had agreed to delete Article 7. When the time came to vote on the amended law as a whole, however, Ferry's republican supporters, who thought the bill was too weak, allied themselves with those on the Right, who considered the bill too strong, to recommend rejection. As president of the commission, Simon summarized the positions of these two groups and, then, presented the reasons that had led him and Voisins-Lavernière to recommend that the Senate reject Article 7, while passing the other nine articles reforming the law on freedom of higher education.

Simon's arguments against Article 7 rested on his conviction that although laicity was an important republican principle, liberty of conscience took precedence. Liberal principle, that is, respect for liberty of conscience, and by extension, for lib-

27. Capéran, *Histoire contemporaine*, 1:187–93.

erty of education, required the rejection of a measure that contradicted republican tradition. Had not republicans written liberty of education into the constitution of the Second Republic and reaffirmed this commitment in their vote on liberty of higher education in 1875? Casting himself as the bona fide defender of the liberal creed, Simon implied that Ferry had exaggerated the principle of laicity and, consequently, had produced a profoundly illiberal bill. Simon's arguments against Article 7 were particularly strong because he was a known partisan of the lay University and because he accepted the rest of the law. Like Ferry, he had always opposed the "mixed juries" that the Law of 1875 had created for examining the students of private universities. Liberty of education, he believed, still might imply substantial State regulation of private education. The right to establish a school did not imply the right to teach doctrines that endangered morality or the constitution, nor did it imply the right to give degrees like the *baccalauréat* by which the State maintained certain universal academic standards. "Complete and attentive inspection, even severe repression, and State diplomas," he insisted, "may all be consistent with liberty." In establishing the "mixed juries," the Law of 1875 had underestimated the prerogatives of the State. Despite his anticlerical sympathies, however, Simon explained to the Senate, he was obliged to oppose Article 7: it was preventive legislation that discriminated not so much against unauthorized religious orders, whose legal status was certainly debatable, as against individual Frenchmen who were breaking no law in belonging to such orders. Jesuits, he agreed, rarely taught their students to admire republican institutions. But the true republican anticlerical policy, which was also liberal, was to improve the rival public system of education and to exercise the legitimate right of surveillance over the teachings of Catholic congregations.

In this speech, as in all his subsequent battles against various aspects of the laic laws, Simon, true to his highly personal liberalism, appropriated the epithet *liberal* for himself. His use of the term, in these years, was therefore partially polemical, for it did not do justice to the moderate Ferry's efforts to balance, in a slightly different way, the interrelated but competing claims of laicity and liberty of conscience.

Article 7 was, in Simon's eyes, not only illiberal and unrepublican but also inefficacious and profoundly impolitic. Intended to reduce significantly the role of religious orders in French education, the measure would result only in a redistribution of regular clergy. Members of the unauthorized congregations would join authorized congregations, become chaplains in private schools, or become secular clergymen. Indeed, far from strengthening the Republic, the measure would weaken it. At a time when republicanism was making great progress, the government should "mollify, reassure, and attract." Governments bent on conciliation should always treat religious questions with an extreme reserve, for "even the most circumspect minds are likely to fall into exaggerations where religious interests or irreligious interests . . . are concerned." The government was unwittingly serving clericals who, in the next elections, would argue that Catholics must choose between their religion and the Republic. Persecution would only strengthen the Church. In such an event, a violent anticlerical reaction would lead to the sacrifice of the liberal elements in the republican party to the more authoritarian ones.[28]

The Senate commenced deliberation on this proposed law on 23 February 1880. Since June 1879, Simon had been working to unite men in the chamber, the Senate, the academy, and the University who shared his general outlook.[29] More recently, he had lobbied tirelessly among the senators of the Left Center to ensure a negative vote on Article 7.[30] Indeed, in the Senate there developed what *Le Temps* called a "dissident Left Center" to which Simon was linked. Concerned about the strength of militant anticlericalism in the chamber, this group began to violate the custom of republican solidarity in the elections of tenured senators by abstaining when the republican candidate was too sympathetic to Gambettist anticlericalism. Although this practice had no effect on the late February election of the journalist John Lemoinne of *Le Journal des débats*, it did lead to closer relations between this group and members of the

28. JS, "Rapport fait au nom de la commission chargée d'examiner le projet et loi relatif à la liberté de l'enseignement supérieur," *Annales (Annexes)* 11 (1879): 3–18; also JS to Gustave Simon, 1879, 87 AP 8.

29. JS to Étienne Vacherot, early June 1879, 87 AP 7.

30. Jean-B. Krantz, Paris, to Louis Denormandie, 12 January 1880, Jean-B. Krantz, Paris, to JS, 27 December 1879, 87 AP 17.

Right.[31] At the same time, the Central Committee of Catholic Education, a Catholic lobby run by the Jesuit Du Lac, was discreetly putting its resources at Simon's disposal.[32]

In his speeches before the Senate, however, Simon was careful to distinguish himself from his Catholic and anti-republican allies. He opposed Article 7, he said on 27 February, for republican reasons rather than religious ones; he was defending not the congregations but liberty. In a nation of thirty million Catholics, no Republic could exist that denied liberty of education to religious interests.[33] All laws dealing with liberty of education should be unequivocal, for they would serve as indispensable barriers against turbulent intolerant forces in the chamber. By this standard, Article 7, which raised serious questions related to the right of association, had no place in a law on liberty of education. Finally, on 6 and 8 March, when he rose in the Senate to reply to Ferry's arguments in support of Article 7, he summed up his previous arguments and drew a sharp contrast between Ferry's illiberal way of maintaining a majority and the liberal traditions of 1789. In those last days of debate, he received a short note signed by a "fond" Jules Ferry awaiting the "knife of Calchas" from the "parricidal hands" of his master.[34] During the hearing, the Senate rejected Article 7 by a vote of 148 to 129; Simon and twenty-eight senators of the Left Center, including Édouard Laboulaye and Jules Dufaure, voted with the Right. Eight others, including the positivist Littré, abstained.[35]

The matter did not end there. To Simon's dismay, the government yielded to pressure from the republican majority in the chamber and decided to try to accomplish by administrative decrees what it had failed to achieve by legislation. Because of numerous uncertainties in the law concerning unauthorized orders, executive measures were bound to seem arbitrary and even dictatorial to many, especially in the wake of a legislative

31. Audren de Kerdrel, Paris, to JS, 19 February 1880, Kerdrel, Paris, to JS, 8 March 1880, 87 AP 4; *Le Temps*, 21 February 1880.

32. Capéran, *Histoire contemporaine*, 1:197.

33. JS, Senate, 27 February 1880, *Annales* 3 (1880): 50–63.

34. JS, Senate, 6, 8 March 1880, *Annales* 3 (1880): 246–47, 251–65. Ferry to JS [1880], Raphael, "Trois lettres inédites de Jules Ferry," p. 86.

35. Capéran, *Histoire contemporaine*, 1:201.

defeat. But the government persisted; invoking laws originating in the revolutionary and Napoleonic eras, the decrees of
29 March declared that (1) the unauthorized Society of Jesus
must disband and evacuate all its buildings within three
months and (2) all other unauthorized orders must request
authorization within the same period, or disband also. When
Catholics sought to question the legality of the decrees before
a conservative judiciary, the government arbitrarily excluded
their pleas from all but an administrative court in which its
interests were well represented.[36]

Up to this time, Simon believed that his differences with
most republicans were primarily political. Committed like
them to the Republic, he differed from them in his estimation
of the measures that would make it flourish. Convinced that
his kind of liberalism constituted the best republican defense
against a monarchist or Bonapartist resurgence, he redoubled
his efforts after the announcement of the decrees to expand the
power of the dissident Left Center, which the vote on Article 7
had shown to hold the balance of power in the Senate. In April,
he set about organizing a Parisian electoral committee that
would serve as a clearing house for men interested in building
up a "Republican Right."[37] A brake upon the anticlericalism
of the Opportunists, the group would offer Catholics a rallying point within the republican movement. Although these
efforts incurred the hostility of most of the Right, often frustrated in their attempts to use this group for their own purposes,
republicans generally ostracized Simon as an apostate. His iso-
lation from the Republican Left and his hostility to Gambetta
deepened his disaffection with Opportunist politics. In the
period between mid-1880 and the beginning of 1883, two more
issues arose to accentuate Simon's sense of distance from his
former allies: (1) the government's demand for full amnesty
for all those detained for participation in the Commune; (2)
the passage of the Law of 28 March 1882 on Obligatory Primary Education, which laicized the curriculum in public schools.
The Opportunists, he came to believe, differed from him not

36. Théophile Roussel, Aufeuillette, to JS, 18 April 1880, 87 AP 18.
37. "La Droite Républicaine," Le Gaulois, 9 April 1879; Le Gaulois,
13 April 1880; "Le Centre Gauche et le Parti Conservateur," Le Gaulois,
19 April 1880.

only in their understanding of the principles of liberal republicanism but also in their complacency toward social forces that threatened the existence of French civilization. With their excessive concern for political expediency, he feared, they would allow their Radical allies to lead them step by step down the path to a godless, freedomless, and proletarian collectivism.

The question of full amnesty for the Communards, a recurrent republican issue since 1876, came before the public once again in June 1880. The chamber, on the urging of Premier Charles de Freycinet, promptly voted the measure and sent it along to the Senate. For Simon, a member of the senatorial commission charged with reporting on the proposal, the Commune symbolized the ever-present danger to liberty and morality posed by social forces that society could contain only through constant vigilance. The enemy, in June 1848 and in the spring of 1871, was always the same: a hard core of inveterate revolutionaries and socialist sectarians ready to make a tiny minority of the working class the instrument of their hatred of the bourgeoisie.[38] Under the empire, Simon had confidently sought to persuade socially conservative notables that with proper, enlightened leadership, the common people, in their basic goodness, would instinctively reject such blandishments. The Commune of 1871, however, raised doubts that he had not known before, especially because it seemed the negation of all national sentiment. After the Commune, revolutionary militants were more threatening, for the people had proved to be more easily misled and to be, perhaps, less attached to traditional morality than he had once believed.[39] Simon had thus opposed Hugo's proposal of 23 May 1876 for total amnesty; and in February 1879, he had only grudgingly voted for Waddington's bill that combined cessation of all further prosecu-

38. JS, *Souvenirs du quatre septembre*, 1:163, 350–53, 384, 417.

39. For Simon's public statements on the Commune, see: JS, "Circulaire relative aux événements (23 mars 1871)," JS, "Circulaire aux recteurs sur la collaboration des membres du corps enseignant aux journaux et receuils périodiques (24 avril 1871)," *Bulletin administratif de l'Instruction Publique*, 23 June 1871, pp. 33–35, 55–59.

For later statements, see: JS, "Discours du 27 décembre, 1871," *Bulletin administratif de l'Instruction Publique*, 17 February 1872, p. 624; JS, *Souvenirs du quatre septembre*, 1:417–19; JS, *The Government of M. Thiers from 8 February 1871 to 24 May 1873*, 1:181–83, 258–533.

tions with pardons for some and amnesty for other specified categories of Communards.[40] For Simon, amnesty was not the proper approach to the problem, for it tended to obscure the moral questions involved. He feared that the more extreme elements on the Left were demanding amnesty, which involved full return of civic rights, not as an act of mercy but as an act of justice. Amnesty implied, in his mind, a condemnation of the "Government of Monsieur Thiers" to which he had belonged. Like his friend Dufaure, Simon preferred to proceed through executive pardons that underscored the Republic's moral condemnation of the Commune and required the returned Communard to undergo a period of probation before he might apply for the rights of full citizenship.

The government presented the bill to the Senate not as a question of principle but as a measure of national conciliation that would consecrate the first celebration of 14 July as a national holiday. While the Senate's commission was deliberating the question, the government moved ahead with the execution of the decree against the Jesuits.[41] On 2 July, the commission, chaired by Simon, submitted a report urging rejection of the bill favoring amnesty. "The question of principle and of national morality dominates all considerations of politics or of persons," wrote the republican *rapporteur*, Honoré de Voisins-Lavernière.[42] On the next day, Simon rose to answer Hugo's eloquent appeal for an amnesty that would demonstrate the "fraternity of France and of all humanity." Executive pardons, "the ornament and the flower of public holidays," Simon declared, would achieve all that amnesty might accomplish. Besides, amnesty would not bring about reconciliation between Frenchmen. The Communards who had been amnestied in 1879 had returned unrepentant, with the same hatreds and demands. How can one give political rights, he asked, to those who "do not regret the rifle or the torch which was torn from their hands, who see their judges, who judged them in the name of the law, merely as armed adversaries?" To such men,

40. JS, Senate, 3 July 1880, *Annales* 9 (1880): 278; Jean Joughin, *The Paris Commune in French Politics, 1871–1880; The History of the Amnesty of 1880*, 1:200–219.

41. Adrien Dansette, *Histoire religieuse de la France contemporaine*, p. 417.

42. Honoré de Voisins-Lavernière, Senate, 2 July 1880, *Annales* 9 (1880): 239.

he would grant pardon but not amnesty. Over Simon's opposition, the Senate eventually passed a modified measure that, combined with a general pardon for all remaining Communards in detention, granted amnesty to all but fourteen.[43]

In his opposition to the amnesty law, Simon also presented a broader critique of Opportunist politics. This law, he believed, like Article 7 and the decrees of 29 March, formed part of a pattern of concessions made to Clémenceau and others on the Extreme Left in the name of a supposedly moderate politics that amounted to little more than a bankrupt effort to appease violent and authoritarian elements in the republican camp. So long as the government chose to seek allies on the edges of the Commune, it would find itself at the mercy of their illiberal initiatives. This criticism expressed Simon's long-lasting distrust of the "unprincipled" politics of Gambetta and his dismay at the influence the tribune exercised over men like Ferry and Freycinet. Gambetta, Simon confided to an English journalist, had no real ability as a politician and statesman for he acted according to no political principles except, perhaps, systematic prevarication. Driven by an insatiable ambition, he had already in 1871 not hesitated to imperil France to benefit his own popularity. The perfect Opportunist, Gambetta was "a man who waits, quietly observing which current of public opinion is the strongest and the most powerful, and then following it, regardless of anything save his personal ambition."[44] Such republican politics, Simon warned Ferry, would alienate men of principle, "men who were honest, firm, impeccable, with both a virtuous and republican past." The false moderation of the Opportunists was no substitute for the true moderation of "liberal politics," which rested not on popular passions but on respect for the law, for the rights of property and the rights of the conscience. Such a view reflected Simon's belief that republicans needed to "cut their tail," to sacrifice Gambetta's more militant followers, in order to save the Conservative Republic.[45]

43. JS, Senate, 3 July 1880, *Annales* 9 (1880): 253–61; Joughin, *The Paris Commune in French Politics*, 2:465.

44. "Portraits in Words, XIV. The Whitehall Review and M. Jules Simon," *The Whitehall Review* (20 September 1879), pp. 436–37; for a similar view, expressed at the time of Gambetta's death, see JS, "Gambetta," *Figures et croquis*, pp. 47–48.

45. JS, Senate, 3 July 1880, *Annales* 9 (1880): 259–61.

Ferry, whose Opportunism was more principled than Simon would publicly admit, was not inclined to take such advice, which amounted to abandoning a large part of republican terra firma for the tepid and uncertain currents of the swamp that covered the French political center. The law on obligatory primary education, submitted to the chamber on 4 December 1880, linked obligation with clauses establishing the legal bases for a curriculum that, in principle at least, did not need to include any form of religious or philosophic spiritualism. Article 1 replaced the Falloux Law's requirement that "religious and moral" instruction should be part of the curriculum, with the stipulation that students should learn "moral and civic" duties. This measure, inserted in the law at the behest of the Gambettist Paul Bert, ensured that the curriculum of French public schools would be non-confessional, laic, or neutral; the catechism would no longer be taught in school. The fate of philosophic spiritualism, however, was much more ambiguous. The debate which occupied the chamber intermittently for the next fifteen months revolved not on the question of obligation, assured of passage, but upon the precise legislative definition of the concept of laicity.

The secularization of the curriculum of public schools, Ferry told the chamber, was but one further manifestation of that laic spirit that had found its first full expression in the French Revolution. True to positivist historical theory, he believed that this "necessary principle presently reaching fruition" would guarantee a laic society against the pretensions of a Roman Catholic Church that, if given even a small foothold in the curriculum, would inevitably assert the right to the ultimate surveillance of French public education. The laic school, however, Ferry insisted, was not necessarily a "school without God"; the curriculum, while emphasizing ethical rather than metaphysical ideas, would nevertheless reflect the spiritualistic convictions of the vast majority of teachers. Without rejecting "independent morality," Ferry (with his secret expectation of its ultimate triumph) assured his parliamentary audience that lessons in ethics would draw on "all comforts, all supports . . . whether they come from idealistic, spiritualistic or even theological beliefs—all supports are good."[46]

46. Jules Ferry, Chamber of Deputies, 23 December 1880, *Annales* 13 (1880): 163–71.

Passed by the chamber on 24 December the law did not come up for debate in the Senate until 2 June 1881. Overwhelmingly spiritualist in composition, and with fewer militant anticlericals, this body found the proposed law dangerously imprecise. Despite Ferry's assurances and the spiritualistic doctrines of contemporary teaching personnel, Catholics were certain that the law would lead to the school without God. As Broglie pointed out, natural religion could only exist in tandem with revelation. In a sardonic reference to Ferry's positivism, he asked the Senate whether it could do anything but oppose "a [deistic] secular religion formulated by the High Council of Public Instruction under the infallible magistery of M. Jules Ferry, who is not even sure that he believes in it?"[47] The Right pressed Ferry to demonstrate his opposition to the "atheistic school" by specifying in the law that French schoolchildren would learn a "religious morality." Ferry refused, assuring the Senate that (1) a curriculum for schoolchildren could hardly have much metaphysical content and (2) that what content it did have would be spiritualist, since the author of the ethics program, Paul Janet, embraced the spiritualist beliefs of the immense majority of the French population. While reiterating that children would learn the Catholic "good old morality of our forefathers," he insisted that these ethics, based on the golden rule, were essentially the same as those of "the honorable M. Jules Simon" and of Kantians, evolutionists, utilitarians, and positivists.[48]

At this stage in the debate, Simon rose to speak for the first time. With a passing dig at Comte whom, he suggested, hardly deserved to be classed with such masters as Kant and Spencer, Simon agreed with Ferry's position that ethics taught to children should not take a strictly metaphysical form. Indeed, in the realm of ethics, the teacher should act like the parent, referring the child to relevant precepts as occasions presented themselves in the communal life of the classroom. But, the author of *La Religion naturelle*, in a profession of faith that was itself an act of worship, called on the government to offer some reassurance to a spiritualist people that felt an irrepressible

47. Albert de Broglie, Senate, 10 June 1881, *Annales du Sénat* 2 (1881): 198.
48. Jules Ferry, Senate, 2 July 1881, *Annales du Sénat* 2 (1881): 439–43.

sentiment of "astonishment and disapproval" in the presence of atheism. The phrase "religious morality" might at some time enable a reactionary government to restore the catechism to the curriculum, but could the government refuse to agree to a clause stating that teachers will teach children their "duties toward God and country?" Once more, Simon was inviting the Opportunists to break with Radicals like Clémenceau and Ranc and to reject an atheism, which in the Commune, had shown itself to be contrary to virtue, social order, and country. The leaders of the Republic should respect God, liberty, and country.[49]

In an effort to defeat Simon's amendment, which despite an unfavorable commission report seemed likely to pass, Ferry addressed the Senate once more on 4 July. Identifying modernity and laicity, he insisted that the State should not officially sanction theological or metaphysical positions: "God is not voted in assemblies." The government did not need to put God in the law as a reassuring gesture, for impartial judges would find in the full range of its policies no sign of animus against Catholicism, the religious sentiment, or the idea of God.[50] Confident of victory, Simon replied only briefly. The State, he conceded, should not endorse an official metaphysical system. But, given its concern for public order and the administration of justice, it had a vested interest in the maintenance of *bonnes moeurs*. It was therefore obliged to give public endorsement to those fundamental philosophic notions, including the existence of God, which formed the basis of public and private morality. As a republican and a spiritualist, he asked the Senate to place the education of the young Republic under the sovereignty of God. By a narrow margin, the Senate passed his amendment.[51]

The Chamber of Deputies, spurred on by Bert, summarily rejected this amended bill, and in the following year the Senate took up the question once more. Simon's chances of repeating his previous success were minimal, for the Opportunist majority in the chambers had been strengthened in recent elections. Yet on 11 March, he attempted again to defend his amendment. The previous vote by the Senate, he remarked at

49. JS, Senate, 2 July 1881, *Annales du Sénat* 2 (1881): 444–45.
50. Ferry, Senate, 4 July 1881, *Annales du Sénat* 2 (1881): 466–70.
51. JS, Senate, 4 July 1881, *Annales du Sénat* 2 (1881): 470–73.

the outset, had signified the majority's desire to emphasize both its acceptance of the principle of confessional neutrality and its rejection of the principle of philosophic neutrality. To place a reference in the law to "the God which all spiritualist philosophies and religions recognize" was to erect a barrier against the spread of impiety, a "moral disease" that, although not yet of critical proportions, threatened social life. Sounding a note of alarm not present in his previous public statements, Simon bitterly protested the "perverting" effects of the sham moderation of Opportunist politicians. "What a series of insanities have been proposed," he cried. "We have to take seriously . . . ideas which well-bred people . . . would have disdainfully ignored a few years ago." Finally, as a republican spiritualist, he declared his repugnance for a law on public education "from which the name of God has been withdrawn; that shocks me, that grieves me, that . . . has saddened my life; I no longer feel that I am in the world and the country where I have worked and combated for so many years."[52] For Ferry, such a protest must have confirmed the old positivist suspicion that the theological and metaphysical mentalities shared a deep common affinity. Simon's protest, he told the Senate, expressed the philosophic preoccupations of a man so obsessed and possessed by the fear of "public atheism" that, contrary to the doctrines of his lifetime, he had resorted, like his Catholic allies, to the secular arm in the defense of his ideas about human destinies.[53] With Simon abstaining, the Senate passed the Law of 28 March 1882 on Obligatory Primary Education.

Hardening around issues like the amnesty of the Communards and the secularization of the primary school curriculum, Simon's continual conflicts with the Opportunists led him to reorder his vision of the principal political problems confronting French society. Until the elections of August 1881, which gave the republicans a huge majority in the country and gave Gambetta's Republican Union the strongest position in the chamber, the notion of republican defense dominated Simon's political thinking. Unlike many Opportunists, however, he believed that republicans posed almost as great a threat to the Republic as a reactionary clericalism. Indeed, his commitment to civil liberties, his philosophic views, and his respect for

52. JS, Senate, 11 March 1882, *Annales du Sénat* 4 (1882): 194–98.
53. Ferry, Senate, 11 March 1882, *Annales du Sénat* 4 (1882): 198–99.

Catholicism led him to attempt to temper the "exaggerated" republican fear of clericalism. In this spirit, he concentrated his primary efforts on moderating Opportunist policies; secondarily, he worked to provide a rallying point for new, hesitant recruits to the republican cause. After the elections, however, the priorities were reversed. The balloting, as well as Opportunist politics of the past two and one-half years, convinced Simon that the most immediate threat to his liberal republicanism came from the Left rather than the Right. Opposing further concessions to the Extreme Left, Simon sought to organize a "Republican Right" made up of previously silent moderates and of men who, ceding to the promptings of reason rather than emotion, were ready to abandon old dynastic hopes and accept the Republic. To regenerate the Left Center, he sought to recruit conservative and practical men, who held "reasonable opinions, to which they are reasonably attached, and which they serve to a reasonable degree."[54] While remaining a loyal friend of the Republic, especially in moments of crisis, Simon finished out the last years of his political career as the liberal advocate of Catholic interests. These new attitudes first found expression in Simon's editorials for Le Gaulois, a newspaper that he began directing in November 1881, and in a book written in late 1882, Dieu, patrie, liberté (1883).

Simon's decision to assume the political direction of Le Gaulois in itself symbolized one aspect of his change in attitude. Le Gaulois, a newspaper directed by Arthur Meyer, had been Bonapartist until the death of the prince imperial in June 1880 and then, with its director, had shifted to the monarchist camp. After the elections of August and September 1881, the stockholders had dismissed Meyer and called on Simon to try to lead the newspaper's readers to a "liberal and conservative republicanism."[55] "We think," announced Simon in his first article, "that a republic which is not liberal is not a republic,

54. JS, "Encore des abstentions," Le Gaulois, 13 December 1881. See also JS, "Introduction," Dieu, patrie, liberté, p. iv. For Simon's attitude toward Raoul Duval's later efforts to form a less resolutely republican "Republican Right," see "Place aux nouveaux," Le Matin, 8 September 1886 and "La Droite républicaine," Le Matin, 22 September 1886.

55. "Lettre de M. Jules Simon," Le Gaulois, 17 July 1882. Simon was political director of Le Gaulois from 29 November 1881 until 17 July 1882. On the evolution of Le Gaulois, see Arthur Meyer, Ce que mes yeux ont vu, pp. 244–51.

just as a government which is not conservative is not a government." Pledging to oppose the constitutional revision demanded by Gambetta and the Extreme Left, and to defend liberty of conscience, he insisted that "the real struggle now is between Jacobins and liberals." He identified Jacobinism with the contemporary anticlerical movement and the campaign for revision. The modern Jacobins dreamed of a "government both omnipotent and servile: omnipotent with regard to the public and private purse, labor, education and the individual conscience, servile before the will of a single Chamber itself subject to the incessant fluctuations of the popular will." For these Jacobins, "progress consisted in absorbing all individual forces in the collective force."[56] Initially "neutral, with a slight tendency to approve" of Gambetta's long-awaited "great ministry," Simon served warning that he would oppose any concessions to authoritarian elements in republican ranks.[57] The time had come, he insisted, to abandon those whose politics rested on ambition, ignorance, and personal rivalry, for "these are neither men, in the most profound sense of the word, nor leaders of peoples."[58]

The dichotomy between Jacobinism and liberalism in politics had its corollary in the moral realm. In *Dieu, patrie, liberté*, a study of the nature and origins of the republican laic campaign to 1883, Simon formally developed a theme that he had previously treated more obliquely.[59] Just as men viewed the eighteenth century as a struggle between philosophy and religion, they would perceive the nineteenth century as a struggle between nihilism and spiritualism.[60] Disturbed by demands from the Extreme Left for the elimination of God's name from judicial oaths, and by the protests against deistic curricula raised by the General Council of the Seine and the Parisian Municipal Council in late 1882, Simon warned that official neutrality might easily slide into official irreligion and official atheism.[61]

56. JS, "A partir d'aujourd'hui," *Le Gaulois*, 29 November 1881.
57. See Étienne Vacherot's article "Encore l'Union des Gauches" which Simon printed (*Le Gaulois*, 10 January 1882); JS, "Aux nouveaux ministres," *Le Gaulois*, 28 January 1882.
58. JS, "La Guerre au cléricalisme," *Le Gaulois*, 19 February 1882.
59. JS, "La Guerre au cléricalisme," *Le Gaulois*, 20 February 1882; JS, "Le Déisme, voilà l'ennemi," *Le Gaulois*, 21 February 1882.
60. JS, *Dieu, patrie, liberté*, p. 27.
61. Ibid., pp. 257–59, 353–57.

Indeed, only an infinitesimal atheistic minority could really favor this proscription of the God of the immense majority of Frenchmen. Unable to believe that such an affront to the consciences of the majority could reflect any real respect for liberty of conscience, Simon suspected that those who were most demanding on the question of neutrality really sought to "seal the lips of believers who might pronounce the name of God."[62] The law neutralizing the curriculum of the primary school, he suggested, may have provoked the recent "explosion of atheism." For although intellectuals might easily distinguish between neutrality and atheism, "the ignorant and the imbecilic," had "a tendency to exaggerate everything, to confuse brutality with power, to seek a kind of glory in impudent negation of all that is respectable."[63] The Opportunists were so afraid of the sacristy that they did not see the threat posed by the ever-present Commune.[64] Only a strict liberalism, his own, could safeguard philosophic and religious spiritualism and the French nation against a corrosive Jacobin nihilism.

Eloquent, sometimes vehement in his public statements, Simon always exercised, nevertheless, a certain parliamentary restraint. In a private letter, apparently unsent, to a sympathetic English ecclesiastic, Simon more freely summed up both his despair and his hopes:

> The vagaries of universal suffrage have brought ignorant and violent men into our assemblies. Although these men constitute a minority, they exercise a predominant influence because of their organization, their violence, and the weak heartedness of the moderates. After having pushed hard, as you know, against spiritualist beliefs and against the restraints of conscience, they have turned to politics in efforts to disarm law and justice. I have tried . . . to oppose this double war, which threatens the foundations of all society, and I have run the risk of becoming a voice crying in the wilderness. I have not tried to combat the anger of the enemies of all eternal and sacred principles, but rather, the criminal cowardice of leaders who, to stay in power, favor enterprises which will, in a short time, lead to the destruction of all authority. I have also combated the no less guilty and no less

62. Ibid., pp. 258–60.   63. Ibid., p. 359.
64. Ibid., p. 413.

detestable complicity of those who abandon their religious
and political creed to keep their advantages and their popularity, or who, discouraged, withdraw from the struggle,
letting the torrent run unopposed, in order to concern themselves with their personal affairs. I have always thought that
in the worst days of the Terror, the Plain of the Convention
was as guilty and as responsible as the Mountain. I have no
hopes . . . of enlightening the criminals, nor even of regen-
erating the cowards, although that was once my principal aim.
But perhaps I will stimulate the younger and the more capable
to make similar and more powerful efforts.[65]

Between the publication of *Dieu, patrie, liberté* and the Boulanger Affair, Simon continued to combat an anticlericalism
that, in his view, had degenerated into a campaign against not
only Catholicism but also the idea of God. He shared with many
French Catholics the conviction that the laic campaign did not
express adequately the real religious mood of the French population. Exploiting the popular horror of "government of priests"
in their own interests, the Opportunists and the Radicals had
stimulated these fears beyond all proportion. The position of
Simon and of Catholic moderates remained weak, however,
because the Church itself withheld the kinds of reassurances
that would have given the moderate position a real credibility.
Despite such a handicap, Simon worked indefatigably in defense of Catholic liberties in debates on legislation concerning
the right of association, judicial reform, military organization,
and private or free education. In 1886, he rose once more in
the Senate to combat the Goblet Law, which laicized, in principle at least, all the personnel in public primary education.
Simon insisted that he had always preferred lay teachers for
his own children. On liberal grounds, however, he protested
against a legislative project that would effectively limit the
possibilities open to parents who wanted congregationist instruction; would deny a certain category of Frenchmen the
right to teach in public schools; and would diminish the liberty
of municipal councils to decide for themselves on the personnel
of local public primary schools. The Goblet Law, like the
Ferry Laws, he concluded, was a law of anger and of revenge,

65. JS, Paris, to Christopher Wordsworth, bishop of Lincoln, 5 July
1883, 87 AP 5.

another example of the inability of the republican leadership to resist the imperious and exorbitant demands of "anticlerical passions."[66]

In this struggle against republican anticlericalism, Simon found reasons to defend some of the remaining elements of Catholic culture embedded in French legislation. Thus, he opposed the National Assembly's decision to abolish the official prayers that inaugurated each legislative year, and he combated Alfred Naquet's legislative proposals in favor of divorce. Finally, while in principle favorable to the separation of Church and State, he reluctantly conceded that the Concordat was, and would be for an indefinite time to come, the best guarantee for liberty of conscience in general, and particularly for the threatened liberties of Catholics. Separation must wait until Frenchmen had acquired the "habits of freedom."[67]

*   *   *   *   *

In the early years of the Third Republic, Simon pursued with single-minded determination the same ideal of a "respectable," republican "government of talent" that had inspired his opposition to the Second Empire. His particular sort of liberalism, rooted in rationalist philosophic principle, served a politics that always bore the imprint of the University. With a professorial conviction that "the false is often only in the way one expresses one's thought, and that if men put a little more clarity in their definitions, the most bitter adversaries would come close to an understanding," the resourceful Simon worked to forge a "governmental" party drawn from those upright and high-minded bourgeois standing in the fissured and fragmented center of the French political spectrum.[68] His feeling for complexity and nuance, his experience in government, and his tastes and sympathies all tended to direct and to deflect his vision toward the men, facts, and events that contradicted the polarized image of "two Frances" endemic to the propaganda

66. JS, Senate, 18, 20 March 1886, *Annales du Sénat* 15 (1886): 384–89, 399–401. On this debate, see Louis Capéran, *Histoire de la laïcité républicaine. La Laïcité en marche*, pp. 178–209.

67. JS, "Introduction nouvelle," *La Liberté de conscience*, 6th ed. (Paris: Hachette, 1883), p. xvii.

68. Auguste Cartault, "Publicistes français contemporains. M. Jules Simon," *Revue politique et littéraire*.

of both the militant Left and Right. To his discriminating mind, the anticlericalism of most republican voters was by no means anti-Catholic and the authoritarianism of clerical defenders of the Church did not signify that the Church and the Republic were irreconcilable. A moderate and spiritualistic France would, he believed, accept a firm leadership that, with the courage of its convictions, defended philosophy and the lay University and, at the same time, permitted the Church a religious liberty broad almost to the point of privilege. In this judgment, Simon seems largely to have underestimated the passionate laic faith and gnawing anticlerical fears of men who not only voted republican but who, as journalists, municipal councillors and committee members, constituted the iron of the republican movement. For Simon, this error was easy to make for his assumptions about political leadership did not dispose him to pay much attention to the demands of electoral committees. Indeed, he conceived of politics in almost exclusively parliamentary terms. For him, the hemicycle was the arena within which a political elite, the designates of universal suffrage, who were chosen for their knowledge, integrity, and general political orientation, decided the affairs of the nation according to principle and conscience. For the stern class-bound moralist, the deputy was less a delegate of the people or an officer of public opinion than a servant of a justice that was both human and divine.

CHAPTER X

EPILOGUE

Jules Simon died suddenly on 8 June 1896 after a short ill-
ness. *Le Temps* soberly reported that on the evening before
his death, he received the last sacraments of the Church from
his friend Abbé Herizog, the priest of the Madeleine.[1] The
government immediately accorded him a State funeral. For in
the years after 1886, Simon had become one of the venerable
elder statesmen of the Republic. As his activity in the Senate
diminished, he gradually returned to the graces of the republican Left. As an early opponent of Boulanger, against whom he
waged an extended journalistic campaign in the Parisian daily
Le Matin, Simon was able to demonstrate to republicans that
his opposition to the laic laws reflected no lack of loyalty to
the Republic.[2] In early 1890, Eugène Spuller, once one of Gambetta's associates, and now minister of foreign affairs in the
moderate Tirard cabinet, appointed Simon to head the French
delegation to the Berlin Labor Conference (15–29 March 1890)
held under the patronage of the Emperor William II.[3] About

1. "La Mort de M. Jules Simon," *Le Temps*, 9 June 1896; Abbé J.-A.
Clamadieu, *Jules Simon*, p. 6.
2. From August 1884 until February 1890, Simon wrote a weekly
article for this Parisian *journal d'affaires*. His articles against Boulanger
began appearing in January 1887. Many of them were republished in a
collection entitled *Souviens-toi du deux-décembre* (Paris: V. Havard,
1889), which came out in the week before the general's election in Paris
on 27 January 1889. Although the collection contained much that was
critical of both Gambetta and Clémenceau and their followers, the
Gambettist *La République française* (24 January) and the Radical *La
Justice* (25 January) praised Simon's work and recommended it to their
readers. See also Gustave Simon, "Notes et souvenirs (Documents
inédits), Partie IV," *La Revue mondiale*, 170, no. 7 (1 April 1926): 217–
18; *Le Matin* articles, 87 AP 14 VI (1).
3. On the Berlin Labor Conference, see Gustave Simon, "Notes et
souvenirs (Documents inédits), Partie V," *La Revue mondiale*, 170, no.
8 (15 April 1926): 318–21; "Conférence ouvrière de Berlin, 15, 29 mars
1890," 87 AP 10 V.

the same time, *Le Temps*, the staid newspaper of the French republican establishment, engaged the republican veteran to write weekly and sometimes biweekly columns on matters of his choice under the heading "Mon Petit Journal." Thus, Simon received full republican pomp and circumstance for a funeral celebrated in the classical Church of the Madeleine, the church that the Second Republic had preferred, for its official religious ceremonies, to the Gothic Notre Dame de Paris. He was buried in the Père-Lachaise Cemetery, where his tomb, by his request, bears the inscription, "Jules Simon 1814–1896. Dieu, Patrie, Liberté."

In his last years, as in his entire adult life, Simon remained a man of firm habit and convictions. From his apartment, located at 10 Place de la Madeleine, where he had lived for over forty years, the elderly politician still viewed the problems of French cultural politics in terms of the same categories and values that had always given his liberal republicanism its particular character. This liberalism rested on a commitment to the principle of liberty of conscience for all—Catholics, Protestants, Jews, philosophic theists, agnostics, atheists. No one should be persecuted for his philosophic or religious views. Simon's particular solicitude, however, was directed at the liberty of the theistic conscience in both its philosophic and religious form, for he considered the spiritualistic cultural tradition the only adequate moral basis for a liberal society. His cultural politics therefore always called for collaboration between philosophic spiritualism and religious spiritualism, between the State-run University and the Catholic Church. Collaboration, however, he warned both clerical and militantly anticlerical critics was not to be confused with capitulation of State to Church. However much he might disagree with the way in which the Opportunists had interpreted and applied the notion of laicity, he still insisted that both liberal principle and the long-run interest of the Catholic faith required that churchmen respect the distinction between the spiritual and the temporal.

In his death "in the arms of the Church," Simon expressed his commitment to a spiritualistic cultural tradition both Catholic and French in origins. Although it is impossible to rule out the possibility of a full and unambiguous assent to Catholic articles of faith, Simon's act probably expressed a more qualified attitude. Both the reticences of Abbé Clamadieu, a priest associated with the Madeleine, and Simon's special attitude toward Catholic "rites of passage" militate against the view that the freethinker's acceptance of extreme unction meant full conversion. Yet, be that as it may, Simon's customary declarations of respect for Catholicism now contained themes expressing a renewed, broader commitment.

This new attitude sharply contrasted with the tone that Simon had set in books like *Le Devoir* and *La Religion naturelle*. In these books, the freethinker, confident that the educated public was inexorably abandoning the Church, treated Catholicism with the detached deference often reserved for grand old institutions in the twilight of their lives. In these later years, however, Simon was not so condescending, although he retained his own habits of free thought.[4] The Church, Simon now believed, was not yet either moribund or anachronistic and still a strong bastion of spiritualism. Indeed, he thought he had formerly exaggerated the progress of dechristianization in France when he had estimated that the "immense majority" of Frenchmen no longer believed the doctrines of the Church.[5] Now, he characterized French culture as Catholic and estimated that between 13.5 and 22.5 million of France's thirty million professed Catholics were Catholics in more than name.[6] Among those whose Catholicism was superficial, few accepted the militant anti-spiritualism of atheists. This sense of the relative vitality of Catholicism grew with Simon's realization in the 1880s that the University, with Cousin's "philosophy of the nineteenth century," had proven itself unable to replace the Church as the primary defender of spiritualism.

The first traces of this intellectual evolution toward a more critical view of philosophic spiritualism appeared in a series of

4. Paul Dresse, *Léon Daudet vivant*, p. 35; Alfred Philibert-Soupé, "Portraits d'Académiques. Jules Simon," *Revue du siècle*; JS, "L'Année philosophique," *Le Journal*, 2 January 1894; Léon Séché, "Jules Simon," *Revue illustrée de Bretagne et d'Anjou*, 18 (June 1896): 255.

5. JS, *Grand Orient de France. Discours de M. Jules Simon et du ∴ F. Bancel*, p. 61; JS, *L'École*, p. 154–59.

6. Simon's statistics varied, often within short time periods. See JS, "Public Education in France," *Contemporary Review* 42 (November 1882): 669; JS, *Nos hommes d'État*, pp. 160–61, 284, 333; JS, *Mignet, Michelet, Henri Martin*, p. 334; JS, "Mon Petit Journal," *Le Temps*, 30 December 1891.

responses to the *universitaire* Paul Janet's sympathetic *Victor Cousin et son oeuvre* (1885). Janet, one of Cousin's former students, was serving with Simon on the High Council of Public Instruction and was playing a leading role in the formulation of spiritualistic but confessionally neutral curricula for primary and normal schools. In his book, Janet saluted Cousin as a great thinker, whose mind had indelibly marked several generations of French philosophers. In two sharp articles, written for *Le Journal des débats,* and then in a full-length portrait, *Victor Cousin* (1886), Simon sought to paint a more comprehensive picture of his former teacher.[7]

In 1873, Simon had erected a monument to Cousin in the courtyard of the Sorbonne and praised the man who had thrilled the Liberals of the Restoration with his defense of freedom of thought.[8] By 1886, however, Simon was in a quite different mood. The Victor Cousin of this new series of portraits is a *"petit grand homme,"* a "great man of the second rank."[9] In addition to calling attention to Cousin's eccentricities—his unrequited love for the seventeenth-century Madame de Longueville and his petty, tyrannical relations with academic subordinates—Simon attempted to diminish his reputation as a thinker. As a philosopher, Cousin was "a free spirit if not a very profound intelligence," a professor and orator more than a deep thinker.[10] His philosophic peregrinations ended not in the establishment of a new metaphysical system, but in an appeal to a common sense that verified the basic tenets of the "old faith of our fathers." As Simon explained, Cousin preserved intact "his belief in [rational] dogmas while giving up systematic explanations of them. This I call renouncing metaphysics without renouncing natural religion. It is hardly disguised skepticism concerning systems, a confident and absolute faith in dogmas."[11] This effort to minimize the metaphysical content of the eclectic tradition while insisting on the philosophic validity of the fundamental verities paralleled Simon's arguments during 1881 and 1882 in the debate about "duties toward God and

7. JS, "Variétés. Victor Cousin," *Le Journal des débats,* 12 October 1886; JS, "Variétés. Victor Cousin et son régiment," *Le Journal des débats,* 23 November 1886.
8. *Bulletin administratif de l'Instruction Publique,* 13 March 1873, p. 98.
9. JS, *Victor Cousin,* p. 137.   10. Ibid., pp. 27, 154.
11. Ibid., p. 73.

country." But these views also expressed Simon's sense of the shortcomings of Cousin's work and his uneasiness about its long-range historical significance.

Simon developed this line of thought more fully a few years later in an article in *Le Temps*. The nineteenth century, he wrote, had been an "age of criticism, the aim of which is to explain everything and to destroy everything in the process." In a century of scientific discovery, philosophers had eruditely uncovered and classified much of the philosophic past but had created nothing. Only a comprehensive system, he had come to believe, could have won the allegiance of the age. A few philosophic and literary movements in the century had hinted at the kind of total vision that he felt the nineteenth century had lacked. Indeed, in the first half of the century, romantics and Saint-Simonians had saved French society from skepticism. Cousin's eclectic school had had verve, but its lack of a system had prevented this enthusiasm from producing a real "faith." "The century is impotent," he concluded, "because philosophers no longer create systems." In retrospect, Simon confessed, he would have preferred a century "a little less civilized and a little more *croyant*."[12]

The corollary of Simon's sense of the failure of Cousin's philosophic spiritualism to sink its roots deep into French cultural soil was a more positive assessment of the contribution that Catholicism had made, and might continue to make to a modern culture. In a lucid article entitled "La Morale enseignée aux enfants et aux ignorants," written in late 1894, he praised Ferry for determining that the "old morality of our forefathers" would be taught in public schools. This traditional "universal morality," although not exclusively Catholic, reflected the predominant role that Catholicism had played in French cultural history. It was the product of a dynamic interaction between philosophic principles and Catholicism, for the historic conflicts between freethinkers and Catholics had led to new philosophic insights. Simon, who had formerly conceived of the development of western consciousness as the gradual triumph of a dynamic reason (philosophy) over a static authority (Catholicism), now believed that it was more proper to describe the

12. JS, "Mon Petit Journal," *Le Temps*, 16 August 1891; see also JS, "*L'Année philosophique*, publié sous la direction de M. F. Pillon," *Journal des savants*, July 1895, p. 416.

process in terms of a collaboration between equally necessary progressive and conservative forces. Educators, he urged, should follow the example of history: just as humanity had passed from an age of credulity to an age of reason, so the young should follow a curriculum that gradually moved from a traditional morality enriched by the associations of a Catholic home toward the full development of the rational conscience. From this perspective, Catholicism now appeared to Simon less as the second best moral basis for nineteenth-century republican government than as an indispensable auxiliary of classroom spiritualism. As long as the French masses received little more than a primary education, this tradition would remain a progressive force in French culture and buttress the cause of liberalism against a Jacobin and socialist Left.[13]

Despite this new, especially favorable disposition toward French Catholicism, Simon never abandoned, even in his last years, his highly personal and tempered laicity. This persistent commitment was evident in his response to the Ralliement, the movement inaugurated by Pope Leo XIII and by Cardinal Lavigerie to induce French Catholics to give up their opposition to the Third Republic and to accept unconditionally a republican governmental form that had won the allegiance of most Frenchmen. As one might expect, Simon greeted this new Catholic direction, first expressed by Cardinal Lavigerie in his famous "Algiers Toast" of 12 November 1890, with unqualified approval. Catholics need not be republicans, he interpreted the cardinal's words to mean, but they owed obedience to the established government. The Church's mission was to teach Christian virtue in this life and to work for the salvation of all men in the next. Charged with the administration of divine laws, the clergy did harm to its cause when it set itself in opposition to human laws. Had it not received the command to "render unto Caesar what is Caesar's"?[14] Unlike many Opportunists, who viewed "Ralliés" very distrustfully, Simon welcomed them to the Republic and held out the possibility of an eventual reform of the laic laws in a direction somewhat more favorable to Catholic religious interests. But, with his

13. JS, "La Morale enseignée aux enfants et aux ignorants," *Journal des savants*, October 1894, pp. 624–34. See also JS, *La Femme du vingtième siècle*, pp. 229, 233.

14. JS, "Mon Petit Journal," *Le Temps*, 16, 24 November 1890.

own ingrained anticlericalism, Simon opposed those who would seek to use political action for specifically Catholic ends. The "Ralliés," like other Frenchmen, enjoyed full rights of citizenship. But they should enter the political arena not as Catholics per se, but as liberals determined to oppose both an intolerant Radicalism and a levelling socialism. Thus, Simon enjoined "Ralliés" not to form "leagues, associations committed to realize religious aims by means of political action"; such Catholic organizations as the *Union pour la France chrétienne* would only compromise the cause of religion.[15] For the same reasons, and others related to their particular legal status under the Concordat, priests should avoid all forms of political involvement.[16] The Ralliement, Simon hoped, would open the way not to a Catholic Republic, but to a lay Republic, under God, with liberty of conscience for all.

15. JS, "Mon Petit Journal," *Le Temps*, 6 August 1891; JS, "L'Église et la politique," *Le Petit Marseillais*, 1 April 1892, 87 AP 13 I.
16. JS, "Mon Petit Journal," *Le Temps*, 28 January, 5 February 1892.

Selected Bibliography

I. Primary Sources

A. *Unpublished sources*

1. Archives nationales

F^{17} 21731[2] Remnants of Simon's personal dossier.
++F^{17} 21753 "État des services de . . . Jules Simon."
F^{17} 9172–9197 Municipal options, 1853–1912.
F^{17} 10900 Protests against Martial Delpit legislative proposal, 1871.
F^{18} 341 *L'Écho universel.*
F^{19} 1330–1331* Registers. Archbishops and bishops, 1802–1901.
F^{19} 1332* Political notes on prelates.
F^{19} 1336* Candidacies for the episcopacy, 1855–1905.
F^{19} 1943 Relations between France and Rome during the Third Republic, 1881–1906.
F^{19} 1947 Roman congregations, 1852–1853.
F^{19} 1954–1956 Question of *nobis nominavit.*
F^{19} 2005 Dumay notes.
F^{19} 2452 Personnel: archbishops and bishops, 1776–1901.
F^{19} 2459 Episcopacy: nominations and transfers, 1803–1912.
F^{19} 2479–2596 Episcopacy: personal dossiers.
F^{19} 2609–2610 Personnel: archbishop and bishops. Candidates.
F^{19} 2611–2646 Episcopacy: unsuccessful candidacies.
F^{19} 2655 Desservants, 1839–1881.
F^{19} 3056 Fortuné Frélaut Dossier.
F^{19} 5610 Reports and notes on the attitudes of the episcopacy, 1872–1906.
F^{19} 6529 Note cards on candidates for the episcopacy (early Third Republic).
BB^{18} 1657 Justice. *Bureau des affaires criminelles et correctionnelles* (*Le Phare de la Loire*).
BB^{18} 1786 Justice. Reports of *Procureurs généraux.* Elections of 1869.
C 1144 *Corps législatif* (1870).
C 3129 National Assembly (1871)—Public Instruction.

2. Archives nationales (Archives Privées)

87 AP 1–21 (21 cartons) Jules Simon Papers[1]

1. Although this collection contains much valuable material, it is on the whole disappointing. A substantial portion of Simon's private papers, recording his activities prior to 1875, disappeared during his own lifetime. Simon turned these papers over to Ferdinand Hérold who was planning to use them as the basis of a political biography. After

3. Archives du Ministère des Affaires Étrangères
   Mémoires et documents: Rome. Vols. 115–17, 125.
   Correspondance politique: Rome. Vols. 1048–49.

4. Bibliothèque nationale
   n.a.fr. 12704–12711   Auguste Scheurer-Kestner, "Souvenirs d'un
   républicain alsacien (1833–1899)"
   n.a.fr. 14634–14639   Bernard Lavergne, "Mémoires (1881–1896)"
   n.a.fr. 20621–20628   Adolphe Thiers Papers
   n.a.fr. 24910   Joseph Reinach Papers
   n.a.fr. 25189   Daniel Ollivier Papers

5. Bibliothèque Victor Cousin
   Correspondance de Victor Cousin. 40 vols.
   Marie Arconati-Visconti Papers

6. Archives de l'École normale supérieure
   Director's Reports, 1833–1836

7. Bibliothèque municipale de Versailles
   MS F 757   Ernest Bersot Papers

8. Musée Victor Hugo
   Victor Hugo Papers

9. Institut de France
   MS 3748   Maxime Du Camp Papers, vol. 33
   MS 1577   Jules Simon Papers (Primary Education)

10. Archives de la Préfecture de police
    B A/1270   Jules Simon Dossier

11. Archives de la Mairie du 8ième arrondissement
    "Suisse dit Jules Simon (François Jules). Déclaration des mutations
    par décès, 5 août 1896," fo. 31, ce. 11, #1253

12. Private Papers
    (a) Jean-Philibert Damiron Papers
    (b) Hachette Archives

---

the "16th of May," Hérold joined the militant republican anticlericals
and abandoned the project. Evidently when Hérold died in 1883, he had
not returned the papers to Simon. In 1886, Simon told Léon Séché that
the papers had been lost. For this reason, the extant collection is heavily
weighted toward the 1880s and 1890s. It does, nevertheless, contain some
valuable information on the earlier periods, particularly letters which
Simon wrote as a student, and papers relevant to his work as minister
of public instruction.

B. *Published Writings of Jules Simon*[2]

Simon, Jules. *Études sur la théodicée de Platon et d'Aristote*. Paris: Joubert, 1840.
————, ed. *Oeuvres de Descartes*. Paris: Charpentier, 1842.
————, ed. *Oeuvres philosophiques de Bossuet*. Paris: Charpentier, 1843.

2. Although there is no complete bibliography of Simon's published writings, several bibliographies are extremely helpful. The fullest bibliographical work on Simon is Hugo P. Thième, *Bibliographie de la littérature française de 1800 à 1930* (Paris: E. Droz, 1933), 2:784–87. Rather than duplicate this work, I refer the reader to its excellent bibliographies of Simon's contributions to periodicals and of the secondary periodical literature on Simon. Another important bibliographical aid is Georges Picot, *Institut de France, Jules Simon, notice historique* (Paris: Hachette, 1897), pp. 88–108.

Between 1901 and 1909, the sons of Jules Simon published three "memoirs" under their father's name: *Premières années* (1901), *Le Soir de ma journée* (1901), and *Figures et croquis* (1909). Simon had already published a substantial amount of autobiographical information both as fact and as historically based fiction. The more factual recollections appeared in his articles in *Le Temps* in the 1890s; the more fictional accounts appeared in the form of *contes* such as those published in *Mémoires des autres* (1890), *Nouveaux mémoires des autres* (1891), and *Les Derniers mémoires des autres* (1897). Although these accounts do include many true facts about the author's past, Simon repeatedly stressed that he felt himself bound to tell the "psychological" but not the literal truth. The posthumous works are, for the most part, simply a conglomeration of Simon's earlier more scattered recollections.

Because of the conditions under which they were published, these works are rather unreliable sources. Simon played some role in the conception of *Premières années* and *Le Soir de ma journée*, which are particularly autobiographical. It is more difficult to estimate the role he played in the actual composition of these two works. Two facts, however, do seem certain. First, the tone of these recollections suggests that Simon's purpose was to entertain as much as to inform; he sought to evoke images of a world which, from the vantage point of the 1890s, often seemed centuries removed. These volumes contain none of the historical seriousness which pervades the memoirs of nineteenth-century figures like Guizot, Rémusat, or Albert de Broglie. Second, Simon could not have read the completed manuscript of *Le Soir de ma journée*, and he may not have read the completed version of *Premières années*. In the third work, *Figures et croquis*, Simon had little or no hand. His sons seem to have spliced together remarks on contemporary celebrities which he had made in the 1880s and 1890s in his articles for *Le Temps* and in other articles. Therefore, these works are primarily useful as sources for many potentially verifiable historical clues about the character of Simon's activities.

————, ed. *Oeuvres philosophiques d'Antoine Arnaud*. Paris: Charpentier, 1843.

————. *Histoire de l'École d'Alexandrie*. 2 vols. Paris: Joubert, 1845.

————, ed. *Oeuvres de Malebranche*. 2 vols. Paris: Charpentier, 1846.

————. "A MM. les électeurs de l'arrondissement de Lannion, 20 janvier 1847." Paris, 1846.

————, Jacques, A.; and Saisset, E. *Manuel de philosophie*. Paris: Joubert, 1846.

————. "Aux électeurs des Côtes-du-Nord." Paris, 1848.

————. "A MM. les électeurs des Côtes-du-Nord." Paris, 1849.

————. *Le Devoir*. 2d ed. Paris: Hachette, 1854.

————. *La Religion naturelle*. 2d ed. Paris: Hachette, 1856.

————. "Élections au Corps législatif, 8ᵉ circonscription. Jules Simon, ancien Représentant du peuple, candidat de l'opposition démocratique." Paris, 1857.

————. *La Liberté de conscience*. 2d ed. Paris: Hachette, 1857.

————. *La Liberté*. 2d ed. 2 vols. Paris: Hachette, 1859.

————. *L'Ouvrière*. 2d ed. Paris: Hachette, 1861.

————. "Aux électeurs de la 8ᵉ circonscription. Candidature de Jules Simon." Paris, 1863.

————. *L'École*. Paris: A. Lacroix, Verboeckhoven, 1865.

————. *Le Travail*. Paris: A. Lacroix, Verboeckhoven, 1866.

————. *L'Ouvrier de huit ans*. Paris: A. Lacroix, Verboeckhoven, 1867.

————. *La Politique radicale*. Paris: A. Lacroix, Verboeckhoven, 1868.

————. "Électeurs de la Teste." Bordeaux, 1869.

————. "Aux électeurs de la 8ᵉ circonscription." Paris, 1869.

————. "Lettre sur la situation politique. Jules Simon, Ostende. 10 août, 1869." Bordeaux, 1869.

————. *Grand Orient de France . . . Discours de M. Jules Simon et de . . . F. Bancel*. Paris: Degorce-Cadot, 1869.

————. *La Peine de mort*. Paris: A. Lacroix, Verboeckhoven, 1869.

————. "Circulaire du 2 mai contre le plébiscite." Paris, 1870.

————. "Jules Simon. Candidat libéral de la 3ᵉ circonscription de la Marne." Reims, 1871.

————. "République française. Ministère de l'intérieur. Jules Simon à Jules Favre, 1 mars, 1871." Paris, 1871.

————. *L'Instruction gratuite et obligatoire*. Paris: Bibliothèque démocratique, 1873.

————. *La Réforme de l'enseignement secondaire*. Paris: Hachette, 1874.

————. *Souvenirs du quatre septembre. Le Gouvernement de la défense nationale*. 2d ed. Paris: Michel-Lévy, 1874. 2 vols.

————. Introduction to *Politique et philosophie*, by Frédéric Morin. Paris: G. Baillière, 1876.

————. *Le Gouvernement de M. Thiers, 8 février 1871–24 mai 1873*. 2 vols. Paris: C. Lévy, 1878.

————. *The Government of M. Thiers, from 8 February 1871 to 24 May 1873*. 2 vols. New York: Charles Scribner's Sons, 1879.

————. *Le Livre du petit citoyen*. Paris: Hachette, 1880.

————. *Dieu, patrie, liberté.* 11th ed. Paris: C. Lévy, 1883.
————. *Une Académie sous le Directoire.* Paris: C. Lévy. 1885.
————. *Thiers, Guizot, Rémusat.* Paris: C. Lévy, 1885.
————. *Victor Cousin.* Paris: Hachette, 1887.
————. *Nos hommes d'État.* Paris: C. Lévy, 1887.
————. *Victor Cousin.* Translated by Melville B. and Edward P. Anderson. Chicago: McClurg, 1888.
————. "Un Normalien en 1832." *Revue internationale de l'enseignement* 16:10 (15 October 1888):374–92.
————. *Souviens-toi du deux-décembre.* Paris: V. Havard, 1889.
————. *Mignet, Michelet, Henri Martin.* Paris: C. Lévy, 1890.
————. *Mémoires des autres.* Paris: E. Testard, 1890.
————. *Nouveaux mémoires des autres.* Paris: E. Testard, 1891.
————. *Notices et portraits: Caro, Louis Reybaud, Michel Chevalier, Fustel de Coulanges.* Paris: C. Lévy, 1892.
————, and Simon, Gustave. *La Femme du vingtième siècle.* 3d ed. Paris: C. Lévy, 1892.
————. *Quatre portraits: Lamartine, le cardinal Lavigerie, Ernest Renan, l'empéreur Guillaume II.* Paris: C. Lévy, 1896.
————. *Les Derniers mémoires des autres.* Paris: E. Flammarion, 1897.
————. *Premières années.* Published by Charles Simon and Gustave Simon. Paris: E. Flammarion, 1901.
————. *Le Soir de ma journée.* Completed by Gustave Simon. Paris: E. Flammarion, 1901.
————. *Figures et croquis.* Published by Charles Simon and Gustave Simon. Paris: E. Flammarion, 1909.

Correspondence Published in Periodicals

Le Goffic, Charles. "Les Débuts politiques de Jules Simon." *Revue encyclopédique* 6(1896):421–25.
Gasté, Armand. "Jules Simon. Maître d'études au collège royal de Rennes," *Nouvelle revue* 51:4(15 August 1896):718–20.
Prou-Gaillard, A. "Jules Simon à l'Ecole normale (1833–1834). Lettres intimes de la vingtième année." *Le Correspondant* 185:4(25 November 1896):589–614.
Gasté, Armand. "Jules Simon. Quelques lettres intimes de sa jeunesse (1831–1846)." *Mémoires de l'Académie nationale des sciences, arts et belles-lettres de Caen* 98(1896):251–64.
Chambon, Félix. "Les Correspondants de Victor Cousin. Une Élection en Bretagne en 1847." *L'Amateur d'autographes* (1902), pp. 207–14.
"Jules Simon à M. Hippolyte Tassel (1852)." *Nouvelle revue rétrospective* 18(January–June 1903):285–87.
Aubry, R. "Lettres inédites publiées par R. Aubry." *Le Temps.* 11 July 1903.
————. "Jules Simon et la nomination des évêques (lettres et notes rédigées en 1872 sur la question du *nobis nominavit*)." *Le Temps.* 28 October 1903.

Quentin, Dom Henri. "Autour de Lamennais. Lettres inédites de Béranger, de Jules Simon et de l'abbé Desgenettes." *Revue des sciences religieuses* 9(1929):1–10.
"La Mortalité dans les fabriques et parmi les enfants en nourrice en 1869. Lettre de Jules Simon à un ami belge." *Études et chronique de démographie historique* (1964), pp. 279–80.

C. *Published Sources*

Adam, Juliette. *Après l'abandon de la revanche.* Paris: A. Lemerre, 1910.
———. *Nos amitiés politiques avant l'abandon de la revanche.* 5th ed. Paris: A. Lemerre, 1888.
———. *Mes angoisses et nos luttes.* 4th ed. Paris: A. Lemerre, 1907.
———. *Mes illusions et nos souffrances.* 6th ed. Paris: A. Lemerre, 1906.
———. *Mes premières armes littéraires et politiques.* 8th ed. Paris: A. Lemerre, 1904.
———. *Mes sentiments et nos idées avant 1870.* 6th ed. Paris: A Lemerre, 1905.
Agoult, Marie d'. *Daniel Stern. Lettres républicaines du Second Empire. Documents inédits.* Paris: Éditions du Cèdre, 1951.
Allain-Targé, Henri. "Autour du 19 janvier. Tiers parti et opposition républicaine (Fragments inédits de la correspondance d'Allain-Targé)." *Revue historique* 179(January–March 1937):135–45.
———. *La République sous l'Empire; lettres, 1864–1870.* Edited by Suzanne de la Porte. Paris: B. Grasset, 1939.
———. "Souvenirs d'avant 1870." *Revue de Paris* 5:17(1 September 1903):5–16.
Barbey d'Aurevilly, Jules. *XIXe siècle. Les Oeuvres et les hommes.* Paris: Amyot, 1860.
———. *Polémiques d'hier.* Paris: A. Savine, 1889.
Bersot, Ernest. *La Correspondance de Voltaire.* Paris: Pillet fils ainé, 1857.
———. *Essais de philosophie et de morale.* 2 vols. Paris: Didier, 1864.
———. *Études sur le XVIIIe siècle.* 2 vols. Paris: A. Durand, 1855.
———. *La Philosophie de Voltaire.* Paris: Ladrange, 1848.
Broglie, Albert de. *Mémoires du Duc de Broglie, 1821–1901.* 2 vols. Paris: C. Lévy, 1938–1941.
Cambon, Paul. *Correspondance, 1870–1924.* 3 vols. Paris: B. Grasset, 1940–1946.
Cartault, Auguste. "Publicistes français contemporains. M. Jules Simon." *Revue politique et littéraire.* 2d series, 14:42(20 April 1878):981–89.
Castelnau, Michel de. *Essai critique sur "la Religion naturelle" de M. Jules Simon.* Paris: V. Sarlit, 1858.
Catalogue de la Bibliothèque de feu M. Jules Simon. 2 vols. Paris: Em. Paul et fils et Guillemin, 1902.
Clamadieu, Abbé J.-A. *Jules Simon.* Paris: Delagrave, 1896.
Clamageran, Jean-Jules. *Correspondance (1849–1902).* Paris: F. Alcan, 1906.

Claretie, Jules. *Portraits contemporains*. 2 vols. Paris: F. Polo, 1873–1875.

———. *La Vie à Paris, 1896*. Paris: G. Charpentier & Fasquelle, 1897.

Claveau, Anatole. *Souvenirs politiques et parlementaires*. Paris: Plon-Nourrit, 1913–1914.

Cochin, Augustin. *Augustin Cochin, 1823–1872. Ses lettres et sa vie*. Edited by Henry Cochin. 2 vols. Paris: Bloud & Gay, 1926.

Coignet, Clarisse. *Rapport présenté au nom de la Commission des dames chargée d'examiner les questions relatives à la réforme de l'instruction primaire*. Paris: P. Dupont, 1871.

Comte, Auguste. *Cours de philosophie positive*. 6 vols. Paris: Bachelier, 1830–1842.

———. *A General View of Positivism*. Translated by J. H. Bridges. Dubuque, Iowa: William C. Brown Reprint Library, 1971.

Cormenin, Louis de. "A MM. les électeurs de l'arrondissement de Lannion, 14 février 1847." Paris, 1847.

Cousin, Victor. *Cours de l'histoire de la philosophie moderne*. 5 vols. Paris: Pichon & Didier, 1846.

———. *Fragments philosophiques*. 3d ed. 2 vols. Paris: Ladrange, 1838.

———. *Du Vrai, du beau et du bien*. Paris: Didier, 1853.

Crémieux, Adolphe. *Gouvernement de la Défense nationale. Première partie. Actes de la Délégation à Tours et à Bordeaux*. Tours: E. Mazereau, 1871.

Darimon, Alfred. *Histoire d'un parti. Les Cinq sous l'Empire (1857–1860)*. Paris: E. Dentu, 1885.

———. *Histoire d'un parti. Le Tiers parti sous l'Empire (1863–1866)*. Paris: E. Dentu, 1885.

———. *L'Opposition libérale sous l'Empire (1861–1863)*. Paris: E. Dentu, 1886.

Daudet, Ernest. *Jules Simon*. Paris, A. Quantin, 1883.

Delord, Taxile. *Histoire illustrée du Second Empire*. 6 vols. Paris: G. Baillière, 1880–1883.

Deschamps, Nicolas. *Le Monopole universitaire*. Lyons: Librairie chrétienne, 1843.

Deschanel, Émile, *Les Conférences à Paris et en France*. Paris: Pagnerre, 1870.

Des Michels, Jules-Alexis. *Souvenirs de carrière (1855–1886)*. Paris: Plon-Nourrit, 1901.

Dictionnaire des sciences philosophiques. Adolphe Franck, ed. 6 vols. Paris: Hachette, 1844–1852.

Dictionnaire général de la politique. Maurice Block. 2d ed. (original edition, 1863–1864). 2 vols. Paris: O. Lorenz, 1880.

Dréo, Amaury. *Gouvernement de la Défense nationale, 4 septembre 1870–16 février 1871. Procès-verbaux des séances du conseil. Publiés d'après les manuscrits originaux de M. A. Dréo*. Edited by Henri Des Houx. Paris: Charles-Lavauzelle, 1905.

Du Camp, Maxime. *Souvenirs littéraires*. 2 vols. Paris: Hachette, 1883.

"Élections de Lannion. Pas de fonctionnaires publics à la Chambre." Paris, 1847.

Fage, Émile. *Causeries limousines*. Paris: P. Ollendorf, 1889.

Falloux, Alfred de. *Augustin Cochin*. Translated by Augustus Craven. London: Chapman & Hall, 1877.

Favre, Jules. *Gouvernement de la Défense nationale du 31 octobre au 28 janvier 1871*. 2 vols. Paris: Plon, 1872.

Féré, Octave. *M. Jules Simon. Oui ou non?* Paris: E. Dentu, 1868.

Ferrari, Joseph. *Les Philosophes salariés*. Paris: G. Sandré, 1849.

Ferry, Jules. *Discours et opinions de Jules Ferry*. Edited by Paul Robiquet. 7 vols. Paris: A. Colin, 1893–1898.

——. *Lettres de Jules Ferry, 1846–1893*. Edited by Eugène Jules-Ferry. Paris: C. Lévy, 1914.

Gambetta, Léon. *Discours et plaidoyers politiques de M. Gambetta*. Edited by Joseph Reinach. 11 vols. Paris: G. Charpentier, 1880–1885.

——. *Lettres de Gambetta, 1868–1882*. Edited by Daniel Halévy and Émile Pillias. Paris: B. Grasset, 1938.

Goncourt, Edmond de and Goncourt, Jules de. *Journal*. Edited by Robert Ricatte. 4 vols. Paris: Fasquelle, 1959.

Gréard, Octave. *La Législation de l'instruction primaire en France depuis 1789 jusqu'à nos jours*. 3 vols. Paris: C. de Mourgues frères, 1874.

Halévy, Ludovic. *Carnets*. 2 vols. Paris: C. Lévy, 1935.

——. *Trois dîners avec Gambetta*. Paris: B. Grasset, 1929.

Haussonville, Joseph Othenin de. *Souvenirs et mélanges*. Paris: C. Lévy, 1878.

Hérault, Alfred. "Les Derniers jours du cabinet Dufaure." *Revue de Paris* 3(1 June 1930):498–521.

——. "Le Ministère de Jules Simon." *Revue de Paris* 3(15 June 1930): 883–910.

Hugo, Victor. *Les Châtiments*. 5th ed. Paris: J. Hetzel, 1870.

Hulst, Mgr. Maurice d'. *Les Maires et les écoles pendant le siège*. Paris: C. Douniol, 1870.

Janet, Paul. *La Crise philosophique*. Paris: G. Baillière, 1865.

——. "Un républicain de la veille; Michel de Bourges." *Revue politique et littéraire*, 2d series, 18:42(17 April 1880):981–91.

——. *Victor Cousin et son oeuvre*. Paris: C. Lévy, 1885.

Lacombe, Charles de. *Journal politique de Charles de Lacombe*. Edited by A. Hélot. 2 vols. Paris: A. Picard & fils, 1907–1908.

Lavergne, Bernard. *Les Deux présidences de Jules Grévy, 1879–1887*. Paris: Fischbacher, 1966.

Lavertujon, André. *Gambetta inconnu: cinq mois de la vie intime de Gambetta*. Bordeaux: G. Gounouilhou, 1905.

Levallois, Jules. "Souvenirs littéraires." *Revue politique et littéraire*, 4th series, 3:11(16 March 1895):327–32.

"Liste d'adhésion au principe de l'instruction gratuite et obligatoire soumise par M. Jules Simon aux délibérations du Corps législatif." Strasbourg, 1871.

Littré, Émile. *Conservation, révolution et positivisme*. Paris: Ladrange, 1852.

——. *De l'Établissement de la troisième République*. Paris: Bureaux de "la Philosophie positive," 1880.

Madelin, Louis. "Les Mémoires de Jules Simon." *Revue des Deux Mondes* 1(1 January 1910):216–28.

Manuel, Eugène. "Jules Simon." *La Vie contemporaine* (13 June 1896): 526–27.

Marcère, Émile de. *L'Assemblée nationale de 1871.* 2 vols. Paris: Plon-Nourrit, 1904.

Meaux, Camille de. *Souvenirs politiques, 1871–1877.* Paris: Plon-Nourrit, 1905.

Mémorial de l'association amicale des anciens élèves de l'École normale (1846–1876). Versailles, 1877.

Meyer, Arthur. *Ce que mes yeux ont vu.* Paris: Plon-Nourrit, 1911.

Michelet, Jules. *La Bible de l'Humanité.* Paris: F. Chamerot, 1864.

———. *Histoire de France.* Edited by Claude Mettra. 18 vols. Lausanne: Éditions Rencontre, 1965–1967.

———. *Lettres inédites à Alfred Dumesnil et à Eugène Noël (1841–1871).* Edited by Paul Sirven. Paris: Presses Universitaires de France, 1924.

———. *Le Prêtre, la femme et la famille.* 7th ed. Paris: F. Chamerot, 1861.

Michelet, Jules and Quinet, Edgar. *Les Jésuites.* Paris: Hachette & Paulin, 1843.

Morin, Frédéric. *Les Hommes et les livres contemporains.* Paris: Michel-Lévy, 1862.

———. *Les Idées du temps présent.* Paris: Michel-Lévy, 1863.

Nisard, Désiré. *Souvenirs et notes biographiques.* 2 vols. Paris: C. Lévy, 1888.

Noël, Eugène. "Variétés. Opinion de Michelet sur Jésus en 1854." *Revue politique et littéraire,* 4th series, 3:23(8 June 1895):731–32.

Nourrisson, Jean. *Voltaire et le voltairianisme.* Paris: P. Lethielleux, 1896.

Pessard, Hector. *Mes petits papiers, 1860–1870.* 2 vols. Paris: C. Lévy, 1887–1888.

Peyrat, Alphonse. *Études historiques et religieuses.* Paris: Michel-Lévy, 1863.

———. *Histoire élémentaire et critique de Jésus.* Paris: Michel-Lévy, 1864.

———. *Histoire et religion.* Paris: Michel-Lévy, 1858.

Philibert-Soupé, Alfred. "Portraits d'Académiques. Jules Simon." *Revue du siècle* 10(July 1896):365–85.

Poitou, Eugène. *Les Philosophes français contemporains et leurs systèmes religieux.* Paris: Charpentier, 1864.

Procès-verbaux du Comité du travail à l'assemblée constituante de 1848. Paris: Bibliothèque de la "Révolution de 1848," 1908.

"Procès-verbaux inédits de la Commission de l'enseignement." *Le Correspondant* 114:5–6(10, 25 March 1879):814–42, 984–1031.

Quinet, Edgar. *Lettres d'exil à Michelet et à divers amis.* 4 vols. Paris: C. Lévy, 1885–1886.

Quinet, Mme. Edgar. *Cinquante ans d'amitié. Michelet-Quinet, 1825–1875.* Paris: A. Colin, 1899.

————. *Mémoires d'exil*, n.s. Paris: A. Le Chevalier, 1878.

Ranc, Arthur. *Souvenirs-correspondance, 1831–1908*. Paris: E. Cornély, 1913.

Raphael, Paul. "Trois lettres inédites de Jules Ferry." *Revue historique* 109(January–February 1912):85–86.

Reinach, Joseph. *Récits et portraits contemporains*. Paris: F. Alcan, 1915.

Rémusat, Charles de. *Mémoires de ma vie*. Edited by Charles Pouthas. 5 vols. Paris: Plon, 1958–1967.

Renan, Ernest. *Oeuvres complètes*. Edited by Henriette Psichari. 10 vols. Paris: C. Lévy, 1947–1961.

Rendu, Eugène. *L'Instruction primaire devant l'Assemblée nationale*. Paris: Hachette, 1873.

Richer, Léon. *Lettres d'un libre-penseur à un curé de village*. 2 vols. Paris: A. Le Chevalier, 1868–1869.

Rousse, Edmond. *Lettres à un ami*. 2 vols. Paris: Hachette, 1900.

Rousset, Gustave. *Code général des lois sur la presse*. Paris: Cosse, Marchal, 1869.

Senior, Nassau. *Conversations with Distinguished Persons during the Second Empire from 1860 to 1863*. Edited by M. C. M. Simpson. 2 vols. London: Hurst & Blackett, 1880.

Silvy, Auguste. *La Délégation du Ministère de l'Instruction publique à Tours et à Bordeaux. Compte rendu présenté à M. le Ministre de l'Instruction publique, des Cultes et des Beaux-Arts*. Paris: Imprimerie nationale, 1872.

Simon, Gustave. "Jules Simon: notes et souvenirs (Documents inédits), Partie I." *La Revue mondiale* 169:4(15 February 1926):339–49.

————. "Jules Simon: notes et souvenirs (Documents inédits), Parties II-V." *La Revue mondiale*, vol. 170, nos. 5–8(1, 15 March, 1, 15 April 1926):3–16, 113–27, 211–18, 315–22.

Spuller, Eugène. "M. Thiers et M. Jules Simon." *Revue politique et littéraire*, 3d series, 8:20(15 November 1884):609–14.

Taine, Hippolyte. *Essai sur Tite Live*. Paris: Hachette, 1856.

————. *H. Taine, sa vie et sa correspondance*. 4 vols. 2d ed. Paris: Hachette, 1902–1907.

————. *Les Philosophes français du dix-neuvième siècle*. Paris: Hachette, 1857.

Thiers, Adolphe. *Le Courrier de M. Thiers*. Edited by Daniel Halévy. Paris: Payot, 1921.

————. *Thiers au pouvoir (1871–1873)*. Edited by Gaston Bouniols. Paris: Delagrave, 1921.

Tridon, Gustave. *Oeuvres diverses*. Paris: J. Allemane, 1891.

Vacherot, Étienne. *Essais de philosophie critique*. Paris: F. Chamerot, 1864.

————. *La Religion*. Paris: Chamerot & Lauwereyns, 1869.

Vermorel, Auguste. *Biographies contemporaines. M. Jules Simon, avec un portrait*. Paris: Administration des biographies contemporaines, 1869.

Voltaire. *Oeuvres complètes de Voltaire*. Edited by Georges Avenel and Émile de La Bédollière. 8 vols. Paris: Le Siècle, 1867–1870.

D. *Periodical Literature*

1. Newspapers

L'Avenir national
Le Constitutionnel
Le Dix-neuvième siècle
L'Écho universel
Le Français
Le Gaulois
La Gironde
Le Journal
Le Journal des débats
Le Matin
Le Moniteur universel
Le National
Le Pays
La Presse
La République française
Le Siècle
Le Temps
L'Univers

2. Journals

L'Avenir, Revue hebdomadaire des lettres et des arts
Bulletin administratif de l'Instruction Publique
Contemporary Review
Le Correspondant
L'Illustration
L'Instruction Publique
Journal des savants
Le Journal pour tous
La Liberté de penser
Le Libre conscience
La Libre recherche
La Morale indépendante
La Philosophie positive
Revue encyclopédique
Revue de famille
Revue de l'Instruction Publique
Revue de Paris
Revue des cours littéraires de la France et de l'étranger
Revue des Deux Mondes
Revue du lyonnais
Revue germanique
Revue illustrée de Bretagne et d'Anjou
Revue internationale de l'enseignement

Revue nouvelle
Revue philosophique et religieuse
Revue politique et littéraire
La Vie contemporaine
Whitehall Review

II. Secondary Sources

A. Books

Acomb, Evelyn. *The French Laic Laws (1879–1889). The First Anticlerical Campaign of the Third French Republic.* New York: Columbia University Press, 1941.

Aquarone, Stanislas. *Life and Works of Emile Littré (1801–1881).* Leyden: Sythoff, 1958.

Avenel, Henri. *Histoire de la presse française depuis 1789 jusqu'à nos jours.* Paris: E. Flammarion, 1900.

Bastid, Paul. *Un Juriste pamphlétaire. Cormenin, précurseur et constituant de 1848.* Paris: Hachette, 1948.

Bellanger, Claude, et al. *Histoire générale de la presse française.* 5 vols. Paris: Presses Universitaires de France, 1969–1976.

Bloch, Maurice. *Trois éducateurs alsaciens.* Paris: Hachette, 1911.

Boutmy, Émile. *Taine, Schérer, Laboulaye.* Paris: A Colin, 1901.

Brabant, Frank. *The Beginnings of the Third Republic in France.* London: Macmillan, 1940.

Brown, Marvin. *Louis Veuillot: French Ultramontane Journalist and Layman, 1813–1883.* Durham, N.C.: Moore Publishing Company, 1977.

Bury, J. P. T. *Gambetta and the National Defence.* London: Longmans & Green, 1936.

———. *Gambetta and the Making of the Third Republic.* London: Longman, 1973.

Canivez, André. *Jules Lagneau, professeur de philosophie: essai sur la condition du professeur de philosophie jusqu'à la fin du XIXᵉ siècle.* 2 vols. Paris: Les Belles Lettres, 1965.

Capéran, Louis. *Histoire contemporaine de la laïcité française.* 2 vols. Paris: Rivière, 1957–1960.

———. *Histoire de la laïcité républicaine. La laïcité en marche.* Paris: Rivière, 1961.

Chadwick, Owen. *The Secularization of the European Mind in the Nineteenth Century.* New York, Cambridge: Cambridge University Press, 1975.

Charlton, Donald. *Positivist Thought in France during the Second Empire, 1852–1870.* Oxford: Clarendon, 1959.

———. *Secular Religions in France, 1815–1870.* London: Oxford University Press, 1963.

Chastenet, Jacques. *Cent ans de République.* 9 vols. Paris: Tallandier, 1970.

Chevrillon, André. *Taine: formation de sa pensée.* Paris: Plon, 1932.

Chapman, Guy. *The Third Republic of France. The First Phase, 1871–1894.* London: Macmillan, 1962.

Collins, Irene. *The Government and the Newspaper Press in France, 1814–1881*. London: Oxford University Press, 1959.

Commission internationale et sous-commission française d'histoire ecclésiastique comparée. *Colloque d'histoiré religieuse (Lyon, octobre 1963)*. Grenoble: Allier, 1963.

Cresson, André. *Hippolyte Taine, sa vie, son oeuvre*. Paris: Presses Universitaires de France, 1951.

Dansette, Adrien. *Histoire religieuse de la France contemporaine*. 2d ed. Paris: Flammarion, 1965.

DeLuna, Frederick. *The French Republic under Cavaignac, 1848*. Princeton: Princeton University Press, 1969.

Dictionnaire biographique du mouvement ouvrier français, Jean Maîtron, ed. 14 vols. Paris: Éditions ouvrières, 1964.

Dide, Auguste. *Jules Barni: sa vie et ses oeuvres*. 2d ed. Paris: F. Alcan, 1892.

Dresse, Paul. *Léon Daudet vivant*. Paris: Laffont, 1948.

Dufeuille, Eugène. *L'Anticléricalisme avant et pendant notre République*. Paris: C. Lévy, 1911.

Duroselle, Jean-Baptiste. "Arnaud de l'Ariège et la démocratie chrétienne (1848–1851)." Complementary thesis, Faculty of Letters of the University of Paris, 1949.

————. *Les Débuts du catholicisme social en France, 1822–1870*. Paris: Presses Universitaires de France, 1951.

Duveau, Georges. *Les Instituteurs*. Paris: Éditions du Seuil, 1957.

————. *La Pensée ouvrière sur l'éducation pendant la Seconde République et le Second Empire*. Paris: Domat-Montchrestien, 1948.

Eisenstein, Hester. "Victor Cousin and the War on the University of France." Ph.D. dissertation, Yale University, 1967.

Falcucci, Clément. *L'Humanisme dans l'enseignement secondaire en France au XIXe siècle*. Toulouse: E. Privat, 1939.

Flint, Robert. *Historical Philosophy in France*. Edinburgh: W. Blackwood & Sons, 1893.

Foisset, Théophile. *Vie du R.P. Lacordaire*. 2 vols. Paris: J. Lecoffre, Lecoffre fils, 1870.

Gadille, Jacques. *La Pensée et l'action politique des évêques français au début de la IIIe République, 1870–1883*. 2 vols. Paris: Hachette, 1967.

Gaumont, Jean. *Histoire générale de la coopération en France*. 2 vols. Paris: Fédération nationale des coopératives de consommation, 1923–1924.

Gay, Peter. *The Party of Humanity*. New York: W. W. Norton Co., 1971.

Gerbod, Paul. *La Condition universitaire*. Paris: Presses Universitaires de France, 1965.

————. *Paul-François Dubois, universitaire, journaliste et homme politique, 1793–1874*. Paris: C. Klincksieck, 1967.

Gimpl, Sister M. Caroline Ann. *The "Correspondant" and the Founding of the French Third Republic*. Washington, D. C.: Catholic University of America Press, 1959.

Giraud, Victor. *Essai sur Taine, son oeuvre et son influence*. 7th ed. Paris: Hachette, 1932.

232/Jules Simon

Gontard, Maurice. *Les Écoles primaires de la France bourgeoise (1833–1875)*. Toulouse: Institut pédagogique national, 1965.

Gouault, Jacques. *Comment la France est devenue républicaine; les élections générales et partielles à l'Assemblée nationale, 1870–1875*. Paris: Colin, 1954.

Griffiths, David. *Jean Reynaud, encyclopédiste de l'époque romantique*. Paris: Rivière, 1965.

Grimaud, Louis. *Histoire de la liberté d'enseignement en France*. 6 vols. Grenoble: Arthaud, 1944.

Grubb, Charles Alan. "The Politics of Pessimism: A Political Biography of Duc Albert de Broglie during the Early Third Republic, 1871–1885." Ph.D. dissertation, Columbia University, 1969.

Guérard, Albert. *French Prophets of Yesterday: A Study of Religious Thought under the Second Empire*. New York: Unwin, 1913.

Guillemin, Henri. *Les Origines de la Commune*. 3 vols. Paris: Gallimard, 1956–1960.

Guiral, Pierre. *Prévost-Paradol; pensée et action d'un libéral sous le Second Empire*. Paris: Presses Universitaires de France, 1955.

Halévy, Daniel. *La Fin des notables*. Paris: B. Grasset, 1930.

———. *La République des ducs*. Paris: B. Grasset, 1937.

Hanotaux, Gabriel. *Histoire de la France contemporaine (1871–1900)*. 4 vols. Paris: Combet, 1903–1908.

Hatin, Eugène. *Bibliographie historique et critique de la presse périodique française*. Paris: Firmin Didot frères, fils, 1866.

Headings, Mildred J. *French Freemasonry under the Third Republic*. Baltimore: The Johns Hopkins University Press, 1949.

Hémon, Félix. *Bersot et ses amis*. Paris: Hachette, 1911.

Himmelfarb, Gertrude. *On Liberty and Liberalism. The Case of John Stuart Mill*. New York: Knopf, 1974.

Isambert, François André. *Christianisme et classe ouvrière*. Tournai: Casterman, 1961.

Joughin, Jean. *The Paris Commune in French Politics, 1871–1880: The History of the Amnesty of 1880*. 2 vols. Baltimore: The Johns Hopkins University Press, 1955.

Krakowski, Édouard. *La Naissance de la IIIe République: Challemel-Lacour, le philosophe et l'homme d'état*. Paris: V. Attinger, 1932.

Lagrange, François. *Vie de Mgr. Dupanloup, évêque d'Orléans*. 3 vols. Paris: Poussielgue frères, 1883–1884.

Langlois, Claude. *Un Diocèse breton au début du XIXe siècle*. Paris: Klincksieck, 1974.

Larkin, Maurice. *Church and State after the Dreyfus Affair: The Separation Issue in France*. London: Macmillan, 1974.

Latreille, André and Rémond, René. *Histoire du Catholicisme en France*. 3 vols. Paris: Éditions Spec, 1957–1962.

Lecanuet, Édouard. *Les Dernières années du Pontificat de Pie IX, 1870–1878*. 2d ed. Paris: F. Alcan, 1931.

———. *Les Premières années du Pontificat de Léon XIII, 1878–1894*. Paris: F. Alcan, 1931.

Legrand, Louis. *L'Influence du positivisme dans l'oeuvre scolaire de Jules Ferry; les origines de la laïcité.* Paris: Rivière, 1961.

Liébard, Th. *Jules Simon et la Bretagne.* Paimboeuf: Coyaud, 1902.

McKay, Donald. *The National Workshops: A Study in the French Revolution of 1848.* Cambridge, Mass.: Harvard University Press, 1933.

McManners, John. *Church and State in France, 1870–1914.* New York: Harper & Row, 1972.

Manuel, Frank. *The Prophets of Paris.* New York: Harper & Row, 1965.

Martin, René. *La Vie d'un grand journaliste, Auguste Nefftzer, fondateur de la "Revue germanique" et du "Temps."* 2 vols. Besançon: Camponovo, 1948–1953.

Maurain, Jean. *La Politique ecclésiastique du Second Empire de 1852 à 1869.* Paris: F. Alcan, 1930.

Monod, Gabriel. *Michelet, sa vie et son oeuvre.* Paris: Hachette, 1905.

———. *Renan, Taine, Michelet.* Paris: C. Lévy, 1894.

Moody, Joseph N. *The Church as Enemy: Anticlericalism in Nineteenth Century French Literature.* Washington, D. C.: Corpus Publications, 1968.

Ollé-Laprune, Léon. *Étienne Vacherot, 1809–1897.* 2d ed. Paris: Perrin, 1898.

Ozouf, Mona. *L'École, l'Église et la République, 1871–1914.* Paris: A. Colin, 1963.

Paguelle de Follenay, Joseph. *Vie du Cardinal Guibert.* 2 vols. Paris: C. Poussielgue, 1896.

Pisani-Ferry, Fresnette. *Le Coup d'état manqué du 16 mai 1877.* Paris: Laffont, 1965.

Planat de la Faye, Mme. Frédérique. *Vie de Planat de la Faye.* Paris: P. Ollendorf, 1895.

Pommier, Jean. *Deux études sur Jouffroy et son temps.* Paris: F. Alcan, 1930.

Powers, Richard. *Edgar Quinet: A Study in French Patriotism.* Dallas: Southern Methodist University Press, 1957.

Prost, Antoine. *Histoire de l'enseignement en France, 1800–1967.* Paris: A. Colin, 1968.

Reclus, Maurice. *Jules Favre, 1809–1880.* Paris: Hachette, 1912.

———. *Jules Ferry, 1832–1893.* Paris: Flammarion, 1947.

———. *Le Seize mai.* Paris: Hachette, 1936.

Rémond, René. *L'Anticléricalisme en France de 1815 à nos jours.* Paris: Fayard, 1976.

Roux, Marie de. *Origines et fondation de la Troisième République.* Paris: B. Grasset, 1933.

Scott, John. *Republican Ideas and the Liberal Tradition in France, 1870–1914.* New York: Columbia University Press, 1951.

Séché, Léon. *Jules Simon; sa vie et son oeuvre.* Paris: A. Dupret, 1887.

———. *Jules Simon. Souvenirs personnels.* Rennes: Simon, 1903.

Sedgwick, Alexander. *The Ralliement in French Politics, 1890–1898.* Cambridge, Mass.: Harvard University Press, 1965.

Sève, Lucien. *La Philosophie française contemporaine et sa genèse de 1789 à nos jours.* Paris: Éditions sociales, 1962.

Simon, Walter. *European Positivism in the Nineteenth Century.* Ithaca, N.Y.: Cornell University Press, 1963.

Sociologie électorale. François Goguel and Georges Dupeux, eds. Paris: A. Colin, 1951.

Soltau, Roger. *French Political Thought in the Nineteenth Century.* New Haven, Conn.: Yale University Press, 1931.

Sorlin, Pierre. *Waldeck-Rousseau.* Paris: A. Colin, 1966.

Spencer, Philip. *Politics of Belief in Nineteenth-Century France; Lacordaire, Michon, Veuillot.* London: Faber & Faber, 1954.

Tchernoff, Iouda. *Le Parti républicain sous la Monarchie de Juillet; formation et évolution de la doctrine républicaine.* Paris: A. Pedone, 1901.

———. *Le Parti républicain au coup d'état et sous le Second Empire.* Paris: A. Pedone, 1906.

Telzrow, Thomas M. "The 'Watchdogs': French Academic Philosophy in the Nineteenth Century. The Case of Paul Janet." Ph.D. dissertation, University of Wisconsin, 1973.

Touchard, Jean. *Histoire des idées politiques.* 2 vols. Paris: Presses Universitaires de France, 1963–1965.

Vandam, Albert. *Men and Manners of the Third Republic.* London: Chapman & Hall, 1904.

Vier, Jacques. *La Comtesse d'Agoult et son temps.* 6 vols. Paris: A. Colin, 1955–1964.

Watson, David R. *Georges Clemenceau: A Political Biography.* London: Eyre Methuen, 1974.

Weill, Georges. *L'École Saint-Simonienne, son histoire, son influence jusqu'à nos jours.* Paris: F. Alcan, 1896.

———. *Histoire de l'idée laïque au XIXᵉ siècle.* Paris: F. Alcan, 1925.

———. *Histoire du parti républicain en France de 1814 à 1870.* 2d ed. Paris: F. Alcan, 1928.

Zeldin, Theodore, et al. *Conflicts in French Society: Anticlericalism, Education and Morals in the Nineteenth Century.* London: Allen & Unwin, 1970.

———. *Emile Ollivier and the Liberal Empire of Napoleon III.* Oxford: Clarendon Press, 1963.

———. *France, 1848–1945. Ambition, Love and Politics.* Vol. I. Oxford: Clarendon Press, 1973.

———. *France, 1848–1945.* 2 vols. Oxford: Clarendon Press, 1973–1977.

Zévaès, Alexandre. *Au temps du seize mai.* Paris: Éditions des portiques, 1932.

B. *Articles*

Allanic, Jean. "Histoire du Collège de Vannes (suite et fin)." *Annales de Bretagne* 18:2(January 1903):234–75.

Auriac, Jules d'. "Jules Simon improvisateur." *La Révolution de 1848* 17(1920–1921):104–15.

Bertocci, Philip A. "Positivism, French Republicanism and the Politics of Religion, 1848–1883." *Third Republic/Troisième République*, no. 2(Fall 1976):182–227.

Besner, A. "L'Esprit public dans un département Breton en 1848." *Nouvelle revue de Bretagne* 2:2(March–April):83–90.

Clarac, Pierre. "Jules Simon en 1871." *Institut de France. Académie des sciences morales et politiques*, no. 30(1971):1–15.

Debauve, Jean-Louis. "Les Origines de Jules Simon." *Bulletin mensuel la Société polymathique du Morbihan*, 1957, pp. 111–18.

————. "Bretons et Parisiens en 1870. Pages oubliées de Jules Simon." *Bulletin mensuel de la Société polymathique du Morbihan*, 1972, pp. 100–103.

Dietz, Jean. "Les Débuts de Jules Ferry." *Revue de France*, 5:19, 20 (1, 15 October 1932):501–21, 608–27.

————. "Jules Ferry et les débuts de la Troisième République." *La Grande Revue* 139:10(October 1932):550–72.

————. "Jules Ferry et les traditions républicaines." *Revue politique et parlementaire*, 159, no. 475(10 June 1934):521–32; 160, nos. 476–78(10 July, 10 August, 10 September 1934):100–111, 297–311, 495–512; 161, nos. 479, 481(10 October, 10 December 1934):122–41, 492–505.

Dupront, A. "Jules Ferry opposant à l'Empire. Quelques traits de son idéologie républicaine." *Revue historique* 177(March–April 1936):352–74.

Eros, John. "The Positivist Generation of French Republicanism." *Sociological Review* 3:2(December 1955):255–77.

Gadille, Jacques. "La Politique de défense républicaine à l'égard de l'Église de France (1876–1883)." *Bulletin de la Société d'histoire moderne*, no. 1(1967):2–9.

Goldstein, Doris. "'Official Philosophies' in Modern France: The Example of Victor Cousin." *Journal of Social History* 1:2(Spring 1968):259–79.

Gontard, Maurice. "Une Bataille scolaire au XIXᵉ siècle; l'affaire des écoles primaires laïques de Lyon (1869–1873)." *Cahiers d'histoire* 3:3 (1958):269–94.

Guiral, Pierre. "Note sur l'anticléricalisme des Saint-Simoniens. *Archives de sociologie des religions* 5:10(July–December 1960):31–40.

————. "Quelques notes sur le retour de faveur de Voltaire sous le Second Empire." *Hommage au Doyen Étienne Gros*, Gap, Louis-Jean (1959), pp. 193–204.

Larkin, Maurice. "The Church and the French Concordat, 1891 to 1902." *The English Historical Review* 81:321(October 1966):717–39.

Liard, Louis. "Notice sur la vie et les oeuvres de M. Jules Simon." *Mémoires de l'Académie des sciences morales et politiques* 21(1898):621–52.

Monin, Hippolyte. "La Dernière leçon de Jules Simon en Sorbonne (décembre, 1851)." *La Révolution de 1848* 3(March–April, May–June 1906):43–52, 115–17.

Monod, Gabriel. "Les Débuts d'Alphonse Peyrat dans la critique historique." *Revue historique* 96(1908):1–49.

Moody, Joseph N. "French Anticlericalism: Image and Reality." *Catholic Historical Review* 51:4(January 1971):630–48.

Oheix, André. "Un Coin de bibliographie simonienne, Jules Simon au *Journal pour tous.*" *Revue historique de l'Ouest* 13(1897):139–57.

Ollivro, Édouard. "Jules Simon, candidat malheureux à Lannion en 1847," *Nouvelle revue de Bretagne* 1:5(September–October 1947): 338–42.

Pichois, Claude. "Voltaire devant le XIXᵉ siècle." *L'École* 43(16 February 1952):346, 351–52.

Pommier, Jean. "Les Idées de Michelet et de Renan sur la confession en 1845." *Journal de psychologie normale et pathologique* 33:71:8 (15 July–15 October 1936):514–44.

———. "Victor Cousin et ses élèves vers 1840." *Revue d'histoire et de philosophie religieuse* 11(July–October 1931):386–408.

Poulat, Émile. "Socialisme et anticléricalisme. Une Enquête socialiste internationale (1902–1903)." *Archives de sociologie des religions* 10 (July–December 1960):109–31.

Pouthas, Charles. "Le Collège Royal de Caen sous l'administration de l'abbé Daniel." *Mémoires de l'Académie nationale des sciences, arts et belles-lettres de Caen* 107(1905):147–219.

Pozzi, Regina. "Un Episodio della lotta ideologica in Francia sotto la Seconda Repubblica. La Liberté de Penser (1847–1850)." *Critica storica* 5:1(31 January 1966):62–103.

Pradon, Jacques. "L'École du *Correspondant.*" *Revue internationale d'histoire politique et constitutionnelle*, n.s., no. 18 (April–June 1955), pp. 97–113.

Raphael, Paul. "L'Affaire Émile Deschanel." *La Revue* 106(1 February 1914):363–77.

Rivéro, Jean. "L'Idée laïque et la réforme scolaire (1879–1882)." *Revue politique et parlementaire* 148:442(1931):367–80.

Saltet, Abbé Louis. "Une Légende et un conte de Jules Simon sur Renan à Saint-Sulpice." *Bulletin de littérature ecclésiastique* 27(1926):210–29.

Séché, Léon. "Un anniversaire. Les Derniers jours de Mgr. Darboy." *Revue politique et littéraire*, 4th series, 13:21(26 May 1900):652–57.

———. "Les 'Premières années' de Jules Simon. Souvenirs personnels." *Revue politique et littéraire*, 4th series, 15:20(18 May 1901):615–19.

———. "Renan et Jules Simon." *Le Temps.* 3 September 1903.

Simon, Walter. "The 'Two Cultures' in Nineteenth Century France: Victor Cousin and Auguste Comte." *Journal of the History of Ideas* 26: 1(January–March 1965):45–58.

Sorre, Maurice. "Les Pères du radicalisme. Expression de la doctrine radicale à la fin du second empire." *Revue française de science politique* 1:4(October–December 1951):481–97.

Vauthier, Gabriel. "Troubles à la Sorbonne en 1856." *La Révolution de 1848* 21(January–April 1925):385–400.

Watson, David R. "Communication. A Note on Clemenceau, Comte and Positivism." *Historical Journal* 14:1(1971):201–4.

Weill, Georges. "Un Éducateur français en Argentine." *Revue univer-sitaire* no. 1 (January 1918), pp. 24–33.

————. "Les Républicains et l'enseignement sous Louis-Philippe." *Revue internationale de l'enseignement* 37:1(15 January 1899):33–46.

Index

A

Abélard, Peter, 53
Abstentionism, 56, 71, 123, 146
Adam, Juliette, 149, 186
Agoult, Marie d', 93, 121
Aladel, 42
Allain-Targé, Henri, 5, 140, 141, 144
Anticlericalism: historiographical overview, 2–3; definition, 3–4, 10–11
Aquinas, Thomas, 53
Aristotle, 45, 84, 96
Article 7, 192–98, 201
Association philotechnique, 129, 137
Aurelius, Marcus, 89–90
Avenel, Georges, 13
Avenir, L', 93
Avenir national, L', 10, 16–17, 26

B

Bacon, Francis, 99
Bardoux, Agénor, 194
Barni, Jules, 112–13, 144
Barodet, Désiré, 170, 187
Barrot, Odilon, 59
Baur, Ferdinand Christian, 25
Béranger, Pierre Jean de, 57
Baudin, Dr., 144
Bédollière, Émile de La, 12, 13
Berlin Labor Conference, 212
Berryer, Pierre Antoine, 123
Bersot, Ernest, 20, 29–30, 63, 66, 67
Bert, Paul, 184, 194, 202, 204

Berthelot, Marcellin, 135
Besson, Louis, 160
Bethmont, Eugène, 79
Blanchy, 148
Blanqui, Auguste, 128
Blot, Alfred, 178
Boissonnet, Louise Marie Émilie, 71*n*59
Bonald, Louis G.-A. de, 64
Bossuet, Jacques Bénigne, 82
Bouillerie, Mgr, François de la, 156
Boulanger, Gen. Georges, 212
Brisson, Henri, 51, 140, 144
Broglie, Albert de: on *La Religion naturelle*, 78, 108–11; mentioned, 113, 123, 147, 173, 184, 187, 188, 203
Broglie, Victor de, 123
Brossays-Saint-Marc, Mgr. Godefroy, 160
Buchez, Philippe-J.-B., 58, 67, 79

C

Cabet, Étienne, 128
Cabrières, François de, 156
Caisse d'escompte des associations populaires, de crédit, de consommation, de production, 132
Candide, Le, 135
Capéran, Louis, 3
Carle, Henri, 135
Carnot, Hippolyte, 55, 121, 123, 147, 149, 161, 178
Carrel, Armand, 57
Catholic party, 51

Caussette, Abbé Jean-Baptiste, 156

Central Committee of Catholic Education, 197

Challemel-Lacour, Paul, 144, 163, 184

Changarnier, Gen. Nicolas, 123

Charles X, 36

Charma, Antoine, 47

Chateaubriand, François René de: use of Le Génie du christianisme, 15, 131; mentioned, 42, 44, 72

Chaurand, Jean-Dominique, 166

Chigi, Mgr. Flavio, 155, 156, 158, 159, 160

Circular of 28 October 1871, 167–70

Circular of 27 September 1872, 178–79

Circular of 7 January 1873, 160

Clamadieu, Abbé J. A., 214

Clarke, Samuel, 120

Clémenceau, Georges, 19, 201, 204

Clerical party, 24, 58, 64, 67, 77, 103, 130, 193

Cochin, Augustin, 107–8, 121, 123, 175

Colet, Mgr. Charles-Théodore, 159

Comité général démocratique de Paris, 147

Comte, Auguste: for positivist republicans, 20–25; on coup d'etat of 2 December 1851, 72; influence, 1860s, 135; cited by Ferry, 186; disparaged by Simon, 203

Concordat of 1801, 142, 154–55, 160, 192, 218

Condillac, Étienne Bonnot de, 95, 97, 98

Congregation of the Index, 30, 106, 112

Constant, Benjamin, 60

Constitutionnel, Le, 194

Convention of 15 September 1864, 140

Cormenin, Louis de, 59, 67

Corne, Hyacinthe, 67

Correspondant, Le, 104, 107–8, 157, 177

Coup d'etat of 2 December 1851: apologies for, 72–73, 75–76

Courrier du dimanche, Le, 122

Cousin, Charles, 185

Cousin, Victor: moderate anticlericalism, 20, 27–29, 30–31; teachings, 36, 37–38, 39–40, 42, 45, 46–47, 48, 52, 81, 84, 103; Simon's portrait, 19, 214–16; criticized by young professors, 62–63; on Voltaire, 29, 63; and Taine, 95, 96–98; and Peyrat, 101; mentioned, 6, 49, 56, 58, 60, 66, 80

Cuvillier-Fleury, Alfred, 179

D

Damiron, Jean-Philibert, 42, 45, 46

Daniel, Jacques-Louis, 46

Darboy, Georges, 157, 159

Daru, Napoleon, 123

Decrees of 29 March 1880, 198, 201

Delescluze, Louis Charles, 145

Delpit, Martial, 168

Descartes, René, 52, 82, 96, 102

Deschamps, Nicolas, 49

Deschanel, Émile, 65, 66, 68–71

Despois, Eugène, 65, 144

Devoir, Le: as political opposition, 54, 71–77; mysticism, 86; worship, 91; overture to Catholic liberals, 106; and Le Siècle, 114; secondary education, 177; quoted by Ferry, 186; mentioned, 7, 94, 130, 214

Diderot, Denis, 83, 95, 99
Dieu, patrie, liberté, 206, 207, 209
Dix-neuvième siècle, Le, 183
Dollfus, Charles, 113
Drumont, Édouard, 33*n1*
Du Camp, Maxime, 127, 135
Dufaure, Jules, 187, 188, 197, 200
Du Lac de Fugère, Stanislas, S. J., 197
Dupanloup, Félix: and Simon, 34*n3*, 155, 157–59, 190; and primary education, 168, 175, 176; and Circular of 27 September 1872, 178–79; and Littré, 185
Duportal, Armand, 163
Duprat, Pascal, 93, 160
Duquesnay, Alfred, 160
Duruy, Victor, 162
Duval, Raoul, 206*n54*
Duvergier de Hauranne, Prosper, 59–61

E

Écho universel, L', 191
École, L', 1, 129
Écoles de France, Les, 135
Enfantin, Barthélemy Prosper, 106
Epicurus, 75
Ère nouvelle, L', 111
Essai sur Tite Live, 96, 98

F

Falloux, Alfred de, 67–68, 108, 113
Falloux Law, 68, 162, 166, 167, 170, 192, 202
Favre, Jules, 135, 140, 160
Faye, Herve-Auguste, 173
Fernier, Louis, 171
Ferry, Jules: positivist republican, 20, 21, 23–24; on Voltaire,

24; at *Le Temps*, 25; concept of laicity, 31–32; and Simon, 144, 147, 148–49, 183–84, 186, 189, 197–98, 201–2; and *Revue politique*, 144; and Freemasonry, 185–86; laic laws, 192–210; mentioned, 1, 5, 6, 8
Fontaine, Marguerite-Vincente, 33*n1*
Fontette, Edmond de, 108
Forcade, Théodore-Augustin, 158, 193
Français, Le, 160, 166, 173, 174, 176, 178
France, Anatole, 145
Freethinker: definition of, 4*n3*
Frélaut, Fortuné, 34, 36, 40, 45, 46, 48
Frères de la Doctrine Chrétienne, 165
Frères des écoles chrétiennes, 192
Freycinet, Charles de, 199, 201
Fribourg, Ernest, 133
Fruchard, Félix, 156

G

Gallerand, Gabriel, 38, 40, 41, 43, 44
Gambetta, Léon: and Simon, 6, 118, 140, 143, 144, 148–50, 152, 164, 167, 169, 174, 188–91, 198, 201, 207; "Belleville Program," 118, 143; and *Revue politique*, 144; on primary education, 161; seen from Right Center, 173–74; freedom of higher education, 185; mentioned, 1, 5, 19, 175
Garibaldi, Giuseppe, 141
Garnier, Adolphe, 42
Gaulois, Le, 206–7
Gay, Peter, 81
Géruzez, Eugène, 111

Girardin, Émile de, 25, 99
Gironde, La, 20, 23, 147, 148, 189
Glais-Bizoin, Alexandre, 59
Goblet Law, 209
Goncourt, Edmond, 18
Goncourt, Jules de, 18
Gounouilhou, Gustave, 148
Gouvernement de M. Thiers, Le, 191
Grévy, Albert, 172
Groups, parliamentary: Left Center, 6, 27, 59, 60, 61, 183, 188, 196, 197, 198, 206; Republican Left, 21, 183, 184, 188, 189, 198; Extreme Left, 58, 59, 60, 61, 183, 201, 203; Third party, 134–35, 140, 144, 153; Republican Union, 183, 189, 205
Guéronnière, Arthur de La, 72, 73, 75
Guibert, Joseph, 155, 159
Guigniaut, Joseph-Daniel, 38
Guizot, François, 59, 60, 111, 175

H

Hachette, Louis, 91, 129
Haussonville, Joseph d', 121, 122
Havin, Léonor, 12, 114, 122, 123
Hébrard, Adrien, 20
Hegel, Georg Wilhelm Friedrich, 96
Hénon, Jacques, 170
Herizog, Abbé, 212
Histoire de l'École d'Alexandrie, 53, 85–86
Hobbes, Thomas, 75
Hugo, Victor, 55, 199, 200

I

Independent morality. See Morale indépendante, La
Instruction Publique, L', 178

International Workingmen's Association, 133, 174, 183

J

Jacques, Amédée, 62, 65, 66, 67, 68, 69, 70
Jacquinet, Paul, 173
James, William, 84, 89
Janet, Paul, 21, 66, 203, 214–15
Jaubert, Hippolyte-François, 184
Jesus of Nazareth: Peyrat's view, 16; Liberal Protestant view, 25; Simon's view, 130, 131; Renan's view, 131; Chateaubriand's view, 131
Johnston, Nathaniel, 179
Jourdan, Louis: Voltairean journalist, 12, 13, 15; religious views, 17, 93; on La Religion naturelle, 114–16; on independent morality, 137
Journal des débats, Le, 107, 179, 196, 215
Journal pour tous, Le, 131

K

Kant, Immanuel, 28, 97, 203
Koenigswarter, Maximilien-Jules, 124

L

La Bédollière, Émile de, 12, 13
Laboulaye, Édouard, 197
Lacordaire, Henri, 42–44, 45, 47, 50
Ladoue, Mgr. Casimir de, 190
La Guéronnière, Arthur de, 72, 73, 75
Lamennais, Félicité de, 42–44, 50, 57, 58
Lamy, Étienne, 194
Larcy, Charles-Paulin de, 123
Laromiguière, Pierre, 95, 96

Laurent-Pichat, Léon, 93, 99
Laurier, Clément, 140
Lavertujon, André: positivist
  republican, 20; on statue of
  Voltaire, 23–24; and Simon,
  147–48, 149, 152
Lavigerie, Charles, 217
Law of 12 July 1875 on Liberty of
  Higher Education, 192, 195
Law of 28 March 1882 on Obliga-
  tory Primary Education, 198, 205
Lebas, Philippe, 57
Le Chapelier Law, 132
Leclerc, Joseph-Victor, 76
Legain, Théodore, 155
Legouvé, Ernest, 133*n*44
Leibnitz, Gottfried Wilhelm, 102,
  120
Lemoinne, John, 196
Leo XIII (Pope), 217
Leroux, Pierre, 58
Leroy-Beaulieu, Paul, 179
Léséleuc de Kérouara, Léopold
  de, 156
Letter of 19 January 1867, 140
Liberal Catholicism: and Simon,
  42–44, 104–12, 121, 147, 173
Liberal Protestantism: and
  moderate anticlericalism, 20,
  25–27
Liberal Union: republican attitudes
  toward, 26–27, 122–24, 134–35
Liberté, La, 119
Liberté de conscience, La, 119
Liberté de penser, La: political
  and philosophic positions, 55,
  56, 62–71; on socialism, 70–71
Libre conscience, La, 135
Libre pensée, La, 135
Libre recherche, La, 93
Ligue de l'enseignement, 129, 170,
  174–75
Littré, Émile: on anticlericalism,
  3; on Voltairianism, 11; positiv-
  ist republican, 20, 21–23; on

statue of Voltaire, 23; opposes
  coup d'etat of 2 December 1851,
  72; in Freemasonry, 185; on
  Article 7, 194, 197; mentioned,
  26, 95, 135, 146
Locke, John, 28, 29, 81, 97
Lorquet, Alfred, 38
Lucretius, 99

M

Macé, Jean, 129, 170
MacMahon, Maréchal Edme Patrice
  de, 6, 187, 189, 190, 191
Madol, 40
Maine de Biran, Marie, 98
Malebranche, Nicolas de, 51
Marcère, Émile de, 188
Maret, Henri, 111
Marie, Alexandre, 134
Massol, Marie Alexandre, 136, 137,
  138, 145
Materialism: among republicans,
  93–94; Simon opposes, 94–95,
  101–2; Barni opposes, 113
Mathieu, Césaire, 14, 160, 173
Matin, Le, 212
Meyer, Arthur, 206
Michelet, Jules: his Voltairian-
  ism, 11, 17–19; Les Jésuites, 17;
  Du prêtre, de la femme et de
  la famille, 17–19, 65, 67; portrait
  of Voltaire, 19; teacher at
  École normale, 57; mentioned,
  30, 68
Mignet, François, 121
Mill, John Stuart, 7, 125
Moizan, Abbé, 34
Monnet, Alfred, 166
Montalembert, Charles de: and
  Simon, 64, 67, 107–8, 111, 121,
  147; and Deschanel, 68; and
  Revue de Paris, 113; and Liberal
  Union, 123
Morale indépendante, La: and

Simon, 89, 136–39; affinity with *Le Siècle*, 115–16, 137; distinguished from positivism, 136; journal, 136–38; and laicity, 202; mentioned, 147

Morin, Frédéric: on *La Religion naturelle*, 79, 111; on Christian democracy, 114; on Simon's influence, 117

Mottu, Jules, 163–64, 174

Municipal councils: choice of teaching personnel, 161–73

N

Napoleon I, 35, 154

Napoleon III (Louis Napoleon), 55, 73, 76, 77, 103, 135, 188

Naquet, Alfred, 210

National, Le, 55, 57, 59, 70, 72

Nefftzer, Auguste: as Liberal Protestant, 20; moderate anticlericalism, 25–27, 31; and Liberal Union, 122; mentioned, 147

Nisard, Désiré, 76

Nouvel, Denis, 155

O

Ollivier, Émile, 140

Opportunism, 198–99, 201, 204–6, 208, 209, 217

L'Ouvrière, 124, 126

P

Pantheism: among republicans, 93; Simon opposes, 81, 94–95

Parieu, Marie de, 69–70

Pays, Le, 72–73

Peine de mort, La, 148

Pelletan, Eugène, 93, 137

Pensée nouvelle, La, 135

Peyrat, Jean-Alphonse: his Voltairianism, 15–17; and

Gambetta, 16; *Histoire élémentaire et critique de Jésus*, 16; and Michelet, 19; and Liberal Union, 26–27, 122; and *La Religion naturelle*, 99–101, 114

Philosophic spiritualism: definition, 28; and Catholicism, 48–54, 77; and republicans, 1860s, 135

Philosophie positive, La, 11, 20, 135

Picard, Ernest, 140

Pius VII (Pope), 154

Pius IX (Pope), 12, 13, 111–12, 141, 155, 157–59, 160, 174, 189, 190

Plato, 47, 75, 84, 96, 102

Plotinus, 86

Politique radicale, La, 118, 137, 140, 143–44, 151

Positivism: among republicans, 21–25, 94, 135; Simon opposes, 83, 101, 203

Positivist republicanism: definition, 21–25

Presse, La, 16, 99, 103, 112, 114

Press laws, 12 and n2, 143

Prévost-Paradol, L.-A., 66, 67, 95

Prost, Antoine, 27

Protestantism: and Simon, 80

Proudhon, Pierre-Joseph, 136

Q

Quinet, Edgar, 65, 68, 160

R

Radicalism, 187, 199, 204, 209

Ralliement, 217–18

Ranc, Arthur, 19, 204

Referendum of 20 December 1851, 55, 72, 73, 75, 76

Reid, Thomas, 98

Religion naturelle, La: discussed, 78–92 *passim*; republican

reception of, 99–104, 112–16;
"Avertissement" to third edi-
tion, 101–4, 105, 106; mentioned,
7, 35, 135, 136, 214
Rémusat, Charles de, 1–2, 59, 111,
121, 187
Renan, Ernest: author of *Vie de
Jésus*, 16, 131; contributor to
La Liberté de penser, 65, 66;
mentioned, 135
Renault, Léon, 194
Rendu, Eugène, 171
"Republican Right," 198, 206
République française, La: Circular
of 28 October 1871, 169; on
Simon, 175, 182–83, 191;
Circular of 27 September
1872, 178; anticlericalism, 184;
on liberty of higher education,
184–85
Réveil, Le, 145
Revue de l'Instruction Publique,
96, 111
Revue de Paris, 93, 99, 112–14
Revue des Deux Mondes, 58, 63–64,
96
Revue politique, 144
Reynaud, Jean, 93, 96, 97, 99,
107–8
Ribot, Alexandre, 194
Rive gauche, La, 135
Robin, Charles-Phillippe, 135
Roman Question, 121–22, 134,
140–42, 147
Romieu, Auguste, 73
Ropert, Abbé, 34
Rousseau, Jean-Jacques, 42, 79,
81, 106, 111, 113
Royer-Collard, Pierre Paul, 60,
98

S

St. Augustine, 87
Sainte-Beuve, Charles, 72, 75

Saisset, Émile, 30, 38, 65, 67
Sébaux, Alexandre, 155
Seinguerlet, E., 144
Siècle, Le (Empire): Voltairean
anticlericalism, 10, 11–15;
statue of Voltaire, 12, 16, 23–24,
26; on Michelet, 24; and Liberal
Union, 26, 122–24; deism, 93,
101–2; on Taine, 99; criticized by
Simon, 103–4, 120–21; on Simon,
114–16, 124; on *La Morale indépendante*, 183
Siècle, Le (Third Republic): Circular of 7 January 1873, 161;
Circular of 28 October 1871,
169; on primary education,
175; Circular of 27 September
1872, 178; and Conservative
Republicanism, 183
Simon, Jules: character of, 1–2,
144–45; member of Academy of
Moral and Political Sciences, 7;
family origins, 33 and n1; at
Royal College of Vannes,
33–34; at École normale, 35–45;
at Royal College of Caen, 45–
47; at the Sorbonne, 47–48,
55, 71; on Saint-Simonianism,
94, 216; and Orleanists, 121–23,
132, 134–35, 146–47, 173–74;
in Government of National Defense, 151, 152 and n2; and
Freemasonry, 186 and n10;
member of *Académie française*,
187; president of council of
ministers, 187–91; and Boulanger, 211 and n2
—liberalism: characteristics,
31–32, 138–45, 195–96, 198–99,
206–8, 210–11, 213, 216–18; and
coup d'etat of 2 December 1851,
55–56, 71; on primary education, 55, 129–32, 174–76, 198,
202–5; and July Monarchy, 56,
57, 60–61; and republicanism

before 1848, 56–61; on popular sovereignty, 60–61, 143–44; on "liberty of education," 63–64, 184, 194–97; abstentionism, 122–23; as Conservative Republican, 181–84, 188–91, 201
—philosophic views: his deism, 74–75, 86–87; positivism, 75, 83, 95, 101; mysticism, 84–86; worship, 90–91; and La Morale indépendante, 135–40. See Religion naturelle, La; Devoir, Le
—Roman Catholicism: Society of Jesus, 4, 31, 49, 64, 67, 77, 103, 120, 195, 197; Voltaire, 30, 120, 143; Voltairianism, 32, 66–70, 101–4, 107, 120–21, 143; his early Catholicism, 34–37; Catholic doctrine, 37, 63–64, 119–20; New Testament, 130; Jesus of Nazareth, 130–31
—secularism: his anticlericalism, 3–6, 20–21, 27–31, 217–18; opposes laic laws, 6, 31–32, 192–210; Roman Question, 121–22, 124, 140, 147; conception of laicity, 138–42, 217–18; Separation of Church and State, 141–42, 210; opposes Article 7, 194–97
—social outlook: National Workshops, 70–71; concept of règle, 75; laissez-faire, 119, 124–26, 132–33, 145; lower classes, 124–33; family, 132; workers' organizations, 132–33; woman question, 133n44, 210; Commune, 181, 199–201, 204, 208
Simon-Suisse, Alexandre, 33n1
Simon-Suisse, Hermione-Françoise, 33, 44
Société coopérative des habitations à bon marché, 132
Société coopérative immobilière, 132

Des Sociétés de coopération et leur constitution légale, 179
Société d'instruction primaire de Lyon, 171
Société Franklin, 129
Société pour l'instruction élémentaire, 129, 148
Society of Jesus: viewed by Simon, 4, 30, 49, 64, 67, 79, 103, 120, 195; viewed by Michelet, 17; viewed by Comte, 24; and Article 7, 31, 192, 193; and decrees of 29 March 1880, 198, 200; mentioned, 12
Society of the Rights of Man, 57
Souvenirs du quatre septembre, 181
Spencer, Herbert, 203
Spinoza, Benedict, 95, 96, 98
Spuller, Eugène, 140, 144, 212
Staël, Germaine de, 73
Syllabus of Errors, 134, 147, 184, 193

T

Taine, Hippolyte: on philosophic spiritualism, 95–98; and Simon, 96–97, 101–3
Tardif, Adolphe, 156, 160
Tassel, Yves, 60
Temps, Le: its moderate anticlericalism, 11, 20, 25–27; and Liberal Union, 122–24; and Conservative Republicanism, 183; Article 7, 194; Simon's column, 213; mentioned, 147, 175, 196, 216
Ténot, Eugène, 12
Thiard de Bissy, Auxonne-Marie, 58
Thiers, Adolphe: and La Religion naturelle, 111; and republicans (1863–1864), 123, 134, 135; and Simon (1871–1873), 151, 153–

54, 156–60, 178, 179, 180;
president of the Republic, 159,
164, 174, 177; influence on
Gambetta, 183, 189, 191; men-
tioned, 59, 161, 181, 200
Tocqueville, Alexis de, 127
Travail, Le, 132
Tribune, Le, 137
Tubingen school, 33

U

Ulbach, Louis, 113
Union pour la France chrétienne,
218
University of France: its moderate
anticlericalism, 11, 20–21, 27–31
Univers religieux, L' (1835), 43,
45
Univers religieux, L': and Simon,
49, 64, 106, 120, 157, 166; and
Liberal Catholicism, 107, 108,
157; mentioned, 115, 155

V

Vacherot, Étienne, 46, 144
Vallès, Jules, 145
Vapereau, Gustave, 66
Vatican Council of 1870, 156,
157, 158, 159
Veuillot, Louis, 64, 77, 78, 101,
106, 108, 120
Victor Cousin, 215
Vilbort, J., 14
Villemain, Abel, 59
Villemot, Auguste, 26

Voisins-Lavernière, Honoré de,
194, 200
Voltaire: *Dictionnaire philosophique*, 11, 13; statue of, 13, 16,
23, 26; in Michelet's *Louis XV,
1724–1757*, 18–19; and Littré, 21–
24, 185; and Cousin, 29, 63;
and Simon, 30, 120, 143; and
Bersot, 29–30, 63, 67; and *La
République française*, 185
Voltaireans, Old: definition,
129*n*33
Voltairianism: definition, 11–19;
after 1870, 19; and positivists,
21–25; and *Le Temps*, 26; and
Liberal Union, 26–27, 122; and
University spiritualism, 30;
at *La Liberté de penser*, 62, 65–
69; and *La Religion naturelle*,
99–104, 114–15; at *Revue de
Paris*, 112–14, and avant-garde,
1860s, 135; and press laws,
12 and *n*2, 143

W

Waddington, Charles, 192, 199
Waldeck-Rousseau, Pierre, 146
Weill, Georges, 3
Walras, Léon, 132
William II, Emperor, 212
Wordsworth, Bishop Christopher,
209

Z

Zeno, 102
Zévort, Charles, 163